Inspiring Innovations in Language Teaching

MODERN LANGUAGES in PRACTICE

Series Editor
Michael Grenfell, *School of Education, University of Southampton*

Editorial Board
Do Coyle, *School of Education, University of Nottingham*
Simon Green, *Trinity & All Saints College, Leeds*

Editorial Consultant
Christopher Brumfit, *Centre for Language in Education, University of Southampton*

Other Books in the Series
Le ou La? The Gender of French Nouns
    MARIE SURRIDGE
Validation in Language Testing
    A. CUMMING and R. BERWICK (eds)

Other Books of Interest
The Age Factor in Second Language Acquistion
    D. SINGLETON and Z. LENGYEL (eds)
Approaches to Second Language Acquisition
    R. TOWELL and R. HAWKINS
Distance Education for Language Teachers
    RON HOWARD and IAN McGRATH (eds)
French for Communication
    ROY DUNNING
A Parents' and Teachers' Guide to Bilingualism
    COLIN BAKER
Quantifying Language
    PHIL SCHOLFIELD
Reflections on Language Learning
    L. BARBARA and M. SCOTT (eds)
Teaching-and-Learning Language-and-Culture
    MICHAEL BYRAM, CAROL MORGAN and colleagues

Please contact us for the latest book information:
Multilingual Matters Ltd, Frankfurt Lodge, Clevedon Hall,
Victoria Road, Clevedon, Avon, England, BS21 7SJ.

MODERN LANGUAGES IN PRACTICE 3
Series Editor: Michael Grenfell

Inspiring Innovations
in Language Teaching

Judith Hamilton

I will not creep along the coast, but sail out in mid-sea,
by guidance of the stars   George Eliot
                                             Middlemarch

MULTILINGUAL MATTERS LTD
Clevedon • Philadelphia • Adelaide

Library of Congress Cataloging in Publication Data

Hamilton, Judith, 1943-
Inspiring Innovations in Language Teaching/Judith Hamilton
(Modern Languages in Practice: 3)
Includes bibliographical references and index
1. Languages, Modern–Study and teaching. I. Title. II. Series.
PB35.H284   1995
418'.007–dc20   95-24252

British Library Cataloguing in Publication Data

A CIP catalogue record for this book is available from the British Library.

ISBN 1-85359-284-6 (hbk)
ISBN 1-85359-283-8 (pbk)

Multilingual Matters Ltd

UK: Frankfurt Lodge, Clevedon Hall, Victoria Road, Clevedon, Avon BS21 7SJ.
USA: 1900 Frost Road, Suite 101, Bristol, PA 19007, USA.
Australia: P.O. Box 6025, 83 Gilles Street, Adelaide, SA 5000, Australia.

Typeset by Action Typesetting, Gloucester.
Printed and bound in Great Britain by the Cromwell Press.

Contents

PART 3   SOCIAL ORGANISATION FOR INNOVATION

PART 4   THE RIGHT PEOPLE FOR INNOVATION

Acknowledgements

This book has been written because of and thanks to a great many people. I have tried wherever possible in the text to name names and acknowledge the authors of ideas, not only in order to 'do the done thing' but because I think individuals matter, and individual teachers rarely get mentioned in books about teaching. I have been lucky to meet a great many innovators in my career, and to have had some great innovators as close friends and colleagues. Innovators are grand people to work with and fun to socialise with, and as I say in the book, 'innovating is a social activity'.

To all those who shared the fun of the innovative days in Scotland, and to those who invited me to share in their innovations elsewhere in the world, go my heartfelt thanks for all I learnt from them.

To David, who has supported and encouraged me, as well as providing me with a wealth of ideas and suggestions, I dedicate this book.

J. H.
Dar es Salaam, 1994

About the Book

This book is the result of nearly 30 years' experience in Modern Languages classrooms. In the course of a highly privileged career, the writer has worked as a languages teacher, researcher and teacher trainer in Scotland and has had the opportunity to see educational developments in many other countries. The book is the product of first-hand experience and the perspectives arising out of that. Its concern is the classroom, in which most of the writer's professional life has been spent, not the policy room, although she has had the opportunity to 'overhear' some of the things that go on there and which impinge on the way in which teachers carry out their work. The events and institutions recalled are presented the way she understood them to be. The reflections and opinions are a result of this understanding. It is important to state at the outset also what this book is not: it is not a guidebook to good practice; it is not an academic doctoral thesis consisting of a review of the literature and plenty well-researched, carefully weighted evidence; it is not an analysis of the phenomenon of innovation; it is not unbiased.

The book is centred on a country whose education system has been recognised worldwide as having something special to offer. Scotland attracts many overseas visitors who export to their own part of the world some of the innovative practices which they have seen in operation there. Developments first pioneered in Scotland have made their way to all kinds of places. The writer examines in some detail some of the innovations which have taken place in modern languages and with which she is familiar. In order to draw conclusions of a wider-reaching nature, work in other countries which has had an impact beyond the confines of these countries, is juxtaposed, either to highlight a trend or to offer a contrasting picture to the Scottish one. From the insights gained from these experiences an attempt is made to identify and analyse the conditions in which they have arisen, to examine the lessons learnt and to reach some tentative conclusions about the organisational structures and training policies which appear to foster innovative approaches.

The volume is in four parts. In each part there is at least one chapter related to the Scottish scene and one or more chapters entitled 'Looking Around' which relate in cameo form experiences from other parts of the world; the last chapter in each part of the book, entitled 'Pause for Thought' attempts to draw some conclusions about the nature, scope and limitations of the aspect of innovation under discussion. Part 1 considers statutory innovation by central bodies, the notion of legitimacy which it carries with it and the relationship between central controls and innovation. Part 2 considers the advantages of the campaign model for a local teacher development project and the necessity for some element of cultural and societal 'fit'. Part 3 looks at organisational structures and how they affect innovation, and describes from the viewpoint of teachers working there a modern languages department organised specifically to encourage innovation. Part 4 looks both at a partnership approach to teacher training and at some sources of inspiration. The concluding 'Pause for Thought' summarises the picture. Its theme is the need to bring together individuals and institutions in order to provide the best possible opportunity for the promotion of innovative practices.

Teachers are busy people who do not generally have time to do much reading. With this in mind, a summary of the argument is given below so that the reader who is interested in a particular field, a particular methodology, or works in a particular country, should be able to dip into the text at that point. The introductions and the concluding chapter to each Part, 'Pause for Thought', expand the argument, while the intervening chapters provide examples from Scotland and elsewhere.

Except for 'General Introduction', where Notes are at the end, all Notes to text references to subsequent chapters can be found at the end of each Part.

A personal note

The author wrote the bulk of this book on the island of Rarotonga in the Cook Islands, at the other end of the world from where most of her work took place. Writing of the book was completed in one of Africa's poorest countries, Tanzania. Inevitably, her experiences of life in what we know as the 'Third World' impinged, and comments relating to development issues will be found throughout the text. Teachers in rich countries are unaware for the most part of the effects that education policies in their countries have on the poor countries in the world, who are led to believe that 'the West knows best' in terms of education as in other matters. Teachers in rich countries may also tend to think, as did the author, that they have nothing much to learn from teachers operating at barely survival level, being paid wages which even in terms of a poor country are barely survival wages. They are wrong.

Summary: The Argument in Brief

General Introduction

Innovation is needed in education in order that the service may be responsive, flexible and self-renewing. Innovation holds the key to raising standards, because it is a driving force which enhances teachers' careers and prevents 'burn-out'. Innovation is the product of analysis and systematic hard work. It needs the right ground to flourish and has to have social and cultural 'fit' to succeed. This entails operating within society, not against it. Innovation has to be legitimised. Teachers need to take control as 'activists', to have confidence in themselves, to reject ideologies and find their own solutions.

Part 1   Legitimising Innovation

Leadership and informal management structures allow for responsiveness and flexibility. Monolithic central controls stifle innovation. Paradoxically, rebellion against these can also be seen to produce innovation.

Example

In the Scottish Primary Modern Languages Pilot teachers and local advisers fought against centralised control in order to determine the shape and direction of work in their area and to achieve a 'fit' with their individual circumstances. The circumstances and the work done in two different regions is described.

Looking around

The national languages policy of Australia is held up by some as a model for other countries, but its economically inspired origins may have produced a potentially harmful confusion between training and education. However, the natural tensions between State and Commonwealth and Australia's previous experience of a different model in the ALL project may mitigate against the worst effects of central control.

Pausing for thought

Policies alone do not produce innovation. Teachers require to be participants in decision-making. A combination of circumstances and people is what produced the innovations described: challenges to be faced, problems to overcome, the fact that teachers were starting from scratch, as well as a creative tension arising where a local authority decided to resist central control.

Part 2   Campaigning for Curriculum Renewal

Campaigns are a way of organising for change: they encourage innovation because they are driven by issues, not ideologies; they have participants, not recipients, leaders not managers. People are free to differ. There are no predetermined outputs, no hierarchies; decisions are taken by those on the spot. The terrain is important and 'fit' is in a business or industrial setting for success.

Example

Lothian's GLAFLL project offers a model of an educational campaign in which the role of the local authority and adviser were crucial in encouraging innovations by teachers in their methodology.

Looking around

The Bangalore project has similarities with the Lothian one. Prahbu's 'operational syllabus' has teachers making decisions and taking control of the content and sequencing of teaching. Teachers' 'pedagogical perceptions' are central to the notion of innovation. Alterations to these are what make teachers innovate.

Projects such as GLAFLL and Bangalore are unlikely to happen in New Zealand, which gives an example of an education service overtaken by an ideology which has isolated teachers, who in the absence of anyone to turn to for advice have been made dependent on consultants and central diktat. The way ahead seeks to reduce all knowledge to a matter of 'units'.

Pausing for thought

The dependency mentality is not limited to developing nations. Teachers can become dependent on central controls and coursebooks. The international aid business has made education reform in poor countries increasingly dependent on help from the donor community, just as teachers have become increasingly reliant on having materials and syllabuses supplied for them by central sources.

While teachers used to have to think and plan for themselves, central control makes teachers increasingly powerless. Campaigning alters the balance of power. An advisory service makes an ideal campaign head-quarters, allowing as it does for maximum spread and social and cultural fit.

Part 3   Social Organisation for Innovation

Although teachers cannot determine institutional arrangements, they can exercise a degree of self-determination within departments, the organisational structures of which can determine their capacity for innovation.

Example

One department, inspired by experiential education in Canada, run on ideals of choice, responsibility and support for creativity is described in detail by the teachers who worked there. Choices made included use of the target language, negotiation with pupils, responsibility training, emphasis on learning and use of drama techniques. The same condi-tions judged necessary for fostering a climate of innovation in a business or industrial setting are seen in operation in the department described.

Looking around

An American example of an institutional approach to innovation is described. Avoiding the bureaucratic hurdles and supporting alterna-tive models for state schools is shown to liberate teachers and encourage innovative practices which 'fit' local circumstances.

Pausing for thought

Features of informal organisations which foster innovations are the same in education as in business: the adjustment of tasks, the unimpor-tance of rank, commitment to the enterprise, a lack of self-interest, a lateral direction of communication and the dissemination of informa-tion and advice, not directives. These resemble the features of campaigning outlined in Part 2. Some trends in school management seem to go in the opposite direction.

Part 4   The Right People for Innovation

Systems are not always in place to provide the necessary conditions for innovation, and besides, systems can themselves induce dependency. Replacing dependence on systems with dependence on self is what should take place during teacher training.

The task for teacher training is to produce an activist, ideology-proof profession; to help teachers incorporate new ideas into their pedagogic perceptions and to avoid superficial cosmetic changes; to ensure that development is a constant feature of teachers' careers over which they themselves exercise control; to instigate in teachers an attitude of inquiry.

Example

Responsibility for this task is shared, in the detailed example given, in a partnership between student teacher, training institution and a group of local authority teachers. Examples are given of student teachers under this system researching and experimenting with unusual techniques.

Looking around

Certain writers have played a key role in teacher training. Ideas act as a challenge to which teachers respond intellectually, in a way different to the way in which they respond to recommended procedures and recipes.

Pause for thought

Teachers welcome the opportunity to analyse and discuss. An extension of the partnership notion to include the important area of research would offer a way of utilising existing resources and institutions. Teamwork and a redefinition of tasks and remits are another way in which room can be made for innovation. In the attempt to examine to what extent teachers can take a proactive role in the development of innovations, certain key factors have emerged:

Legitimacy is crucial to innovation: However, the balance of power between central authority and local autonomy requires to be maintained, so that domination by the centre does not stifle initiative and deskill teachers. Legitimacy can be conferred by movements and campaigns, by colleagues, and professional organisations.

Spread is crucial to innovation: Spread depends on legitimacy and hence on institutions. It is not just a case of enabling teachers to become informed about developments; it requires a teaching force which is sufficiently activist to react to new ideas and reject new ideologies.

Organisational structures are crucial to innovation: Informal structures allow for flexible responses and encourage initiative.

Individuals are crucial to innovation: We need to identify potential leaders; to support and encourage enquirers and risk-takers; to give a platform to those whose ideas inspire.

General Introduction

Society needs innovation. The capacity to innovate is what keeps institutions, industries, economies, public service departments and businesses flexible, responsive and self-renewing.[1] This capacity is also essential to the education service. Innovation holds the key to raising standards in that it promotes a sense of well-being in the teaching profession.

Innovation is hard work. It is pragmatic, modest and advances often quite slowly. It is not the grandiose scheme, nor is it the one-off, short-term flash of intuition or inspiration, but rather the product of two things: analysis and organised, systematic, often tedious work. Innovation, however, is not the same as excellence. A teacher may be an excellent teacher without being an innovative one. The reason why the innovative teacher outvalues the excellent teacher in the long run is that innovation is a driving force which enhances a career and makes it constantly self-renewing and worthwhile. Excellence *per se* may be a dead-end. The teaching profession is littered with 'burnt out cases' which illustrate just that.

The responsibility for innovation is shared between the teachers themselves and those who create the organisational arrangements under which they operate. These arrangements effectively determine whether or not innovation, which may be initiated by an individual, has the potential to spread.

Innovation needs the right ground in order to flourish – and an innovation that is not embedded in the existing terrain, one that lacks social and cultural 'fit', will not succeed.

Innovators rarely just 'happen' – most good teachers have something of the innovator in them, although this potential all too often lies dormant. It should be the role of decision-makers in the field of education to ensure that the opportunity is provided for the emergence of the innovator within all those for whom they have responsibility. It has been found in industrial studies that informal organisation structures are most likely to foster innovative practices, which are themselves the key to the productivity of the enterprise. Education may be no different in this respect.

Innovation therefore requires good management practices. In the best of all possible worlds, treating people properly would be the first consideration of those responsible in any way for their fellow humans. Even those of a more pragmatic viewpoint tend to agree that to get the best out of people requires good management. The question of what constitutes good management, of teachers and their pupils, as well as of those who manage and train teachers, lies at the heart of much of this book, since unless the possibility for innovation is built into the structure of an institution, it will become an affair of chance, left to the individual teacher, whose good efforts, lacking a supporting framework, wither on the vine. Some of the trends in the management of education over recent years have, wittingly or not, worked against the development of innovative teaching. This is why it matters that those who regard innovation as important to the future of the education service examine critically the premises on which present management training and practices are based.[2]

It is society that requires higher standards in language teaching. Society requires people who can get on with speakers of other languages, whatever their level of grammatical competence. Society requires people who can *behave* in a variety of foreign languages, not just a few who have very good French. What we need to learn as teachers is how to help our pupils be confident, ambitious risk-takers who can make language work for them. To do this we need to have confidence in ourselves and in our ability to function properly.

We know that much of what is presently taught in school language classes is soon forgotten, and that what needs to be addressed is how best to foster skills and attitudes in language learning that will last for a lifetime. We also know that for this to take place a shift in public opinion is necessary, and that we alone in our classrooms are not capable of effecting it.

Teachers are members of society and schools are of society, not outside it, and innovation is a social process. For this reason teachers need to operate with others, not against others. Outright rebellion, in teaching terms, has never paid off, yet changes are essential, not least because of the rapid changes within society. Those who over the years have promoted alternative ways of schooling, or de-schooling, society, have been as voices in the wilderness, because their ideas have lacked the approval of society. Innovation, if it is to take root, has to be legitimised.

The use of the term 'innovation' needs to be distinguished from other, related concepts. In this book the term is used to mean the instigation and implementation of a new way of doing or thinking which has some potential for diffusion. What is described in this book as innovative is not change which is determined by others; nor is it the act of inventing or creating[3] something new: the crucial thing is the seeing through of the whole process from instigation through implementation, including assessment, evaluation, revamping and restructuring. Innovation also has to be recognised – it is not a flower to 'blush unseen, and waste its sweetness on the desert air.'[4] On the contrary, the whole point is that it is a shared experience. Innovators in education, while perhaps not a recognisable 'type', are essentially highly social animals.

Perhaps because of this, innovations often occur within clusters and among groups of people who have social, not merely professional, relationships. Innovations are frequently the product of behaviour that is not ends-means driven; behaviour that is not based on notions of what is most efficient or indeed most logical; behaviour that is not 'rational'. Rationality, proceeding in measured, predetermined steps from A to B, tries to rule out the taking of risks, the following up of new ideas and fresh insights, the chasing of rainbows. Rationality is the watchword of bureaucrats, forward-planners and, all too often today, of policy-makers and managers.

Rationality would not suggest that a teacher whose class seems to be performing well enough but who do not cohere as a group should take himself off to the hills with them and allow himself to be guided by them, blindfolded, across the moors; it does not suggest that teachers give up their little spare time to write a syllabus designed for all levels of language learning when it has been decided nationally that only the brightest pupils ought to continue with the study of a language; it does not suggest that a student teacher should undertake to do what the class teacher says cannot be done, and introduce complex ideas through songs and poetry to pupils whose previous experience of language has been limited to a few 'useful' set phrases.

A Culinary Approach

The view taken of innovation in teaching by the writer sees teachers determining for themselves what they teach. Rather than accept some-one else's package of reforms, they have instigated their own. To take an analogy from the way in which households organise their eating: some rely on the TV dinner, the carry-outs, the instant cans of this or that as their staple fare; others are keen on following recipes prepared by experts; a few, however, decide what makes for healthy and enjoyable eating, search out the best and freshest ingredients and combine them in such a way as to produce meals of 'cordon bleu' standard all the time. The dedicated gourmet would, given the choice, opt to dine with the latter. Of course in real life, even very good cooks may rely from time to time on the pot noodle approach! But as every discriminating eater knows, it is the ability to throw away the recipe book that distinguishes the best from the merely competent cook. And the person who really loves to cook will be happiest when creating, or recreating, some dish whose flavours offer something new and stimulating to the palate even although the risk of failure rises with every new ingredient.

Those who take charge also take responsibility and 'engage' in a way that necessarily entails risk. Without this risk there is no commitment. By taking charge themselves, teachers create a dynamic of ongoing professional development with its own action research dimension and one which belongs to them. It is precisely the experiential, the time-consuming act of learning that makes us better at our jobs. It is not something that others can do for us.

The handing over of someone else's recipes, in the form of curricular product, aims and objectives, targets, templates or whatever, is not the way to educate teachers and improve the quality of education, just as the mere handing over of a body of knowledge is no way to educate children. Learning about teaching, like learning about anything worthwhile, entails personal involvement and no small degree of hardship. The problem for teachers is that if they themselves do not control what is on the menu, if they do not take charge of what happens in their classrooms, then someone else will do it for them.

Notes

1. See Drucker, P. (1986) *Innovation and Entrepreneurship*. Pan Books Ltd.
2. For a summary of the kind of thinking behind some management practices, see Appendix 1.

3. Rogers, E.M. (1954) quoted in West and Farr (eds) (1990) *Innovation and Creativity at Work: Psychological and Organizational Strategies*, defines creativity as '... the emergence in action of a novel relational product, growing out of the uniqueness of the individual on the one hand, and the materials, events, people, or circumstances of his life on the other.'
4. *Elegy Written in a Country Churchyard*, Thomas Gray.

Abbreviations

AACLAME	Australian Advisory Council on Language and Multicultural Education
ALL	Australian Language Learning
CEI	Center for Educational Innovation (New York)
CILT	Centre for Information on Language Teaching and Research
EC	European Community
EIS	Educational Institute of Scotland (the largest teachers' union, comprising primary and secondary teachers)
ERO	Educational Review Office (New Zealand – replaces inspectorate)
ESL	English as a Second Language
FE	Further Education
FCA	Foreign Conversation Assistant
FTE	Full Time Equivalent
GDP	Gross Domestic Product
GLAFLL	Graded Levels of Achievement in Foreign Language Learning
GOML	Graded Objectives in Modern Languages
HT	Head Teacher
HMI	Her Majesty's Inspectorate
INSET	In-Service Training
IST	In-Service Training

L1	First Language
L2	Second Language
LOP	Level of Performance (Lothian Region's GLAFLL project terminology)
LOTE	Languages Other Than English
MBA	Master of Business Administration
M.Ed.	Master of Education
NPL	National Policy on Languages
NZQA	New Zealand Qualifications Authority
OHP	Overhead Projector
PALE	Peripheral Audio-Active Language Equipment
P7	Primary 7 (the final year of primary school, aged 11–12)
PT	Principal Teacher (Head of Department)
RCCC	Regional Consultative Committee on the Curriculum
RSGML	Regional Study Group in Modern Languages
SI/II, etc.	Secondary I/II, etc.
SALT	Scottish Association of Language Teachers
SCCC	Scottish Consultative Committee on the Curriculum
SCCML	Scottish Central Committee for Modern Languages
SCL	Scottish Campaign for Languages
SCOTVEC	Scottish Vocational and Educational Initiative
SEB	Scottish Examinations Board
SED	Scottish Education Department
SNP	Scottish National Party
SOED	Scottish Office Education Department (new name for SED)
S-O-S	Structural Oral Situational pedagogy
TPR	Total Physical Response
U/c	Understand and communicate (Lothian Region's GLAFLL project terminology)

Part 1
Legitimising Innovation

Introduction to Part 1: Legitimate Visions

'The cardinal points of education in a native society such as Tikopia are its continuity in both a temporal and a social sense, its position as an activity of kinsfolk, its practicality – not in the sense of being directed to economic ends, but as arising from actual situations in everyday life – and its non-disciplinary character. A certain subordination to authority is required and is sometimes impressed by forcible and dramatic methods, but these are sporadic and the individual is a fairly free agent to come and go as he likes, to refuse to heed what is being taught him. All this is in direct contrast to a system of education for native children wherever it is carried out under European tutelage. Such consists usually of periodic instruction with segregation, intermitted by intervals of relaxation and rejoining of the normal village life, and imparted not by kinsfolk of the children but by strangers, often from another area, even when non-Europeans. This instruction is given not in connection with actual situations in life as they occur, but in accord with general principles, the utility of which is only vaguely perceived by the pupils. Moreover it is disciplinary, the pupils are under some degree of direct restraint and may even suffer punishment for neglect of appointed tasks.*

The divorce from the reality of the native social life, the staccato rhythm of instruction and the alien methods of restraint undoubtedly are potent factors in retarding the achievement of the aims of so much of what is rather falsely termed 'native education'.

In Tikopia we have an example of a people largely free from European influence, where education is not an imagined preparation for social life but is actually a vital part of it, hinging upon the participation of the child in all ordinary activities from early years, and arising out of the inevitable lacunae in its knowledge when called upon to face practical situations....

Specific spheres in the education of a child are instruction in the manners and moral rules of the society, training in its arts and crafts and imparting *knowledge of traditional lore and ritual formulae. Formal lessons are rarely given in these departments, but advice, explanation and commands tend to cluster around the performance of any activity, or the onset of any social situation.*[1]

The above quotation from Raymond Firth's classic of anthropology, *We, the Tikopia*, suggests that the way in which one educates should reflect the lives of those one purports to be educating. The introduction of European ideas by the missionaries failed in Tikopia, as elsewhere in the Pacific, because they ignored the importance of legitimacy, which in this case had not been conferred by local society. Those who would innovate have to take into account the prevailing conditions in the area in which the innovation is to take place; they have to ensure that those people who have a vested interest in that area are part of the innovation process; they cannot simply rely on their dream, their vision of a better future. Too many excellent ideas end up being jettisoned, or are simply 'one-off' efforts, because of a failure to take this into account.

Dreams and visions are part of the vocabulary of change. In religions, they are used to authenticate new interpretations of existing beliefs; in politics they are meant to reconcile the public to present hardship in the hope of a better future. The 'blessing' of change by the high priests is crucial if change is to become part of the established creed. The visionary is therefore normally dependent on authority for its blessing, unless she or he has either the necessary charisma or the big battalions to mount a campaign. 'Blessing' thus enables the change to become part of the orthodoxy; when the high priests withhold their blessing, it can lead to the formation of a rival sect.

Some people – priests, witch doctors, educationalists, politicians – are not only permitted to have visions that will inspire the rest of society, they are even expected to do so. It is, as it were, in their job remit. They may also have the power to legitimise the vision of humbler people.

In the field of education there is a problem which is more often perceived than discussed: those who have the power have no responsibility; those who have the responsibility have no power. Having a vision is one way by which those without power may seek to get their own way. It is also of course used by those in power to get those with the responsibility to agree to do things that mean more work, less pay, longer hours or similar uncomfortable things, like making a change in their methodology.

The power to 'bless' an innovation belongs with the authorities without whose blessing an innovation is unlikely to spread. Some authorities like to see themselves as the sole instigators and orchestrators of innovation, and woe betide any usurpers or dissidents. This leads to a certain amount of tension, the effects of which may or may not be creative: whereas a small degree of obedience to ground rules is compulsory, in most societies education is a broad church, whose members are not expected all to chant the same creed. Organisations in education are not merely vertical: the Head Teacher is still seen by many, although less often than before, as *primus inter pares*. Even when an innovation is instigated from on high, by government or education authority, there is no automatic guarantee that those responsible will implement it, not even when they make all the proper, expected responses.

This is not just because teachers as a group can be awkward people, dissenters and non-conformists, nor even that teachers of languages are the most awkward of the lot; it is also because there is no shared belief about what precisely education is meant to be doing. Probably at no time more than the present is there greater disagreement about what should be happening in schools. It was all a great deal simpler when what was needed was plenty of docile clerks and some soldiers for the Empire. Legitimacy therefore, is likely to be harder and more difficult to establish in educational circles than in others such as the armed forces where there is common agreement from the most senior general to the lowliest private that the job is about keeping the Queen's peace – even if it means going to war.

Apart from questions of who is in charge or who should be in charge of innovation, account must also be taken of the importance of peers, since in many countries (Germany for instance) differences of rank are non-existent or slight, and the notion that one educated person is as good as another, and certainly as entitled to their own opinion as another, holds sway: colleagues, too, confer legitimacy. Lateral spread therefore has to be taken into account. The high priests of course know this, and the trick is to pass things down in such a way that the lateral spread of the approved doctrine is maximised. Thus there is an emphasis on the importance of 'communicating', 'networking' and 'cascading', and one can see the attraction of databases and modems – and possibly one of reasons why the money can often be found for the technology which enhances the opportunity to do the communicating, networking and so forth. Lateral spread is of course not limited to approved doctrines: too much of it and the authorities may be in for a period of industrial action. Teachers do not always receive with open arms and willing hearts the word from on high.

This part of the book starts off by considering two examples where innovation flourished under a centrally directed initiative. As part of a nationally instigated development within the Scottish context, two very different regions, while profiting from the legitimacy and funding conferred upon them by their association with the 'good and great', took the reins into their own hands and developed projects which were quite at variance with what was originally proposed. The development is described in some detail in Chapters 1, 2 and 3. What the two, superficially very different, projects demonstrate is that teachers themselves do have the power to withhold the legitimisation of doctrines from on high. Given the right support, in this case from their local authorities, teachers can feel sufficiently confident to take off in directions not considered and not necessarily approved of centrally.

From Scotland, attention turns to the opposite end of the globe, at another attempt at innovation from the centre. Australia's much admired and much discussed National Language Policy is likely to be the forerunner of other such policies elsewhere, and Chapter 4 gives a brief outline of the policy and raises some questions. What will be of particular interest there in future will be the way in which national commonwealth policy and local state initiatives interact. Given Australia's federal system and the independent nature of the states, it seems reasonable to speculate that the combination may well make for the kind of healthy disequilibrium conducive to a climate for innovation which was a characteristic of the Scottish Primary Pilot experience. On the other hand, if the politicians have their way, the emphasis on vocational training in economically 'relevant' languages, rather than language education in pedagogically and culturally more accessible languages, may undo much of the progress already made in language learning in Australia.

Chapter 5, 'The Limitations of Policies' suggests that innovation stems from individuals rather than from systems and questions the suitability of the 'top-down' model. It suggests that the 'high priests' from Her Majesty's Inspectorate may not themselves be the best source of visions or indeed for the implementation of the visions of others, although on the other hand they may provide the focus for creative tensions out of which innovations may arise. Local advisory services, which work alongside teachers, appear to be in a far better position to support and inspire innovation. A strong local government can play a fundamental role in the promotion of innovation because it is rooted in the local reality.

Textual note   It is always extremely hard to convey the flavour of life at the chalkface. The written word so often masks what those who work in schools know really matters. Since much is made in this book of the need to take into account the social and cultural realities which most top-down models of reform ignore, an attempt has been made by the inclusion in the text of short, scene-setting vignettes, to replicate the missing evidence of the sights and sounds of classrooms, the buzzing of staffroom chatter, the zany unpredictability of the kids – the very stuff of teaching. These vignettes and other devices of a similar, whimsical nature are indicated in the text *by italics*.

1 Grass-roots Legitimacy: The National Pilot in Modern Languages in the Primary School

This material and the material in the two succeeding chapters deals with the National Pilot in Modern Languages in the Primary School in Scotland. In this chapter is traced some of the background to the Pilot, which illustrates that authority in itself cannot ensure the blanket adoption of the word from on high. In this instance, teachers, backed by their local authorities, withheld their consent to carry out a centralised initiative as determined by the centre, to develop schemes in tune with their own localities.

The four children did not notice the visitor as she peeked round the door of the otherwise empty classroom. Heads bent over the ghetto blaster, they were intent on checking the previous recording.

   'It's not loud enough, we'll have to do it again.'
   'I think Sarah should be the narrator. She says "Walpurgisnacht" the best'.

Next door, some 18 children, all shapes and sizes, were scattered round the room, some at tables, others squatting on the floor, with cards, illustrated books and dice. Somewhere in their midst would be the teacher – yes, that was her, over in the corner, with the little sandy-haired chap and the two smallest girls.

   'What's German for "cake" again, Miss?'
   'Du kannst das auf Deutsch, Kenny. Wie…'
   'Oh, aye … wie sagt man "cake" auf Deutsch?'

The group of four lads, of between eight and 10 years old were arguing over the board game. It looked awfully simple – the numbers from 1 – 100 were written

in childish handwriting, big, on red A3 card, and the boys had been throwing
the dice as they made their way with counters round the board.

'Darf ich mitspielen?' I asked.
'Ja, OK.'
'Wer ist dran?
'Jimmy – Jimmy, es ist ... no, no ... em ... du bist dran ... hier.'

The dice passed to Jimmy.

All you had to do was to keep throwing and the one that was ahead at the end
won. Well, that was an easy game to make – and to understand. There were
other variations, too, involving cards, penalties and the like. The lads seemed to
like it fine as it was.

A witch appeared at the door.

'Miss, wir sind fertig.'

To Begin at the Beginning

It was by the initiative of the then Secretary of State for Scotland, Malcolm Rifkind, that Modern Languages were reintroduced into Scottish Primary schools in 1989.[2] Six secondary schools and their feeder primaries were chosen, each one (coincidentally?) in the constituency of a Scottish Conservative Member of Parliament. Local authorities had earlier been asked by the SOED (Scottish Office Education Department) for a list of schools which might be chosen as part of a pilot scheme to introduce a modern language into the primary school, but their selections were largely ignored. The most blatant example of this was the inclusion in the pilot project of Paisley Grammar School, threatened with closure by the Labour-controlled local authority. It certainly had not been on the authority's list.

The best laid plans

What SOED intended was a controlled and cautious start, bearing in mind the problems associated with the previous attempt at primary languages (though not all the findings of the Burstall[3] report applied to Scotland). Six schools in the first year, another six in the second year, a gradual move towards Primary 6. Start with French and German, Spanish and Italian would come next time.

Anxious not to raise hopes in parents on the one hand, and overload both the primary curriculum and the primary teachers on the other, SOED adopted a policy of *festina lente*, announcing that a field officer would be appointed to coordinate projects and that the pilot would be the subject of properly funded and conducted research to assess implications for its extension. SOED failed to take account of the national mood, however, and the largest authority, Strathclyde, went ahead with its own, much larger, scheme.[4]

Coming as it did just after the much publicised Scottish Campaign for Languages[5] and just in time for 1992 with all of the publicity about the European Economic Community, it was inevitable that many other schools and parents, let alone local authorities, would want to get involved in a scheme which, from early on, was the focus of a good deal of media attention. There was concern on the part of the teachers' unions as well as from primary Head Teachers that however educationally desirable this might be, it would create an extra workload on staff in both sectors. The main teaching union, the EIS (Educational Institute of Scotland), expressed concern and there was, for a while, talk of a boycott.

Of course other countries elsewhere in Europe were thinking in similar terms. The French do it rather differently from the Scots. There the minister announces any new move and it is a *fait accompli*: let there be primary foreign languages – and thus it is. Teachers and inspectors alike describe the situation as chaotic, as everyone rushes in and sometimes, though not always, it works.[6]

Mixed messages

By having delivery provided by the secondary school, the SOED could of course argue that primary teachers were not being asked to do anything extra. This, however, was not strictly speaking the case, as from the beginning it was clear that eventually the teaching would have at some unspecified time to devolve onto the primary teachers, 'as they became more competent'[7]. Moreover, the primary teachers were expected to be part of the language classes – this was not like having visiting PE or music specialists who would take the class on their own. Time would be needed for liaison, for planning and for materials making.

Though taught initially by secondary teachers, the aim was to have the teaching reflect the child-centred methodology of the primary school, not the way things were done in the subject-oriented secondaries. It was evident to those teachers and advisers who attended the introductory meeting held by SOED, that the Modern Languages inspectors themselves had no idea of what a child-centred methodology was: they suggested as suitable material a textbook produced for secondary schools under SOED funding.

Fortunately, a period of time – to be decided by each school on its own – was given for preparation, development of materials and liaison. Some schools, despite the fact that the initial meeting took place in May, started actual teaching between the October holiday and Christmas. Most secondary teachers spent a considerable time in primary class-rooms, getting a feel of the ground and getting to know their new colleagues. Some local authorities granted generous time, giving class cover by supply teachers to enable the teachers from each sector to decide together the kind of programme they wanted. One secondary school, however, went ahead with its plans without a single visit to their feeder primary schools before they began teaching there.

In the course of the first two years of the project, local authorities all over Scotland started up additional schemes of their own, often under pressure from parents excited by the reports in the national press relating to the pilot in other schools. These decisions, while they led to some conflict with the SOED, were in fact taking the national project in the way in which it was ultimately intended to go, if somewhat prematurely in SOED eyes. The problem, seen from the SOED perspective, was that they had no actual mandate to declare primary languages a success in advance of the findings of the research team. Once it had been set up, and after a suitable period of investigation, a national policy decision could be taken in the light of its findings.[8] In 'jumping the gun', the local authorities were responding to enthusiasm generated among their officials, teachers, parents and the general public alike. In effect, there was the 'official' and the 'unofficial' pilot – sometimes in operation within the same school, where it had been decided locally to extend the experience to children in P6.

A key figure

Whatever mistakes SOED made, it made one crucially important decision correctly, certainly in the eyes of those operating the project on the ground. The appointment of Alison Hurrell, Principal Teacher of Modern Languages at Broxburn Academy, as Field Officer for the project ensured that the voices of teachers and local authorities would be heard at SOED. Hurrell's role was an almost impossible one, putting her as it did in the firing line of the discontent of practically everyone involved. Without any executive power to alter things, the role could have become one of merely reporting on progress, absorbing complaints and trying to keep everyone happy.

Hurrell did much more. A committed and talented teacher herself, one of the first in Lothian Region to use the target language as the medium of teaching, she already was a respected figure among her secondary colleagues in the country. Her personal qualities included the ability to relate well to others without compromising her integrity or seeking too much to please, and an invaluable sense of humour and appreciation of the ridiculous, born of her experience of teaching in the rougher areas of Edinburgh. Her years of working with underprivileged children stood her in good stead with the primary teachers, who immediately recognised someone who was at home in the classroom, and whose advice, if sought, would be based on reality, not an idealised world.

Although Hurrell had been actively involved in the writing of *Tour de France*, the coursebook dear to the hearts of HMI, who had lavished considerable sums in its direction, it was not she who put pressure on teachers to use it. On the contrary, she was at pains to support those schools who, while they might not have totally formed plans about how to proceed, wanted to experiment for themselves in the course of the following years.

Hurrell's achievements in the Pilot were considerable, despite increasingly bureaucratic demands and an immense workload, with a great deal of travel involved. This, however, did enable her to be the bearer, to those who wished to hear of them, of tidings from one end of the country to the other. Somehow the SOED never did follow up their original promise to arrange further meetings of the first pilot schools.

In terms of methodology, Hurrell was able to demonstrate by her own behaviour in primary classrooms with the children, that the target language could be used to communicate even with complete beginners and those having severe learning difficulties. While in the classroom, working with the pupils, she used the target languages almost exclusively, even when some of the secondary teachers were using English, leading quietly and unobtrusively by example. She also showed the extent to which a limited language resource could still be used, since she had to operate in some classes in German, not a language she had studied. This was precisely the kind of experience the primary teachers were having, and Hurrell's attempts to speak German persuaded many hesitant and unsure primary teachers to try this themselves.

The 'message' Hurrell conveyed was one of support for teacher initiative. At no time was she seen as the mouthpiece of SOED. It was, as can be imagined, a balancing act. She meant to leave schools feeling the better for her visits, information and advice about work elsewhere were given when sought, not gratuitously offered. Hurrell was thus both information broker for the project and a model from whom teachers could learn.

Although an extremely efficient person, Hurrell never conveyed the idea that efficiency was a goal, or that her time was too precious to 'waste' on what some might consider idle chatter. Her demeanour would best be termed 'non-threatening', her manners in other people's classrooms immaculate.

One of the mistakes believers in systems make is to think that none of this is important. What they fail to see is that the dissemination of information is only effective if the medium if acceptable. Teachers are no different in this respect than other humans. If the messenger is unlikeable, they often reject the message.

Politics

Politicians, both local and national, as has already been seen, played a crucial role in the Primary Pilots. In Scotland supporters of the Labour Party like to say that the Tory government does not have a mandate to govern there, since in the 1993 general election the Conservatives, with 25.7% of the vote, only won 11 of the country's 72 seats.[9] The result of this is that no opportunity is lost for the non-Tory councils to tweak the tail of central government. Education on occasion serves as a convenient battle-ground. The present Conservative government likes to think that by various means it has given more control to the parents and the schools, at the same time ensuring 'quality' by wresting them from the control of the 'bolshie' local authorities. Labour, staunch supporters of local democracy as they see themselves, view these moves as confirmation that what the government intends is a free-for-all, with the wealthy winning out at the expense of the poorer areas. Not one of the schools chosen initially for the National Pilot could be said to be in a deprived area. On the contrary.

In Scotland, the SOED shares with the local authorities the responsibility for the implementation of the policies established by the government of the day. Given that local authorities tend to be Labour controlled, and the government Conservative, there is a certain amount of tension – not altogether a bad thing. The fact that there is a buffer between central government and its arm, Her Majesty's Inspectorate, and those who have to carry out government policy in the schools, means that debate takes place, each side moves some, and it is possible to avoid the worst excesses of either because of this built-in system of checks and balances.

From the point of view of those schools implementing the National Pilot, the fact that there were two institutions involved meant that no one methodology could be imposed. This may be one of the reasons why the pilot has been so fruitful in the area of educational innovation. Had the Inspectorate alone had absolute authority and control, the results would almost certainly have reflected a more conservative approach to curricular and methodological matters. At the same time, since it was the case that the implications of any expansion of the pilot were considerable, in terms both educational and financial, and with memories of the previous ill-fated 'French in the Primary' project, there was an argument for the *festina lente* approach.

2 Doing the Impossible in Dumfries and Galloway

In Dumfries and Galloway Region teachers tackled what seemed an impossible task: how to teach German to primary pupils in the absence of trained German teachers.

Es war einmal ein kleiner Elefant. Der kleine Elefant war sehr traurig. Er hatte eine klitzekleine Nase und er wollte eine große lange Nase haben.[10]

Dumfries and Galloway local education authority was placed in an apparently impossible position by the SOED's selection of Annan Academy and its feeder primaries. No one, it was felt, could have possibly chosen it on rational grounds, and yet, strangely, this apparently ill-favoured decision produced one of the most successful educational outcomes.

Miles to go – and no Teachers

Lovely as the little country lanes around the peaceful town of Annan are in early summer, with the meadowsweet as high as the car roof, they do not lend themselves to the Brands Hatch style of motoring. At any time a tractor can appear round a bend, a covey of young partridge may be taking the air in the middle of the road, or a herd of cows ambling their way to a new field.

Whereas all the other secondary schools selected had only three or four feeder primary schools, Annan Academy had 11, with a distance of 18 miles between Carrutherstown in the north and Springfield in the south. There was also a shortage of staff in the secondary which ruled out the diversion of the secondary teachers to teach part-time in the primaries, as was the initial intention. With some 13 primary 7 (P7) classes, of which seven were composite P6/7 classes, and a primary teaching force in the main devoid of German qualifications, it could not be done according to the original intention. The authority would have to consider something different.

Der kleine Elefant ging zuerst zu der Giraffe.

> *'Guten Tag, kleiner Elefant. Warum bist du so traurig?'*

> *'Ich habe eine klitzekleine Nase und ich möchte eine große lange Nase haben. Kannst du mir helfen?'*

> *'Nein', sagte die Giraffe.*

> *'Geh zu dem Affen!'*

Wer kann hier Deutsch?

Of the 13 class teachers initially involved, three had a university qualification in German, three had 'Higher' German, the remaining seven had mostly studied French at school and were complete beginners in German. This was a start, at any rate.

Despite the unfavourable odds, the decision was taken by the authority to explore the idea of having the primary teachers themselves deliver the German to the pupils, with support. If the project was worth doing, and the authority, to their eternal credit, did not doubt it, an innovative arrangement had to be made. The question remained of how to do this. The way to deal with the problem of the distances could be handled by appointing someone – perhaps as a peripatetic teacher of German, who could go round the classes and give them 'a taste' of German.

This would not fit the bill, because it would lack grass-roots support, since it failed to involve the primary teachers. What was needed was a primary teacher, perhaps one who already had German, to carry out that role. But primary teachers are not easily persuaded out of their schools to move from class to class and teach only one subject. Though those who had some German were prepared to share materials and to help others, this did not mean a wider commitment. The project was only a part of their job – and with the wisdom of having seen scores of projects come and go, the teachers were wary. After all, why should a primary Head Teacher agree to what was effectively, a demotion?

Der kleine Elefant ging zu dem Affen.

> *'Guten Tag, kleiner Elefant. Warum bist du so traurig?'*

'Ich habe eine klitzekleine Nase und ich möchte eine große lange Nase haben. Kannst du mir helfen?'

'Nein', sagte der Affe.

'Geh zu dem Zebra!'

Fortune Favours the Brave

Someone who could lead the project, not just teach classes, was needed – a Tutor Trainer, who as well as a teaching role, would also have responsibility for the production of materials and the ongoing training of the primary teachers. Some concession as to salary could be afforded by the region, say, a senior teacher's pay level. (Since the SOED were paying a Full Time Equivalent salary in any case, all that had to be found would be the extra responsibility payment).

The authority was very lucky. Fortune for once favoured the brave. In response to their advertisement the ideal candidate appeared, a primary specialist, Annelise Swanston, with additional qualifications from her homeland in Denmark as a teacher of foreign languages and art.

There has been a tendency of late to play down personality in the professional field, while playing up the specific job function. It is as if to say that if the candidate is suitably qualified and experienced, the job description and remit correct, performance will follow. Systems, not the personal qualities of any one individual, are what matter most.

Those whose day-to-day job has them in constant contact with others know that this is nonsense. Getting on with people is absolutely essential, especially when there is learning involved. If children find it hard, or sometimes impossible, to learn from a teacher they really hate, adults also cannot work productively at their best when threatened by others in the same area. Hence the appointment of people who enjoy good personal relationships is an essential part of the management of any project involving real, rather than cosmetic, curricular change.

Leadership

Dr Valerie Stewart, in a paper entitled 'Cows, Dogs and Playing Fields' given in New Zealand to the Institute of Personnel Management Conference in 1991,[11] identified 12 characteristics shared by inspiring transformational leaders she had worked with. These were:

(1) They have a divine discontent – things must change.

(2) They hate waste and always look for opportunities to do things better.

(3) They trust their intuition.

(4) They are excited by living with uncertainty.

(5) They have long-term vision.

(6) They are hard-working and expect others to be so too.

(7) They are clear, exciting and urgent communicators.

(8) They are not afraid to surround themselves with able colleagues and subordinates.

(9) They use status where necessary, but do not feel the need to pull rank.

(10) They never stop learning.

(11) They are clear about their values.

(12) They are loved.

As I said, Dumfries and Galloway struck it lucky. Where they would have been glad simply to have found someone qualified, they got a leader.[12]

Der kleine Elefant ging zu dem Zebra.

'Guten Tag, kleiner Elefant. Warum bist du so traurig?'

'Ich habe eine klitzekleine Nase und ich möchte eine große lange Nase haben. Kannst du mir helfen?'

'Nein', sagte das Zebra.

'Geh zu dem Löwen'

Needed: a visionary

Leaders cannot function in a vacuum. They require backing and support from those at the top of the enterprise, whatever its nature, in education as much as in business. To return to Dr Valerie Stewart:

'Leaders, however, will have a difficult time in organisations that do not have a visionary and exciting person at or near the top of the enterprise, because it is from the top that the values, vision and authority must emerge. Organisations must examine their criteria for picking top executives and ensure that leadership is a quality existing in large measure along with the more traditional abilities previously sought'.[13]

From a teacher's perspective, for 'top of the enterprise', read 'adviser' – for the most part, the teacher's sole contact with the education authority. Crucial to the way the project developed was the local secondary Adviser, Martin Prowse, from whom the 'values, vision and authority' were initially to come. By appointment a General Adviser, secondary, he was in fact a Modern Languages specialist.

Vision

The project, as Prowse envisaged, was to go far beyond the teaching of bits and pieces of the German language. It was to have German integrated into the curriculum in such a way that it could naturally be part of any of the normal activities of the school day – PE, art, music, language, science or number work.

It was characteristic that one of the first In-Service training experiences offered to the primary teachers was conducted on the theme of 'Drama in language teaching' by the group 'Pilgrims'. The tone was set for something rather different and rather ambitious.

Values

Some people value the completion of a task or job above getting on with others. They come busily into one's classroom, executive briefcase or filofax in hand and look for something to measure or record. An example of this occurred one day as I visited one of the schools in the Annan area in which someone 'important' was engaged in evaluating something in the classroom in which I found myself. He was too busy to greet a newcomer (in any case, he had ignored the class teacher and pupils), and sat at the back of the room, writing in a big black book, symbol of authority, while the pupils and the other adults engaged, with considerable enthusiasm in a lion hunt, choreographed by the Tutor Trainer. Not once did he enquire of one of us what was taking place.

'Just look at him,' the teacher whispered, 'he looks up now and then and kind of licks his lips – like a big fat toad.'

It was clear what he regarded as important. In total contrast was the assessment by the teachers of the contribution of Prowse to how they felt about the project. Mention was made, time and again, of how good it was to have him visit the school. 'What excellent manners, I wish they were all like that', remarked one teacher nostalgically.

Some people and institutions value power, above all else, and in education one way of exerting it is to demand ever-increasing communication by paper. The amount of form-filling generated on account of the Pilot Project by the SOED was one way of letting teachers know who was in charge. The Advisory Services, both in Dumfries and Galloway and in Lothian, functioned very differently, and generated hardly any paperwork for teachers.

One can only give credit to employers who realise the value of having, in any area of teacher development work, people whose human virtues make them welcome, people who know how to behave on someone else's turf, people who trust the competence of others by the way in which they behave, and do not waste their time asserting their 'authority' by the imposition of meaningless paper tasks.

Organising informally

Der kleine Elefant ging zu dem Löwen.

'Guten Tag, kleiner Elefant. Warum bist du so traurig?'

'Ich habe eine klitzekleine Nase und ich möchte eine große lange Nase haben. Kannst du mir helfen?'

'Nein', sagte der Löwe.

'Geh zu dem Krokodil.'

One of the characteristics of informal organisations to which we will return later is that documentation is likely to be light, since those involved, sharing a common task and common aspirations, communicate easily and readily. In the early days of the Dumfries and Galloway project there was in fact very little by way of documentation. This apparent shortcoming was in the course of time amended, no doubt due to the imminent visits of teams of researchers and the mass of documentation required by the SOED. But there is really very little requirement for much documentation within a project where those who are carrying out the work are the team who are themselves developing the project. This was no 'curriculum package' handed down complete from above. The frequent meetings initially, both formal and informal between directorate and advisers, advisers secondary and primary, as well as between all these and school Head Teachers and teachers, meant that liaison between those making policy decisions and those responsible for the planning and implementation related to the policies was conducted without fuss. Moreover, the unique role and her interpretation of this role by the Tutor Trainer, with feet as it were in both camps, made for effective leadership.

Essential to an understanding of the project is the size of the area, the fact that people tend to know each other well, despite the distances between their schools, the fact that those in the education authority are known also, as former colleagues, or people 'you might meet in the pub'. There is not, as elsewhere, a sense of distance between the 'officials' and the teachers, This is no faceless bureaucracy – and for the most part teachers felt no hesitation in expressing their opinions and feelings directly to those they perceived as being 'in charge' – i.e. the advisers and members of the directorate. The project, though part of the National Pilot, was clearly felt to be a local one. Primary education in Dumfries and Galloway's small country schools reflect what Firth described of pre-missionary education in Tikopia: it is

> not an imagined preparation for social life but is actually a vital part of it, hinging upon the participation of the child in all ordinary activities from early years, and arising out of the inevitable lacunae in its knowledge when called upon to face practical situations....

The sense that all were involved in breaking new ground and that no one person held all the answers, allowed for a sharing of experience that, unlike much In-Service teacher training, was truly needs-related. Moreover, the avoidance of dogma about methodology meant that no one need be hamstrung with a formulaic approach. Indeed, the Adviser and Tutor Trainer were keen to explore and encourage a whole variety of approaches, while providing at the same time a degree of support for the less confident teachers.

The sharing of experiences, as well as of materials, became part of the structure of the project. The 'German Club' released teachers every two weeks in school time for two hours' training by the Tutor Trainer. The 'Club' provided much more than a language training opportunity by allowing for the teachers to consult and support each other, as well as for the planning and distribution of materials prepared by the Tutor Trainer in consultation with the teachers.

It took place in the secondary school, which had allocated a spare classroom to the primary project. This had happened somewhat by chance, the original plan having been for the Tutor Trainer to be situated in a primary school. As it happened, it was extremely useful that the base was in Annan Academy. It allowed the secondary teachers to see the materials that were being produced, to talk to primary colleagues during their visits, and meant that the pupils in the secondary were also still in touch with the Tutor Trainer.

The room took on the appearance of a primary classroom, with a permanent display of the books and materials at one end, groups of chairs and tables, posters and children's work on the walls. It was home to the project, its library, its showcase, its nerve-centre, a counselling service for weary teachers, a coffee bar and an office.

Projects, whatever their nature, need a team-spirit and a sense of identity. Outsiders have to accommodate to and fit in with the team norms and goals. It can be in little as well as big things. For instance, if the 'team' holds it important to relax over coffee and cakes, there is no point in rushing for the list of important 'Things to do'. Similarly, if the team likes to work to an agenda in the shape of a formal meeting, this also requires similar adaptation and respect. In some cultures, business is only conducted after due attention has been paid to the 'inner person'. In teacher training in Pacific Islands, the demands of 'morning tea' (a sumptuous repast of gargantuan proportions) take precedence over any and all other business. But all meetings, however small, start and end with a prayer. To ignore the importance of these rituals would be to risk losing legitimacy in the eyes of the participants. In a sense, all these activities can be seen as a kind of blessing, without which there will be no proceedings.

Often the 'coffee and cakes' provide not only the necessary social setting for discussion, they also serve as the vehicle for the emergence of things regarded as highly important that would otherwise not see the light of day. Whatever it is that gives the sense of team identity needs to be understood by outsiders and given its place.

Der kleine Elefant ging zu dem Krokodil.

'Guten Tag, kleiner Elefant. Warum bist du so traurig?'

'Ich habe eine klitzekleine Nase und ich möchte eine große lange Nase haben. Kannst du mir helfen?'

'Ja', sagte das Krokodil.

Fitting in

An educational innovation may arise from a perceived need in response to a purely local situation; it may also arise, as in this case, in response to what are perceived as national needs. In either case, if an innovation is to be accepted by pupils and parents, not to mention teachers, it has to find a way of accommodating to and blending in with the existing scene.

The 'fit' in terms of the learning environment was very apparent in Dumfries and Galloway. These were country children, very unsophisticated and very 'young' in comparison with pupils in an inner city or in a well-off middle class suburb like Balerno, the next example. Many of the parents were farm workers; the countryside, animals, the weather and the seasons mattered in their lives. The activities and materials were such that undoubtedly appealed to their interests and ages. There were things to handle, such as card and board games which were very popular, movement games to music, lots of simple songs and dances.

In order to demonstrate a way in which German could be integrated into the curriculum, the Tutor Trainer would base her lessons and the materials to be used in her absence, on a unit of work that was common to the curriculum in all schools. All children, and many adults, love a good story, but this requires a good command of the language, as well a the knack of putting it over well. Story-telling became almost the signature of the project. It 'fitted' not only the nature of the children and the area, but also the personality of the Tutor Trainer, who developed the stories, with actions for the children to follow, based loosely on a topic the children would be doing with their class teacher. Work sheets, reading materials, card games and cassettes would also be given to the teacher, so that pupils could, in the course of 'project work' carry on with their German if they or the teacher so chose. But the story itself was the springboard to learning. Even two years later, secondary pupils could recall, word for word, stories encountered in primary – and tell them using all the gestures and sound effects.

Some teachers worked by setting aside particular periods for German, others allowed pupils to select for themselves when to use the materials. To encourage the use of books, picture dictionaries and picture books were much in evidence – very much the kind of book one sees in large bookstores which are popular as Christmas or birthday presents. One could not help but note the family atmosphere in these small village schools, where children of a variety of ages were all learning in the same class with the same teacher. Children could help themselves to these books in most classrooms and made free use of them, sometimes to copy drawings and words, sometimes simply to leaf through, sometimes to check up on a particular word, often encouraged by the teacher. The smaller children in these composite classes would sometimes be found sprawling on the floor, a book open in front of them, quietly engrossed. While to secondary teachers this apparent free-for-all might seem distressingly informal and unstructured, research into literacy suggests that simply the provision of plenty of stimulating materials, on its own, can be sufficient to improve reading skills.

'Good learners' equals 'good teachers'

Und das Krokodil öffnete seinen großen Mund, und nahm die Nase des Elefants zwischen seine scharfe Zähne. Und es zog, und es zog, und es zog ...

Projects in education come and go, and while some have a lasting impact, many have only a transitory effect. Prabhu,[14] the leader of the Bangalore project described later in Part 2, identifies what he calls the teacher's 'pedagogic perception' as the most crucial element underlying real, as opposed to purely cosmetic, changes in a teacher's behaviour. Perhaps the most significant success of the Dumfries and Galloway project was that for a substantial number of the region's teachers, real, as opposed to cosmetic, changes did in fact take place.

By encouraging the development of a methodology peculiar to the project, based on that of the primary school, not that of conventional modern languages pedagogy as originally envisaged by SOED, the project enabled teachers to work out for themselves a way of operating in the classroom and gave them the chance to gain some understanding of this operation. In other words, teacher development was driven by their own classroom experience.

Thus teachers with prior experience of how modern languages had been taught to them were able to develop a fresh perception of second language teaching and learning born from their new experience as learner/teachers. Some commented that they were glad that they were not in fact using the French which they had learnt at school or university. Learning German at the same time as learning the techniques for teaching it in quite a different way meant that they did not bring unsuitable habits copied from a previous experience into their classrooms.

Some of the following quotes from primary teachers show to what extent they had internalised a way of thinking about language and language learning that many language specialists would regard as revolutionary.

- 'German should not be something they should think too much about but something they should be doing.'
- 'I set high standards and give credit for what they are able to do. They'll be able to do what they want to do – there's nothing too difficult.'
- 'The children are so enthusiastic about learning German that they wouldn't mind which or how many school activities are tied to German.'
- 'They just love listening to stories in German and I often hear them quoting from them among themselves – and doing the actions along with the story.'
- 'This is not meant to be a structured language course – the children are learning the language naturally because they are doing things in it.'
- 'I try to talk German all the time because if they see me trying, they'll try too.'
- 'I use German in PE, drama, Art, music and maths – I slide what I know into those areas already but would like to slot in a lot more.'
- 'Baking and cooking, prayers, playground language – I see opportunities for linking German with most aspects of school life.'

Wherever the teachers had a relaxed attitude to the learning of German, the pupils had too and were totally unworried by visitors speaking to them in German. Only in classrooms where German seemed to have become a formal 'lesson', where it mimicked a secondary class, was it possible to detect some anxieties – and these seemed to stem from the teacher's own worries about 'getting them ready for the secondary'.

Interestingly, from classroom observation, some of those teachers who knew no German at the start of the project sometimes seemed more inclined to use their limited German with their pupils than those who had formal qualifications in the subject. It would seem that along with the qualification had gone the attitudes towards foreign language learning, and perhaps German, as an elitist and 'difficult' language in particular, that led to worries about gender, agreements and verbs. Those new to the language, whose experience had been mostly through contact with and teaching by the Tutor Trainer, had picked up her own relaxed attitude to language learning and to error in particular. Perhaps because primary teachers in Scotland see themselves first and foremost as teachers of children, rather than of subjects and syllabuses meant that learning German was seen as no harder than learning anything else. The fact that the pupils made errors in German was, after all, to be expected – they made errors in all the other aspects of the formal curriculum as well!

Research in Canada into the 'good' language learner[15] by H.H. Stern, which understandably seems to crop up in most books about language teaching and learning, indicates the following characteristics of the good learner.

Positive strategies:

(1)   A personal learning style or positive learning strategies.

(2)   An active approach to the learning task.

(3)   A tolerant and outgoing approach to the target language and its speakers.

(4)   Technical know-how about how to tackle a language.

(5)   A methodological flexible approach, developing the new language into an ordered system and constantly revising this system.

(6)   Constantly searching for meaning.

(7)   Willingness to practice.

(8)   Willingness to use the language in real communication.

(9)   Self-monitoring and critical sensitivity to language use.

(10) Development of the L2 more and more as a separate reference system and learning to think in it.

Personality traits:

(a) An element of insight and self-awareness.

(b) Frustration tolerance.

(c) A low level of anxiety (self-reliance).

(d) A high level of achievement and motivation (perfectionism, goal consciousness).

(e) A social (integrative) orientation.

(f) Task orientation (professionalism, technical know-how).

(g) Cognitive flexibility (adaptability, lack of rigidity).

In this project there were two groups of language learners: some of the teachers, all of the pupils. While no specific research into this aspect of the project was done, observation of classrooms over a prolonged period tended to suggest that the presence of a teacher who was a 'good learner' seemed to produce well-motivated pupils who used the language themselves unselfconsciously.

Und der kleine Elefant hatte jetzt eine wunderschöne, große lange Nase.

3 Integrating Times Three in Lothian

In the suburbs of Edinburgh the local secondary school, together with its three feeder primaries decided to work out ways of providing a language learning experience in tune with the very different backgrounds of each school, which would enable the pupils, despite differences of lesson content, to come together later in secondary with learning experiences in common.

The project as conceived by the teachers at Balerno High School and its three feeder primaries of Ratho, Kirknewton and Dean Park, had many features in common with the Dumfries and Galloway experience. Here, too, the aim was to make the project fit into the primary school curriculum, to make decisions together, primary and secondary teachers, about the content of the teaching, and to link what was done in languages to the ways and experiences of the pupils which differed quite markedly from school to school.

The two uniformed moppets with matching ponytails approached the visitors.

  'Good morning. Can we help you?'

The two secondary teachers asked to see the Head Teacher.

  'This way, please.'

The teachers could see a great future for this pair in the hospitality industry. The entrance was a showcase to the high standards of the pupils' work. Only the very best for Dean Park Primary.

                              * * * * * *

The wind blew the umbrella inside out and both teachers were soaking as they arrived in Ratho Primary. No one was to be seen as they entered. No one ever seemed to answer the phone either. In this school it was 'all hands on deck'. They headed towards the maximum noise. The school was open-plan, so there was a fair amount of it. A tiny child rushed towards them, pursued by a teacher. They caught the infant who seemed bent on its own devices and watched as the teacher cajoled it back into the class. The P7 class was waiting.

> *'You the French teachers?'*
> *'Are youse from the secondary?'*
> *'Parlez-vous français?'*
> *Clearly there was no lack of confidence here.*

          * * * * * *

Leaves blew around the playground. The school clock showed 10:05. It was early afternoon. The head was seeing to some matter involving the boys' toilets, so the secondary teacher headed towards the classrooms. Twenty small heads swivelled round.

> *'Bonjour', she said. They looked aghast.*

From next door came the strains of:

> *Ye cannae shuv yer grannie aff a bus*
> *Ye cannae shuv yer grannie aff a bus*
> *Ye cannae shuv yer grannie*
> *For she's yer mammie's mammie*
> *Ye cannae shuv yer grannie aff a bus...*
> *Ye can shuv yer ither grannie aff a bus!*

It was easy for the teachers to see how the Ratho and Kirknewton children would be swamped when they came to secondary. Outnumbered, undersized in comparison to the sleek suburbanites; country cousins – no wonder there were problems when these groups arrived together at the High School, fresh from their very different primary experiences.

What the secondary teachers had to do, in a very short space of time, was to learn enough about the children, the teachers and how they operated, to produce a languages programme that would reflect these very different realities. More importantly, they had to establish a positive and fruitful relationship with the primary teachers, whom they had so far met only occasionally. Tentatively the teachers started visiting the primary schools during normal classes to 'get the feel of things'.

It was clear from the start that what would work really well in one primary school would be out of place in another. Attitudes, expectations, experiences, levels of literacy, range of vocabulary – on each and every criterion, including the style of the class teacher with whom they would soon have to work, the schools could not have offered greater contrasts. The decision was made to customise all methodology and materials to the needs of the individual schools. Fortunately, given the excellent reprographic facilities of the High School and Lothian Region's help with the mass-production of 'home-made' cassettes, there was no real problem with the technical job of customising materials for the different schools and classes.

Support

Assuming the will and the ability of the teaching force to 'do the job', there are two essentials for any educational innovation – time and money. The project at Balerno was exceedingly fortunate in these respects. Lothian Region's directorate, as well as Adviser Peter Wheeldon, took a first-hand interest in the project, attended meetings of teachers at the schools, freed teachers from both sectors to work together, and provided the framework of support that offered the maximum freedom for innovation. The management plan, as designed by Wheeldon, had the pupils and teachers at the centre – the roles of the education authority, advisorate, the Head Teachers were clear – all these were focused on what management books call 'optimising the human resources' – in this case the actual teachers.

A few key meetings laid down the guidelines. Agenda, minutes, discussion papers were prepared and disseminated in advance. Secretarial help from the secondary school ensured that everything was distributed to all on the mailing list. As befits something run from Lothian's showpiece school, the approach was businesslike, efficient. Meetings were addressed 'through the chair'.

Essentially though, this differed little from the relaxed, one might say 'laid back' ways of Dumfries and Galloway. While the superficial differences exaggerated the different natures of the places, the actual structures mirrored how things were done in each area. The formality and paperwork involved in the Lothian scheme gave status and legitimacy to the project, and underlined the official backing it would receive from the region. In Dumfries and Galloway, the same message as to support and intent could be passed in an informal way that was equally reassuring to those taking part. The needs of the teaching team in both areas were seen as paramount.

These were considerable. The SOED, who vetted all the materials the schools wanted for the project, had to be persuaded of the need for listening equipment, hundreds of blank audio cassettes, masses of dictionaries and a large duplicating budget rather than the requisition of class sets of the 'approved' coursebook. Agreement was slow in coming and it was important that those in the directorate who were responsible for passing on requisition requests understood why such things were needed. The fact that the Divisional Education Officer in charge of Primary Education, Jim Morrison, had made a point of attending the early meetings of the Primary Steering Committee and had familiarised himself with the intentions of the group, meant that he, at least, needed no persuading.

Finding a way in

There were two essential things for the teachers to learn. One was of a social nature: how to work in harmony, two teachers in one class; the other was methodological: how to reach a stage where the teachers of French could use the language to teach something other than the language.

Roles and Relationships

In their efforts at finding answers to the second question, the teachers arrived at a way of working together, two teachers to one classroom. Role definition was to be the key to a harmonious approach. The classroom and class 'belonged' to the primary teacher. The secondary teacher could have ended up like any visiting specialist, of music, say, or physical education, teaching something quite separate from the normal work of the class which the primary teachers would not expect ever to have to do themselves. The intention was, however, that the primary teachers would also share in the teaching of French. For this to happen, there had to be a rough allocation of roles and responsibilities. Below is an approximation of what emerged over the first 10 weeks which were given over entirely to planning:

Primary teachers responsible for:	Secondary teachers responsible for:
Classroom organisation	Materials preparation
Decoration: posters, artwork, handcrafts	Foreign assistant
Checking on work done etc	'Dynamics' of lesson
Reminders – notices to class	
Commands generally	
Setting up the lesson	

Individual learning problems
Monitoring/evaluation

Joint responsibilities
classroom harmony
creating a stress-free atmosphere
building a cooperative working pattern together
lesson content
one-off disciplining
planning
identifying problems
relationships with pupils

In addition to the above, the Principal Teacher of Modern Languages in the secondary school had overall responsibility for the running of the project.

By working together on planning and implementation proposals outside the classroom, both sets of teachers, primary and secondary, arrived at a *modus operandi* for the classroom that was to make for harmony. The meetings to prepare the materials, the sharing of experiences, the sheer amount to be learnt took several weeks. Lothian Region generously gave class cover for the primary teachers, while the SOED had already provided an FTE (Full Time Equivalent) to enable the secondary teachers to teach the additional classes. For the first three months, no actual teaching was done at all, while detailed proposals were worked out and materials made.

The integrated day

The primary school was seen straight away by the secondary teachers as the ideal place to attempt an 'immersion' approach. Having the pupils all together with the one teacher in the one room, with few timetabling constraints, means that language learning can spread across all curricular areas. Primary pupils are accustomed to an activity-based style of learning within an integrated day, in which artificial subject boundaries disappear so that maths, science, creative writing, art work and the social sciences can merge under one topic heading. The way of learning in this respect mirrors closely the way children learn naturally. It is task-based, and it can be seen as another version of the Tikopia model 'arising from actual situations in everyday life'. In such an environment the 'immersion' approach would be in harmony with existing experience.

How primary teachers organised their work was a revelation to the secondary teachers. How the secondary teachers viewed language learning was equally a revelation to the primary teachers, who had experienced a very different kind of approach.[16] At first, it was hard to grasp exactly what the 'integrated day' meant for foreign language teaching. The secondary teachers studied teaching plans, and saw how, for example, at Dean Park, the topic of 'Shelter' allowed for a whole host of different activities covering all formal subjects. To give a few examples:

SHELTER

How people live

my room	maths, creative writing, art
using space	maths
housing	geography, maths
long ago	history
other lands	geography
heating	science
homelessness	social science, drama

How animals live

habitats	nature study, zoology
keeping warm	biology
animal families	biology

Activities:
a zoo visit with illustrated talk, note-taking
drama simulation on the theme of homelessness
art-work – a street 'frieze'
drawing a plan of 'my bedroom'
making a model house/village

The above is a simplification of an actual plan used. Individual teachers tended to add their own favourite items to such a theme. What each class did would vary, and not all classes did the same themes. Under 'Shelter', for instance, one class eventually tackled a unit about the Norman Conquest, 'fought' the Battle of Hastings and made model Saxon and Norman houses to see for themselves the changes the Normans effected.

Teachers could see how pupils with an *existing* knowledge of French could deal with some of the 'Shelter' topics *in* French. The problem was, what areas could be used to start pupils off learning French. Ideally what was wanted was something that allowed concrete referents and plenty of activity so that all pupils could contribute. For one class it was decided to start with animals and their habitats. The following games[17] were used at the beginning, as an introduction to French through the medium of French, in order to develop a confident attitude to the language:[18]

Games	movement games:	grab a group
		the circle game
		find your animal family
	card games:	pelmanism
		happy families
	miming games:	animals and their sounds
	guessing games:	which animal am I miming
	Kim's game:	with animals
	word games:	crosswords, puzzles

As a whole class activity, a visit to the zoo was prepared for and carried out with a question sheet in French, accompanied by the French Conversation Assistant, Véronique Longbottom.[19] Edinburgh Zoo, having been briefed, was keen to cooperate.

Inspiring the Pedagogical Approach

The inspiration for the immersion approach was the work the PT had seen on a study tour of Canada and the USA some 10 years previously. As a result of long-term ongoing research in Canada, much information has come to light to enable teachers to learn from experiences there. Several important notions have emerged from the Canadian experience. Firstly, about the need for context in the learning of a foreign language; allied to this is the need for concrete referents; it was later perceived that while pupils in immersion schools had a near native-speaker level of understanding of the language, there was not a correspondingly high achievement in the productive skills. Attention had to be paid to what Swain calls 'comprehensible output' by the learners, in terms of speech and writing, to which an activity-based methodology[20] seems to provide one answer.

Lowering the affective filter: using games and TPR

Virtually every lesson started with movement – games, TPR (Total

Physical Response) techniques, sometimes in the gym, sometimes in the class, even just sitting at a desk. TPR was not used 'classically' as conceived by Asher *et al.*,[21] in order to actually *teach* the language, but as a warm-up activity to get pupils to the point where they reacted automatically to the language. It also allowed the teachers to see how far pupils could go with structures of the language that might be needed later.

For example, TPR would begin with simple commands, such as 'avancez!' 'reculez!', 'retournez-vous!'. The teacher would do the action, the pupils would copy as a class, then as individuals or groups. Commands might then involve parts of the body: 'levez la main droite' and particular groups: 'les filles aux cheveux blonds – touchez le pied avec la main gauche', and 'si vous avez les cheveux blonds, levez la main droite'.

A not-so-simple fact

Because teachers wanted to integrate French with the normal content of the primary curriculum, there was an immediate need for extremely rapid progress in decoding, both to motivate pupils so that French seemed 'easy', and to enable them to follow confidently enough a variety of different topics, using what they had learnt in one context in another, different context.[22]

The simple fact is that French is a very easy language to follow given two factors:

(1) A good understanding of English words of Latin origin.

(2) That the learner is only required to read it.

This 'simple fact' is of course totally eroded by the fact that the sound system makes French totally incomprehensible to the average British child. It was therefore decided to attempt a 'code-breaking' approach to listening, by giving pupils some rules against which to test their hypotheses about the meanings of what they were hearing.

To help the pupils learn to identify the different sounds of French, sound charts were developed by Brigitta Murray, one of the secondary teachers on the project, showing how to link the French sound to the English sound. The ending -tion, for instance, is not easily recognised by the beginner's ear, but once it has been, it vastly increases the ability to process.

Posters[23] were made and stuck on the classroom wall as and when new words were encountered. The primary teacher would 'collect' those which had caused difficulties, and write them quickly in capitals. They would be on the wall before the end of the lesson. Words like 'problème', 'difficile', 'question' were essential for the identification of difficulties encountered by the pupils. Similarly a few key words and set phrases which the teachers needed regularly were highlighted, illustrated and put on the wall: 'compris?', 'tu as compris?', 'concentration', 'nécessaire'.

Selection of language

The workbooks and worksheets were written in French, using a great many words similar to English which helped reduce the difficulty level of the texts. Consider the following, part of the 'Shelter' topic, which used the history of the Norman Conquest to explain differences in house construction in England after the invasion:

> Guillaume a préparé une invasion. Il a assemblé une flotte avec une énorme quantité de bateaux. Il a assemblé une immense armée. L'armée s'est embarqué pour l'Angleterre.

Even without a dictionary, a learner already familiar with the story is likely to understand the gist of the paragraph.

Lowering the lexical bar[24]

Those who survived the teaching of Latin will recall the promise 'it will improve your English'. French, it was found, can serve the same purpose. Where words were used which were identical to English words which the pupils did not understand, the problem of the 'lexical bar' became explicit for the primary teacher, who would make a point of using the same word or words as a basis for English language work later in the day. Learning *about* language addressed a need which the pupils had already felt for themselves.

An eclectic approach

Recent work on learning styles has emphasised the way in which individuals differ, some benefiting from a kinaesthetic approach, some from a visual, some from an aural approach and so on. Since it is proba-bly not feasible to test a class for their preferred learning styles, it makes sense to offer a wide variety of approaches so that those who find it easier to learn by one method have the chance to do so. Teachers could keep track of who had done what through 'activities sheets' on which each pupil ticked off work done.

From what has been written already about the methodology used, it will be realised that teachers had not followed the 'acquisition only' path made famous by Krashen and others. There was a tendency to feel that it would be helpful if certain language could be 'acquired' by the pupils sooner rather than later, if certain skills could be learnt. There were deliberate attempts to identify and teach those skills which would help decoding processes. A series of pedagogical decisions had to be taken from minute to minute within the classroom: whatever worked to convey meaning would be used, as long as that did not entail the use of English. The teachers had already agreed that one of the principal tasks of the primary teachers was to put themselves in the place of the pupils and let the secondary teachers know what was not clear, or who was having particular problems.

Materials

Cassettes

Each pupil had his or her own homework cassette containing the text of the listening and pronunciation exercises in the customised class workbooks. There was also a self-access class cassette library which could be used individually or in a group using a listening centre with six headsets. Some of these were 'learning' cassettes, teaching the alphabet, for example, others were for pronunciation, others were songs and rhymes, yet others were to help with decoding activities – with tasks such as 'find the odd word out' and 'listen and do'.

Customised workbooks and topic related materials

Pupils had their own workbooks, almost exclusively written in French, individually designed for each class, with the cover chosen by competition among the pupils. Materials at a variety of difficulty levels, colour coded on card, were made to accompany the integrated project work according to the choice of each primary class teacher. No particular piece of work had to be 'covered' by every pupil.

Dictionaries

Learning how to learn was an important feature of the work, hence all pupils had dictionaries, and work was done regularly in short, intense, concentrated bursts, with the whole class or with groups and individuals, on how to make the best use of them, both for decoding and encoding[25].

Grammar by dictionary

An ambitious technique was the use of dictionaries to identify parts of irregular verbs which would appear from time to time in texts they were reading: to take the example of 'ira' – future tense of 'aller', this cannot be found in the pupils' small dictionary – what it says is 'voir aller'. Pupils were taught as follows:

'voir' means you look at the verb table at the back to find 'aller'
look for 'ira' – it will be in a numbered column
look for the key to the numbers at the front of the verb list that will tell you the tense

Clearly not all pupils could make use of this information, but those who could made considerable progress. Several pupils started to write in French of their own accord, using the technique in reverse. Peer-tutoring happened automatically in Dean Park – once a few pupils could do this with confidence, they were only too keen to 'teach' their friends.

A spin-off – science through French

The class teacher and the Head Teacher in Kirknewton Primary had been very concerned about the introduction of French into the curriculum, taking up as it did 160 minutes of class time a week. Knowing the problems that the pupils were likely to have in the High School, where the Dean Park pupils predominate and often cause less confident pupils to feel unsuccessful, they were particularly anxious that pupils should not miss out on science teaching as a result of so much time being given over to a language. In order to solve this problem, the teachers decided to attempt to teach the normal science unit through French.

It was an act of faith, bearing in mind that most authorities on the subject suggest that learners need a great deal more exposure to French than in the case of the Kirknewton pupils, if they are actually to learn something new *through* French.[26] The teachers had to ensure that the scientific concepts were being properly covered. Immersion in its 'pure' form was sacrificed initially, since the class teacher did, quite often to begin with, though decreasingly, use English[27] to check the children's understanding of the science, in particular with the slower learners.

Science as such, however, was only taught during the French period and not at any other time.

Without any objective research into the work, all one has to go on is the personal judgement of the primary teacher, who had taught this science unit for some years to her P7 classes. It was her belief that this class had learnt more about science than any previous class, and that they had done so precisely because they had been concentrating throughout on meaning. There was also some evidence that they had learnt a considerable amount of French[28].

4 Looking Around: Innovating Policies from Australia

The Australian ALL (Australian Language Learning) Project is an example of how top-down reforms can accommodate genuine teacher involvement and innovation. The National Policy on Languages further demonstrates the country's commitment to improving the status of languages and investment in language education. It remains to be seen whether economic or educational priorities will determine future directions.

Those people who have an interest in language policy have been following developments in Australia, where more than a decade of work on various aspects of language teaching and learning has resulted in the formulation of a National Policy on Languages (NPL[29]). In adopting the Policy, Australia is addressing problems experienced by many other countries:

- the demands of a multilingual, multicultural society;
- the ensuing need for national unity;
- its own domestic, economic, educational and social needs as well as the needs of its inhabitants for educational, economic, political, technological and social development within a multilingual society.

In order for Australia to progress, it was felt that it had to address the educational problems faced by many of its population. Among these are problems of illiteracy and poor command of English, both within the English-speaking community and the immigrant and Aboriginal populations; the lack of second-language skills of the English-speaking population; the imminent loss of the remaining heritage languages; the lack of sufficient language support services, including interpreting and translating, libraries and language testing; the lack of sufficient emphasis within the existing language provision of practical communication skills.[30]

The Policy aims to support:

(1) Improved English for all: English is the national official language, and provision is made for support for ESL (English as a Second Language) programmes for adults as well as for children.

(2) Aboriginal languages and those of the Torres Straight Islanders: a significant change of heart has taken place within the country with respect to the importance placed on these heritage languages. The loss of about 250 languages over two centuries has left Australia with only some 20 indigenous languages likely to survive the end of this century. Urgent work is taking place in preserving these for the future.

(3) Expansion of the provision of Languages Other Than English (LOTE): This involves both the provision of a first foreign language for speakers of English and the maintenance of the mother tongue for those of a non-English-speaking background.

The Commonwealth Government has backed its Policy with considerable funds and set up a network of institutions all over the country to service and support its implementation. Approximately $94 million was allocated between 1987–88 and 1990–91. Among other measures, the government set up the Languages Institute of Australia under Jo Lo Bianco, author of the original report, whom I met in the course of a visit to Australia in 1992. The remit of the Institute is 'To contribute to improving the quality and relevance of language education in keeping with the goals and principles of the NPL and Australia's social, economic and cultural needs.' This includes the provision of professional development activities for teachers, the creation of a database/clearing house on language education issues and the dissemination of information from these, research to improve practice in language education and the provision of advisory and consultancy services to government and other agencies on language issues. It is also responsible for the provision of a language testing service, for the measurement of language proficiency and the organisation of special purpose vocational language teaching, both of these on a cost-recovery basis.

Large sums of money have gone to Research and Development programmes on Language and Society ($150,000 to Monash University), Language Acquisition Research Centre ($150,000 to Sydney University, and Language and Technology ($100,000 to the University of Queensland).

The government also established in 1988 the Australian Advisory Council on Languages and Multicultural Education (AACLAME), an advisory body whose role is to monitor the effectiveness of the NPL and to act as a forum to discuss national needs and priorities. AACLAME plays a key role in the dissemination of information through publications, in particular of VOX, a journal of extremely high quality, distributed free of charge biannually.

A Spin-off

One of the issues I discussed with Lo Bianco was bilingual education, and in particular the problem of 'code-switching' which bedevils much of language learning.[31] Australia has conducted a great deal of research in the Pacific on English medium education, and on the problems experienced by pupils having to learn a new subject at the same time as learning a new, sometimes even a third, language. One innovative scheme initiated in Western Samoa bears a mention in this respect.

The project which Lo Bianco described[32] was the use of trainee teachers to alert classroom teachers to what they were in fact doing in the course of their lessons. The system is extremely simple. It consists, after some initial consultation, of allocating a trainee teacher to a volunteer practising teacher with the aim of discovering to what extent the teacher uses code-switching. The trainee teacher simply records by means of a horizontal or vertical notation which language is being used – noting each change of code. A time code can also be included at the head of the paper to show the pattern of change, and if necessary refinements can be added to identify what provoked the change of language – what functions are carried out in which tongue, for example. This served to raise awareness within both teacher and trainee through actual relevant experience, about something of which many are unaware. This use of trainees as researchers in collaboration with classroom teachers is one to which I return later in Part 4.

NPL's Precursor – Australian Language Levels[33]

The National Policy on Languages did not appear from out of a clear blue sky when it was adopted in 1987. Australia had been concerned for some time about the neglect of languages – indigenous, community and foreign. The Australian Languages Levels Project, known as ALL, was set up in 1985/6 by the federal Curriculum Development Committee in Canberra and the South Australia Education Department. Its aim was to improve the quality of the teaching of Languages Other Than English (LOTE) of which there were some 20–30 being taught in the education system. These included, in addition to the 'traditional' European languages, languages of commercial importance such as Indonesian and Japanese, as well as the languages of various immigrant communities – Serbo-Croat, Vietnamese, Chinese and various Aboriginal languages. Initially ALL was conceived as a 'top-down' model to construct a graded syllabus for school language learning based on levels and stages, using one template (in English) for each language taught, to be followed by assessment schemes and examinations on a common model.

A small project team was formed, including from Scotland John Clark, at that time Assistant Adviser in Modern Languages for Lothian Region, Director of the Regional GLAFLL Project (see Part 2). The team found two major problems with the initial remit: firstly, that it was impossible to lump all languages together under one model, given the different purposes for which they were being taught, the different socio-cultural uses of the language within the speech communities and the vastly different proficiency levels of the learners; secondly that such a wholly 'top-down' approach was in fact not sensible. More teacher participation was required if the project was to be adopted by the classroom teachers; there would have to be room for individual interpretation to allow teachers to tailor materials produced to the needs of their pupils.

The project team was faced with the difficult task of involving teachers in something which was already under way, which had been initiated over their heads and where some critical decisions had already been taken. To quote Clark:[34]

> The project has highlighted the difficulty of finding an appropriate pathway between the danger on the one hand of producing an over-prescriptive set of curriculum documents created by a project team and handed down to teachers to implement, and the danger on the other hand of producing a series of abstract principles of procedure that would be too vague to be of much use to teachers in their work.

What ALL eventually produced was a framework of interlocking stages for a language curriculum, with some commonality in the expectations of all the languages and some continuity in terms of the progress of learners. Curricular guidelines were produced to enable teachers to work together on the creation of their own syllabuses, schemes of work, observation and evaluation procedures. A set of guidelines for In-Service Training (INSET) was also produced to indicate how support might be offered to those using the curriculum guidelines.

Teachers were thus encouraged with the assistance of In-Service trainers to renew their own curriculum in groups in the light of a number of principles of procedure drawn up by the project team. Given that specification was light, there was considerable room for teachers to determine their own objectives and design their own materials and assessment instruments. The fact that the guidelines were intended for a variety of languages meant that a great deal of help was given to teachers of Asian languages, where the shortage of teaching materials went hand-in-hand with a scarcity of trained teachers.

This project understandably attracted a great deal of interest and attention and ultimately involved a huge number of teachers in a continuing programme of focused teacher development throughout Australia. It produced a cohort of teacher trainers and teachers who educated themselves through participating in the design of syllabuses, materials and assessment instruments and formed a basis on which future developments can build. Those teachers, who had already come together in groups to produce work on the basis of ALL guidelines, are likely to continue to take responsibility for what happens in their schools and to shape the way ahead for themselves. Thanks to this and to the fact that States and Territories have drawn up their own language policies and programmes, which reflect what the AACLAME document calls a 'symbiotic' relationship with national developments, the negative effects of reforms totally dominated by the centre may well be avoided in Australia.

Enthusiasm and Economics

There is much that is admirable in what is happening in Australia, and clearly what takes place will influence language provision in other countries. Many people from other less fortunate parts of the world would like to see their countries emulating the Australian government's initiative. It was clear from the press and from my discussions with members of the general public that the learning of languages enjoyed a high profile, while much interesting and innovative work including schemes for immersion and bilingual education, was taking place in schools.

Australians have been engaged for some time in a process of determining a new national identity, one which has their country far more closely linked to nations on the Pacific rim and in Asia than to European countries. Many Australians rejoice in belonging to a cosmopolitan community in the definition of whose identity each will have a role to play. Part of the interest in languages can be seen to stem from this. Another related part of this interest is also to do with the economic ascendance, within the area of which Australia now sees itself as a key member, of countries in the North Asian region. One of the main reasons behind the NPL is therefore that it is seen as having the potential to improve the country's economic situation.

Take the position of Australia's foreign trade during 1988–89, quoted in the AACLAME document. These cover the top 12 countries to which Australia exported and from which Australia imported goods in that period (Table 4.1).

Table 4.1 Top 12 countries Australia imported from and exported to in 1988–89

Countries Australia imports from	Imports %	Countries Australia exports to	Exports %
USA	21.52	Japan	27.27
Japan	20.75	USA	10.16
UK	7.34	New Zealand	5.09
Federal Republic		Korea	5.01
of Germany	6.27	Hong Kong	4.38
New Zealand	4.19	Taiwan	3.60
Taiwan	4.08	UK	3.5
Italy	2.94	Singapore	3.41
France	2.71	People's Republic	
Korea	2.68	of China	2.79
Singapore	2.32	Federal Republic	
Canada	2.27	of Germany	2.87
People's Republic		USSR	2.33
of China	2.18	France	2.24

Now let us compare the above with the numbers studying languages in Australian education institutions in 1988 (see Table 4.2).

Table 4.2 Students learning languages in Australian education
            institutions in 1988

Language	Secondary schools	Higher education
French	146,491	3,827
German	78,087	3,154
Italian	71,905	2,763
Japanese	31,832	3,436
Indonesian/Malay	18,041	883
Greek	12,619	855
Chinese	6,692	1,224
Spanish	3,501	882
Vietnamese	2,081	202
Arabic	1,615	135
Russian	504	464
Hindi	Nil	48
Thai	Nil	30
Korean	Nil	12

It is understandable that one of the conclusions drawn from these
figures would be that too much attention is being paid to the teaching of
French. This predominance of French as the first foreign language is
generally deplored and certainly there is a strong argument to be made,
in educational as well as practical, economic terms, for diversification.
The grounds for so much French teaching are historical: with France
now at the bottom of the table as a trading partner there would seem
little to justify the large number of school children learning the
language. It would, however, be foolish and uneconomical to ignore the
expertise of many teachers simply because their qualifications did not
extend to languages deemed 'more relevant' to prevailing conditions. It
might also be foolish to overlook the fact that some languages are far
harder to come to grips with than others, some cultures more difficult
than others for a particular set of people to approach.

Looking at these tables, one might note with pleasure that many
students are now learning Japanese at school and college or university.
The numbers have increased considerably since the publication of these
figures, which is not surprising given Japan's position as Australia's
number one export partner. What was surprising to a number of people
in Australia was the announcement in December 1992 by Prime Minister Paul Keating that in future the teaching of Japanese would be made
compulsory in all the nation's primary schools. At this point even the

most committed teachers of languages began to ask themselves whether in fact all this enthusiasm might not be getting out of hand.

If the learning of Japanese starts in the primary it will take six to eight years. To produce language speakers of high calibre, another period of tertiary education would add a further three to four years onto the above. Let us say then, a minimum of eight and a maximum of 12 years. A lot can happen to both the Australian economy and world trade figures in 12 years. If Japan today, what price Korea tomorrow? Now that figures show that the economy to watch is that of China, are the pupils in Australia's primary schools going to have to deal with the problems of Chinese characters, as well as the diversity of Chinese languages? Is there not likely to be chaos in teacher supply?

There seems to be a confusion in the mind of politicians as well as of the public about the nature of what happens in schools. Emphasis is all to do with the benefits of language *training*. Most teachers, however, believe that training is what happens in tertiary education or in the workplace. Training is a matter of adapting the workforce to existing conditions. They hold the view that education is about transforming society through increasing individual potential.[35]

What is strange in this reliance on Japanese as part of the solution to Australia's economic problems is that this is a reform within the public sector. Yet it is the *private* sector – big business and tourism – which needs to have access to lucrative Japanese markets. For a government that believes in letting demand drive the economy, it might make more sense to leave to the private sector the job of training those people in Japanese who need to, or will need to use it. The government's role might better be relegated to the provision of loans to individuals or tax incentives to industry to undertake the funding of training schemes.

The Australian National Policy on Languages is likely to succeed partly because of the groundwork within those areas of the country where teachers have been used to taking decisions about syllabus, assessment and methodology for themselves. It would be a pity if the same politicians who backed the scheme in the first place were to endanger it by an overemphasis on short-term expediency. There is probably a case to be made here for a *festina lente* approach.

In Scotland already in the light of the success of the Primary Pilot, and the announcement that henceforth the learning of a foreign language in primary school will be phased-in throughout the country, concerns are being expressed about the proper training of teachers who will have to implement the policy, about the ability of secondary schools to ensure continuity of the language taught in primary and about the potential effect of this on diversification. In the end, in both countries it will all boil down to the question of implementation, and the quality of the teaching force which will have to bear the burden for the visions of the politicians.

5 Pause for Thought: The Limitations of Policies

This part of the book has been concerned with innovations which resulted from policy initiatives. Not all new policies necessarily produce innovations, although they may lead to changes. For instance, the extension of existing language provision into the primary school is not innovative *per se*, although innovation may arise there coincidentally as it might with any change of circumstances. Policy changes might in fact stifle rather than encourage innovation, depending on the policies themselves, how they are interpreted and how implemented. The policies described are not in themselves policies to encourage innovation – they are policies merely to widen the range of languages taught or the ages at which they begin, in the hope that this will produce better linguists in future.

On the other hand, ALL in Australia changed its policy with respect to the implementation of its scheme to improve language provision by replacing a 'top-down' model with one which could be seen as both 'top-down' and 'bottom-up', deliberately handing over the responsibility for syllabus and assessment schemes to teachers. This policy of encouraging a flexible implementation of central proposals has laid the basis for a creative use of the facilities which have been set up under the National Policy on Languages. One would expect therefore to see innovation flourish as a result, since the kind of networks which are in place are almost bound to encourage the exchange of ideas, discussion and creative thinking.

Innovating is not in fact a comfortable activity. Frustrations and disagreement are often seen to be present, particularly at the outset. This leads me to speculate as to whether the opposite also pertains. Is it that there can be too much consensus, so that in the absence of strong emotion and room for dissent and debate, innovation is less likely to flourish?[36] Is it perhaps the case that the presence of a certain amount of disharmony, of what Schumpeter, quoted by Drucker calls 'dynamic disequilibrium' can be seen as fruitful? Drucker also identifies controversy as a feature of many successful innovations in commerce and industry.

The two Scottish examples given illustrate the importance of individuals and groups of individuals. They show that where there is a chance of making things better by themselves, and where there is support, teachers will put in hours of extra work rather than have things decided for them; they demonstrate that teachers can rise to a challenge and enjoy doing so.

There are several identifiable reasons why the two Scottish schemes produced innovative practices which had nothing whatever to do with policy, but which may help us to understand more about the nature of innovation. If innovation can make for a motivated, activist and effective teaching force, then the more we know about what seems to encourage it, the better.

Innovation is always possible where there is a firm belief in the importance of the individual as opposed to the importance of the system, even when this entails all the untidiness which is inherent when it is a case of people dealing with other people, suggesting, negotiating, hesitating, advancing often by trial and error and sometimes just muddling through. But when people engage in this kind of activity, they learn. It is truly developmental, as were both pilots.

Both regions encouraged teachers to produce their own materials and provided the technological back-up for them to do so. By not falling back on existing material and not depending on a coursebook they allowed for both the localisation of the teaching and the development of their teachers as they experimented with things previously unknown.

Both schemes rejected the ready-made approach and in fact took a long time to arrive at their individual solutions. Those who had to carry out the work were participants in the decision-making process, not recipients of the decisions of others. On the contrary, in Balerno the secondary teachers had to adapt to the primary teachers' existing curricular requirements. Thereafter the decision was taken to determine the nature and content of the course as a team, secondary and primary teachers working together. Clearly in the case of Balerno with secondary teachers taking the lead in teaching, the methodology itself may have had more in common with secondary practices, but it was never a question of asking the primary teachers to rubber-stamp a decision which essentially had already been made.

One of the most important reasons for what took place in these regions was the fact that both schemes decided to start from scratch and do their own thinking, working out their own strategies for delivery. They did not accept that SOED should do this for them. They both considered their areas, what was or was not feasible in terms of logistics, what the strengths were, and where the weak points might be. In Dumfries and Galloway, logistics certainly played a part in determining the fact that primary teachers would have to take a far greater role than elsewhere in the delivery of the subject. The decision to appoint a primary teacher as Tutor Trainer rather than a secondary teacher was the key to what led to a very special experience, one in which only primary methodology came to be used, and one which belonged therefore to the primary teachers.

One cannot of course ignore the chance combination of circumstances. In the Balerno pilot, had all three primaries had roughly the same kind of population, the variety of experiences offered would perhaps not have occurred. The individualisation of workbooks to suit each class and school, the different nature of the subjects dealt with in French, would not have been necessary. It was the challenge of such different environments which resulted in the range of experiences offered.

Similarly in Dumfries and Galloway, had there been ample staffing in the secondary school, a secondary-oriented course could have been delivered on a reduced time basis to each primary school. It would have worked, even with the distances involved, because there were enough primary teachers with some German to at least get some limited scheme off the ground – at the very least some kind of 'taster course'. Necessity and chance certainly played a considerable part in turning the teachers in both areas into pioneers.

Both sets of teachers decided to go for the best possible solution, even although it meant a great deal more work than the original scheme. This could be because of the nature of the people involved, or the combination of certain individuals. It could also be to do with the fact that challenge often brings out the best in people as long as they have some control of events themselves.

A view of pedagogic change that rejects statutory innovation necessarily entails faith in the ability of the teaching force to work things out for themselves. While the trend at present is towards more central control of what teachers do in their classrooms, many of those who work in teacher development are concerned that the removal of the responsibility for thinking and its replacement by central planning and routinisation will lead to a serious de-skilling of the profession: teachers will eventually conform to whatever the authorities determine, goaded by the changes the authorities make to the system. This conformity, however, may be a purely cosmetic exercise and can mean that what takes place is empty routines devoid of significance which are unlikely to enhance learning, since the teachers do not have any commitment to them.

We also have to consider the unique circumstances of the Scottish system. Those arise from the perennial battle for control between the centre and the regions, which mirrors the differences between the two main political parties.[37] In both projects described we saw how local authorities played a crucial role in backing the innovative approaches of their teachers. In Chapter 1 I showed how conflict between the advisory services and Her Majesty's Inspectorate was already there at the start. This was to continue throughout the course of the pilot. What SOED were really aiming at, it seemed, was a feasibility study of a particular model for implementing government policy. They were at no point trying to find out what teachers might do if given free rein to work out their own solutions, which explains in part why the pilot created such acrimony. To quote Lothian Region's Adviser, Peter Wheeldon on the subject:

> Basically the Pilot was saved and made a success by the people on the ground responsible for the delivery, the teachers and the directorates in the regions. Lothian Region fought like mad for extra FTE (Full Time Equivalent) time, and exchanged some brutally worded letters in order to get adequate funding for the materials, which were not what the SOED had in mind at all. Another good example is the risk-taking Dumfries and Galloway model, which the SOED deplored in the early stages. All credit should be given to the Dumfries and Galloway directorate and Martin Prowse, the Adviser, for sticking to their guns. The usual SOED view always came through – 'if it's not our idea, it can't be any good'.[38]

Fighting talk – and as teachers recognise, just the kind of talk which encourages them to set up alternatives. The sense of helplessness felt by individuals and small groups faced with large and powerful organisations may act as an incentive to innovate, since in this way they can assert their uniqueness and right to self-determination. This leads me to wonder whether perhaps the SOED has in fact a vital role to play in innovation.[39] It is at least worth considering whether the primary pilots in Dumfries and Galloway and in Balerno owed some of their success to the very tensions which existed between centre and region, to the fact that the teachers were determined to 'make a go of it' if only to prove the SOED wrong.

The developments described in Scotland appear therefore to be the result of a combination of circumstances rather than a result of policy. Certainly the SOED in setting up the pilot were not looking for innovative teaching. At one point while generally applauding the Balerno experience, they cheerfully dismissed it as 'not replicable'. If indeed it was a combination of circumstances and people which produced the outcomes described, what we need to consider, if we think that innovations such as these are to be encouraged, is how to create the right circumstances in which innovation can flourish. While serendipity and human nature will always ensure that innovation will take place randomly in any case, it would be helpful to see how one might harness the forces which bring it into being, if we are to use it as a means of enhancing teachers' careers and pupils' experiences. The next part of the book will consider one way of doing this.

Notes to Part 1

1. Firth, R. (1963) *We, the Tikopia* (pp. 134–5) Boston: Beacon Press.
2. The announcement took place in January 1989. The initial six projects, teaching French and German, were extended in April 1990 and June 1991. In 1993 they involved 76 primary schools and 12 secondary schools. Spanish and Italian were added in year 2 of the project.
3. Burstall, C., Jamieson, M., Colen, S. and Hargreaves, M. (1974), *Primary French in the Balance*. Slough: National Foundation for Educational Research.
4. In Strathclyde by 1993 the regional project involved 30 secondary schools and their associated primaries.
5. See Appendix 2.
6. Since 1988 France has poured money into education and rapidly expanded its system by 40% in cash terms. As a proportion of GDP, total spending has risen from 5% to 6.6%. This has resulted, among other things, in an improvement in baccalaureat results. The 'bac', which determines entrance to university education, is now passed by over 50% of French pupils. The target officially is to have 80% of school pupils capable of sitting the examination by the year 2000. The public remains unconvinced, however, still rating education as second bottom in order of the quality of their public services. (*Source: The Economist* 18–24 September 1993).
7. In 1993 it was decided to phase the teaching of Modern Languages into the primary curriculum in Scotland. At the time of writing, concern is generally

being expressed at the lack of funding and the resources for the proper training for primary teachers (see notes 10 and 13 below).

8. In January 1993 the Secretary of State announced a new language programme for primary schools, to 'build on the projects which have been running since 1989'. The intention is that the teaching be done 100% by primary teachers, unlike in the pilot study. A training programme, consisting of 160 hours of training and offering 415 places, is aimed at achieving one trained teacher per primary school (around 2400 teachers) after three years. The budget of some 3.75 million, even with a 'top-up' of a further 100,000 for 1993–94 is regarded generally as wholly inadequate, and the largest teachers' union, the Educational Institute of Scotland has voiced its concern on several occasions, while welcoming the initiative in itself.

9. In early 1994 poll ratings for the Conservative Party were at an all-time low of around 13%.

10. I am indebted to Annelise Swanston for her permission to use this story, which is one of those she prepared for the project.

11. Stewart, V. (1992) 'Cows, Dogs and Playing Fields', paper given to the Institute of Zealand Personnel Management Conference in 1991, quoted in Human Resources: *An Introduction to Best Practice*. New Zealand Employers Federation.

12. Henry Kissinger, on the subject of leadership says: 'The task of a leader is to get his people from where they are to where they have not been.'

13. See note 11.

14. Prahbu, N.S. (1987) *Second Language Pedagogy*, Oxford University Press.

15. Stern, H.H. (1974) What can we learn from the good language learner? *Canadian Modern Language Review* 31, 308–18.

16. The work of Stephen Krashen has become familiar to many language teachers, who find notions developed by him which coincide with their own experiences. Some of the premises on which the methodology was based stemmed from his work, and was adapted to fit the classroom experiences. It was important that the primary teachers, whose experience of learning languages was totally different from what happened in the pilot, understood the rationale for some of the methodology. What follows is a summary of the explanation they were given as to why the secondary teachers were operating as they did. As can be seen, it owes much to Krashen.

Meaningful input: Apart from a few set phrases which they can use at will, what pupils hear and what they read should be directed at them, for them to respond to as they would had what been said been said in the mother tongue. The language they will find easiest is language about the here and now. TPR offers such a context, as do games and the telling of familiar stories.

Learning and acquisition: To make a distinction between these can be helpful: acquisition is a largely unconscious process which takes place in response to meaningful input. Learning, on the other hand, means the intervention of a conscious process. The language which is 'acquired' by learners is readily available, whereas that which is 'learnt' has to be consciously retrieved. It is as if they were stored in different compartments of the brain and accessed by different routes.

Order of acquisition: It is likely that there is a natural order of language acquisition in both mother tongue and foreign language learning. In most coursebooks language is still presented much as it always has been, despite superficial changes. In fact certain structures regarded as 'difficult' often present no problem at all, while others deemed 'easy' cause unending problems. Although not enough is known for teachers to programme all their 'output' so as to take advantage of this, the idea is seductive and bears investigation. At the very least, using what the pupils understand and learn easily is a good rule to follow when producing language learning materials.

The right to be silent: In order to make sense of meaningful input, learners need time to process what they are hearing. It can take months, sometimes longer, before they are ready to use the language themselves. Forcing production has negative effects, therefore teachers should incorporate silent periods into their lessons, particularly at the beginning of a lesson, and not demand instant feedback. Listen and Do exercises are a good way to achieve this.

Error: Order of acquisition means that certain errors are inevitable and these should be seen as part of the learning process. Correction should be avoided – it is demotivating and unlikely to lead to improvement.

The 'monitor': What Krashen calls the 'monitor' – a kind of linguistic conscience which becomes activated when one has 'sinned' linguistically speaking, or is about to 'sin'- intervenes as a result of one's conscious learning. It accounts for hesitations in speech as learners struggle to apply rules learnt. It has more positive effects in the case of written work where there is time to reflect. Too much monitor impedes performance, too little may mean highly inaccurate speech, as in examples of some immigrants whose second language has become 'fossilised' once it has served its initial purpose.

Proficiency: According to Krashen, 'acquisition is it '. We become proficient in a language through processing meaningful input. This is the way towards fluency. When we 'learn' in the conscious sense, what we learn can only be retrieved by conscious effort. Invoking the 'monitor' by conscious effort causes 'interference' with the contrastingly natural process of acquisition.

'Meaningful output': Merrill Swain suggests that useful as Krashen's description is, it omits the problem of production: it is hard to get production by pupils of language which 'means' in the same way as the mother tongue would 'mean', particularly in sustained speech. One way of 'cueing' speech of this kind is through the actual teaching of a new subject area combined with an activity-based methodology.

17. Some of these games and other, similar ones, can be found in: Hamilton, J. and McLeod, A. *Drama in the Language Classroom*, CILT, and Hamilton, J. and Reid, S. *In Play, A Drama Resource for Language Teachers*, Nelson.

18. A reading of note 16 should make it clear why the 'normal' approach of asking personal questions 'round the class' about pupils, to which teachers in any case already know most of the answers, was not applied.

19. The role of the Foreign Conversation Assistant and the additional time allocated by the regional authorities for her participation in the project made the burden on the teachers considerably lighter. Longbottom was to become a fully participating team member, whose ability to design attractive materials increased the speed at which these could be produced. This in turn was useful to her too, as she subsequently entered teacher training college and became the first of her year to be employed.

20. Observations of immersion classes indicated that less than 15% of students' utterances were of more than clause length. A substantial proportion of these – 40%, consisted of one or two word responses to the teacher. Swain refers to the programme developed by Florence Stevens (1976) in which an activity approach was taken, where students worked on projects of their own choice individually or in small groups. On a comparison of the French proficiency of these pupils with those in 'traditional' immersion classes, it was found that on measures of speaking and listening the groups came out the same, while in reading and writing they were almost equivalent – this despite the fact that the activity-based learners' programme occupied only 40% of the school day, whereas the 'traditional' programme occupied 80%. A visit by Lothian Region's then Adviser for Modern Languages John Clark a long time earlier first set the department at Balerno thinking about 'comprehensible output' some years before the start of the Primary Pilot. Swain has written extensively on the subject: my source is 'The immersion experience in Canada: is it relevant to Hong Kong?' Merrill Swain, 1990, The Ontario Institute for Studies in Education, Toronto.

21. Asher, J.J. (1969) The Total Physical Response approach to Second Language Learning. *The Modern Language Journal* (p. 53).

22. Swain in the paper 'Two ingredients to the successful use of a second language as a medium of instruction in Hong Kong', suggests that 'If the second language threshold level is to be attained through using it as a medium of instruction, then the faster it is attained the better.'

23. I am indebted to Leni Dam of Denmark for the idea of using posters as prompts in this way.

24. Corson, D. (1985) *The Lexical Bar*. Corson developed Bernstein's restricted and elaborated code theory to show how a lack of the understanding of words of Greek or Latin origin is an impediment to learning. Cummings uses a similar theory in discussions of bilingualism. He shows that while many bilinguals appear to have a fluent command of their second language (eg in the case of American children of Puerto Rican parents), this may be only at the level of 'Bics' – Basic Interpersonal Communicative Skills. At the level of 'Calps' – Cognitive Academic Language Proficiency, they may be totally lacking, which goes a long way to explaining the school failure of many bright bilingual children.

25. Some very basic things can go wrong when pupils first use a dictionary. The notion of a dictionary in two sections may be hard to grasp. Pupils who do not have access to books at home often find it hard to turn the pages swiftly in order to find a page with a particular number. They will turn to the wrong section, and search for the English equivalent of a French word in the English section. They will copy out the phonetic transcription of the word for which they are searching. Homonyms will inevitably confuse: good dictionary users have to be able to identify the part of speech they want – and then as a matter of course recheck by looking up the word in the corresponding section. Competitions, quizzes and 'fun' worksheets were used to encourage effective use, along with simple things like starting a lesson by getting pupils to find the first word beginning with a particular letter of the alphabet, or the first word on a certain page, etc. Short worksheets on dictionary use were designed by Murray in response to problems as they arose and pupils were directed towards the ones which

could help them solve their problems.

26. Experts on bilingual education vary and change their minds about the amount of exposure necessary before actual learning of another subject can profitably take place. Most consider the advantage of the methodology to be on the side of the language-learning, not the subject matter.

27. Bearing in mind work on bilingualism which suggests that code-switching can be to the detriment of pupils, I had to decide what mattered most: the confidence of the primary teacher or the sanctity of the theory. It was not a difficult decision: considerations of what makes people feel comfortable are far more important than any linguistic theory.

28. For an account of some of the activities, see *Jet Magazine for Teachers of English*, Theme Pack Science: Sounds (1991).

29. Otherwise known as the 'Lo Bianco' report, after its author, Jo Lo Bianco.

30. 1990 Report to the Minister for Employment, Education and Training. The National Policy on Languages, December 1987 – March 1990. AACLAME Secretariat, GPO Box, 9880, Canberra, ACT. 2601.

31. Code-switching refers to the practice of using two, sometimes three languages in the classroom and switching between them. It can be harmful to learning, particularly in countries where it is education policy for pupils to be educated in a medium which is not their mother tongue. It has been shown that inconsistent switching of code can have the effect that learners 'block out' the language in which they feel less competent, and thus fail to learn that language and material taught through it.

32. See Lo Bianco, J. (1990) Language in bilingual classrooms – Samoa as an example. *In Vernacular Languages in South Pacific Education*; and Lo Bianco, J. and Liddicoat, A. (1991) Language use in classrooms in Western Samoa.

33. Clark, J.L. 1987 *Curriculum Renewal in School Foreign Language Learning*. Oxford: Oxford University Press; Clark, J.L. 1987, Communicative competence and foreign language learning. *Annual Review of Applied Linguistics*, Vol. 8, 1988, Cambridge University Press (pp. 85–96); Clark, J.L. (1988) Curriculum development across languages and across sectors of education. In Bickley, V. (ed.) (1988) *Languages in Education in a Bilingual or Multilingual Setting*. Institute of Language in Education, Education Department, Hong Kong (pp. 438–49).

34. Clark, J.L. (1988) Teacher development is curriculum development. Paper given at the Hong Kong University Symposium on Curriculum Development and Continuing Teacher Education.

35. Many teachers, who would like to see a return to something closer to a broad, liberal arts education, wonder when the present emphasis on relevance and vocationalism is likely to end. UNESCO's Final Report of the International Conference on Education, 43rd Session, Geneva 1992, underlines this worldwide concern: 'Some speakers expressed a certain amount of anxiety over what they considered to have been an undesirable trend in recent years towards an emphasis on science and technology at the expense of other subjects.' (p. 5).

36. While some kind of internal unbalance seems to be present as one of the prices society pays for innovation, this is not to say that it can flourish in any circumstances in any ground. The case of the 'alternative' school or the 'progressive' teacher who fails to gain the confidence of parents is a regular occurrence. It is not simply the case of an idea whose time has not yet come.

Many talented individuals fail to take note of the need to embed reform within the framework of society and the prevailing culture.

37. Teachers in Scotland are employed by the local authorities, not by government. Local authority education departments, staffed mainly by former teachers, still push, by and large, for a liberal, transformational educational system, or at least one which has that potential. The present central government tends to follow the line that the state education system needs to deliver appropriately qualified people for the country's workforce.

The odds are now on central government as winner, since their plans for the abolition of Scotland's large and powerful regional authorities will effectively reduce local control by limiting local budgets. Limited local budgets will mean that the new smaller authorities will no longer be able to afford an advisory service, for example. This represents a considerable threat to innovation in education.

38. Personal communication.

39. While they may inadvertently contribute to innovation by providing a focus for rebellion, it is surely an anomaly that inspectors, who by training and inclination are firmly on the side of tradition, stability and the *status quo*, should have a major say in determining educational innovation simply because they hold the purse strings. Inspectors see their role principally as maintaining or raising standards in ways which accord with the priorities of the government of the day – they are neither setters of standards nor pace-makers; on the contrary. Few inspectors have any interest in theory of any kind, and tend to dismiss it – one Chief Inspector in Scotland was heard to boast that he had never read a book about Modern Languages in his life. It is almost impossible for HMI to promote innovation in schools themselves because their stock-in-trade has to be equilibrium and optimisation: keeping controversy to a minimum, maintaining the balance, keeping the politicians, teachers, parents, pupils, industry, the universities, and any other interest group happy means not engaging in risky enterprises. The environment in which HMIs work is a traditional one, inimical to change; their jobs are ones in which bureaucratic skills are paramount; they are selected because they are unlikely to rock the boat, not for their charismatic and leadership qualities; they have neither the predilection nor the ability to take risks – and taking risks is a large part of innovating. Worst of all they may neither understand nor appreciate the entrepreneur – and are likely to disapprove of innovation as something which diminishes their capacity to control.

Part 2
Campaigning for
Curriculum Renewal

Introduction to Part 2:
The Campaign Spirit

A campaigning model offers a possible framework within which teachers can determine the direction of their own development. Such a framework allows for flexibility and innovation while discouraging dependency.

Organising for Change

One of the ways in which society organises for change is the campaign. In education we rarely use the word, tending to opt for change on the basis of a rational model. Campaigns are not rational – they are unpredictable and uncontrollable. Yet some curricular innovations can be seen to have many of the characteristics of the successful campaign.

> Campaigning is a strange mixture of idealism and emotion combined with ruthless attention to detail, a matter of working with the people to address a commonly perceived problem... Campaigning is not a matter of listening to the people and then trying to supply the means of their satisfaction. In successful campaigns ... people are participants not recipients; the campaign belongs to everyone and all have a role to play.'[1]

The military model

It might seem that to have recourse to military terminology in order to illustrate successful curricular development initiatives would suggest that teachers should be viewed as unthinking automata ripe for orders and a touch of discipline. On the contrary, as long ago as the time of Bismarck, the Prussian General Staff under Helmuth von Moltke transformed current thinking on warfare by insisting on a level of involvement, understanding and expertise at all levels of the army. To quote General Bronsart von Shellendorf:

> Every fresh campaign brings with it astonishing phenomena not previously dreamed of, in the face of which a Commander who is not accustomed to think for himself in peace stands confounded. But the man who has learnt by ceaseless toil in time of peace to rely on his own judgement, and has altogether abstained from the use of 'normal' formations and 'models', will be able to deal effectively with unexpected and unprecedented incidents.[2]

Staff training under von Moltke aimed at producing such commanders. But before the training came the selection, and the selection of the right kind of people for training as officers on the General Staff was based on observation over a number of years, not on an examination or, unusually for these days, family background.

Selection of the right people is also important for successful companies: reliance on one's own judgement and abstaining from the use of models, thinking for oneself, are behaviours which are stressed by management writers. These are things which, many seem to think, the business schools with their MBAs which now predominate in boardrooms everywhere fail to provide for.

Issues, not ideologies

People campaign for reasons which are as much emotional as intellectual. They campaign out of enthusiasm, and it is issues that drive them to campaign, not ideologies. Ideologies in education have been responsible for producing some of the silliest of outcomes. They still do, as illustrated in the example given later in Chapter 8 about New Zealand's potentially fatal flirtation with public choice,[3] where, to quote one prominent educationalist: 'All learning is being transformed into unit standards'. For teachers to be 'ideology proof' requires the kind of professional development that encourages analysis and a consequent reliance on their own judgement.

Se retirer pour mieux ressortir

An important campaign characteristic is the ability to take account of experiences, to reconsider and to reform, regroup as necessary. Participants in campaigns and movements need to have a responsibility for action which enables them to respond to fresh situations.

> Any organisation that proposes to train people to do better ... ought not be overly burdened by established norms and ought to have the

freedom to move in untested directions. The need for individual freedom and opportunity to take risk increases when the goals sought and the means of accomplishing them increase in ambiguity.[4]

Cycles within a campaign can be identified, so that far from being finite, campaigning can, by its very flexibility, be a self-renewing experience – that is to say, given resourcing and support. Some organisations can be seen to operate on the basis of perpetual campaigning, such as public health organisations, whose priorities may have to change suddenly to accommodate new problems as they arise, such as the AIDS epidemic. It seems to me that this kind of organisation is well suited to education, where, as in public health, no sooner has one problem been tackled than another 20 raise their heads. In public health, as in education, attention to detail is needed, matched by the ability to turn one's hand to a whole variety of tasks.

The kind of campaign I have so far described is one which is organised in advance – where campaigning is planned from the start. There is another kind of campaign, with much the same features and strengths, which starts in a much smaller way, and which tends to become a campaign almost before the participants are aware of it. It may never in fact be called a campaign at all.

Recently in England in frustration against a highly controlled, centralised package of curricular and examination reforms, influential figures in language teaching have suggested that there is a need to 'Bring back GOML' (Graded Objectives in Modern Languages).[5] GOML was a national teachers' movement which arose in order to increase the motivation of learners by making language learning more relevant to their needs and at the same time giving them short-term goals in the form of graded tests. The call for the return of GOML is not purely due to a desire for more Graded Tests as such, it is certainly also a reflection of a groundswell of opinion against centralised control and the consequent lack of involvement of which teachers, teacher trainers and curriculum developers increasingly complain. It is interesting that it is to the campaign model that the call is being made. Developments here will bear watching. GOML was the last time language teachers in England really felt they were influencing events.

Leadership

A characteristic of successful innovative developments and of successful campaigns is the combination of particular individuals and particular times. Innovation is propelled in the first instance by passionate belief. While conditions may be ripe for change, it takes individuals with vision to put something new in place. This is not a role that can be taken by a 'manager' – it requires a leader.

Looking again at the characteristics shared by inspiring leaders, as identified by Stewart (already referred to on page 32), we see characteristics which inspire and challenge people, not those which would 'manage' them:

- They have a divine discontent – things must change.
- They hate waste and always look for opportunities to do things better.
- They trust their intuition.
- They are excited by living with uncertainty.
- They have long-term vision.
- They are hard-working and expect others to be so too.
- They are clear, exciting and urgent communicators.
- They are not afraid to surround themselves with able colleagues and subordinates.
- They use status where necessary, but do not feel the need to pull rank.
- They never stop learning.
- They are clear about their values.
- They are loved.

But leadership is not fashionable in education. The days of the charismatic Head Teachers, thinkers who were prepared to stand up and be counted, and who shaped their schools and gave them a clear sense of purpose, have virtually gone. 'Efficiency and effectiveness' thinking has replaced them with the ubiquitous 'person in a grey suit', mouthing the latest policy document, quoting from the mission statement, or checking the performance indicators.[6]

Self-interest, encouraged by managerialist doctrines which would turn teachers into unthinking cogs only interested in pleasing those who have a say in their eventual promotion, wreaks havoc in organisations such as those which make up the education service, and which rely on a sense of public spirit. The education service can ill afford to nurture only the 'yes' people; it can ill afford to lose people with principles for which they are prepared to stand up. There are few enough of them in any sphere of life, and if they are to be cherished at all, where else will they be found, but in the traditional breeding grounds of a society's democratic spirit, its schools? The drive for conformity in order to please those in authority is dangerous, and if it continues at its present rate, will ultimately damage the education service of any country, because it will kill off the spirit of adventure, the spirit which welcomes, indeed, seeks out challenge and applies to it innovation and entrepreneurship.

Free to differ

In the previous part of the book the question of controversy was raised. With increased control of schools and education generally, disagreements are becoming less and less welcome, certainly when they come from the teachers. Yet organisations which succeed in effecting innovation are characterised by a spirit in which 'differences of opinion are welcomed, mistakes are seen developmentally, rather than causes for punitive behaviour, risk takers are rewarded, and the leader's role is one more of supporter than of enforcer'.[7] People who are looking out for themselves are usually unwilling to give voice to a personal opinion in case it gives offence. They are even less likely to fight for a matter of principle. In schools in New Zealand 'looking out for yourself' has had to become a way of life for many teachers – there is no one else likely to do it for them. Education officials, advisers and such-like have all been 'rationalised' along with other such 'unit costs'.

Structural Considerations

New Zealand's education reforms have totally altered the structure of their education system. A doctrinaire approach based on economic theory has effectively left the teachers at the mercy of an unproven ideology. The new structure put in place by the proponents of this ideology has destroyed links between teachers and education officials, curriculum specialists and advisers, leaving the teachers isolated and unsupported in professional matters. The question for the subject of this book is, once all the dust has settled, where innovation will come from, if it is to come at all. Campaigns require a staff organisation, and this is not to be found in the market place. It is the product of selection and long-term training. Attitudes of service to something other than self have to be formed. A staff organisation is not a committee, to be assembled at the drop of a hat in order to complete a particular task. Nor can what it does be carried out by consultants.

Informal organisation

Most changes in education move from a policy decision (often at a political level, as we have seen in Part 1), influenced by public opinion or a pressure group, though not always. These policy decisions are handed down mostly by means of planned implementation through In-Service Training which is organised to follow a logical structure involving inputs and outputs. Those doing the training know in advance, from many planning meetings, what the outputs of the training should be. It is all very well organised, very well 'managed', and in most cases rarely makes any difference to actual classroom practice.

An alternative to the above is to consider a model which is not 'rational', one that has a lot in common with the campaign, called, in organisation theory, the 'informal organisation'. This reflects a horizontal rather than a vertical structure. It is one which has been seen to work well in industry as well as in other institutions,[8] and one in which teachers used to operate in Britain before the proliferation of hierarchies, management teams and Boards of Studies, and it is in fact how many teachers still prefer to operate.

An interesting study from industrial management may give an idea of what I mean in another context: Burns and Stalker[9] in an analysis of the success and failure of small firms in Scotland, came up with the identification of informal organisation as the key to the success of individual firms. Successful firms were characterised by:

(a) The adjustment and continual redefinition of individual tasks with others.

(b) Problems may be posted upwards, downwards or sideways as being someone else's responsibility.

(c) The spread of commitment to the firm beyond any technical difficulties.

(d) Knowledge about the technical and commercial nature of the here-and-now task may be located anywhere in the network, this location being the *ad hoc* centre of control, authority and communication.

(e) A lateral rather than a vertical direction of communication through the organisation; and communication between people of different rank, resembling consultation rather than command.

(f) A content of communication which consists of information and advice rather than instructions and decisions.

Notice that in (d), the centre of the operation is with the holders of the knowledge, and how that location becomes responsible for 'control, authority and communication'. This is quite at variance with present practice but very similar to the modes of operating to be described in this part of the book. As important for an alternative model to promote developments in teaching are (e), consultation rather than command, and (f), information and advice rather than instructions and decisions. The kind of characteristics which emerged from the Burns and Stalker analysis are of course also present in a successful campaign, as indeed they were in the case of the GLAFLL project.[10]

A Crucial Command Decision

Earlier I mentioned the importance of selecting the right people. Successful businesses invest time and money both on research and development and on the training of key staff. An employing authority which rates research highly, and which puts a premium on human resource development, deserves to reap rewards, as does a commercial firm. It must be a consideration of those who would see teachers innovate and think for themselves rather than simply copy the accepted model, that this is unlikely to be achieved without investment.

The selection of a very few key serving teachers for special training is what in fact happened, some years before the inception of the GLAFLL (Graded Levels of Achievement in Foreign Language Learning) project, also known as 'the Lothian project' to which we will now turn our attention. The training which these people received was crucial to the way in which this project developed. The decision was made to second a small number of Modern Languages teachers, one per year, to study for the Diploma in Applied Linguistics at the Department of Applied Linguistics at the University of Edinburgh, a Department whose work and reputation rank among the best in the world. One of the many lessons of the project, and one which is generally not recognised, is the crucial role of long-term planning which good employers play in the whole process of teacher development. For what was a very small investment by the then Edinburgh District Council, Lothian Region[11] ended up with two future Advisers in Modern Languages, whose thinking was characterised by academic rigour, and whose view of teacher development was non-directive, long term and sustaining.

What Fits

Successful campaigners have to consider the terrain. This was a characteristic of the Lothian project as well as of a related curriculum development project in Bangalore State in India. Poor countries are often the victims of so-called 'development'. Their economies and growing populations force them to be recipients of foreign aid which they can ill-afford to refuse, which, however, brings with it the necessity of applying foreign solutions to local problems. One of the prices to be paid for foreign aid is the presence of whole hosts of foreign advisers, often of 20 or more different nationalities, each one of which has her or his own 'perfect solution' to the problems of that country – in education the Americans will push for affirmative action and school boards, the British will go for computers, the Germans for early selection, the Japanese for discipline and rigorous training, the Scandinavians for 'gender awareness', the New Zealanders for 'user pays', even in countries where the vast majority of people are unwaged, and so on. These countries then have to include all the various fads of the donors in their education programme if they want to continue to receive aid,[12] although in point of fact, of every dollar spent on the aid given by the developed world to the developing countries, on average only about 5 cents actually ever reaches these countries – the rest returns to the donor countries to purchase equipment and to pay for consultancies.

This dependency on often quite unsuitable foreign solutions entails the necessity of paying for rich country technologies, computers being only the latest of these – the demand for textbooks from the better off countries is inexhaustible. There are strong feelings among some nationalists that post-primary education in developing nations is held back by the subsidy which the English language receives at the expense of the language of the country. Kiswahili in Tanzania is a case in point. While it is the official language which unites the whole country, and the language of primary education, English remains the medium of instruction in secondary and tertiary education, despite the fact that pupils understandably fail drastically as a result of having to learn in what may for them be a third language.[13]

The cost of aid is the dependency mentality, the expectance of handouts, people who have lost the ability to make do and mend. There is a corollary with the expectations which underlies certain kinds of thinking about the training of teachers. The teaching 'package' is perilously close in nature to the 'aid package'. Simply open and administer.

What is particularly heartening about the Bangalore project is that it is precisely the opposite. It illustrates the application of local resources to solve local problems within a restricted local budget. The project attracted a great deal of attention at one time, most of which was to do with methodology and issues of syllabus design, communicative methodology, task-based learning and so on. I have also dwelt on these, as these concerns seem to match those of GLAFLL. Less, it seems to me, has been written about the potentially liberating effect on teachers, not only in the developing world, of determining their own programmes, of making their own 'aid packages' which match the cultural environment and fit with the local society. It is not possible for me to gauge at this remove of time and space what the liberating effect may or may not have been and I have not attempted to do so. It is the self-sustaining nature of the project that seems to me to have a message for teachers, the sense of harmony with its surroundings. This notion of harmony, of fit, is likely to be present in a great many successful innovations in education.

6 GLAFLL: A Regional Campaign

The Lothian GLAFLL project is an example of a grass-roots campaign for improving language learning which highlights the role of informal organisation in innovation.

The Lothian Region GLAFLL project was, in point of fact, more a movement rather than a project. GLAFLL stands for: Graded Levels of Achievement in Foreign Language Learning. The name, which belies its subsequent influence in methodology, was derived from concerns of the time with the grading of materials and assessment instruments and with the development of appropriate levels of performance criteria.[14] Most teachers of Modern Languages in Lothian participated to a greater or lesser extent and the project influenced work both inside and outside Scotland, in the rest of Britain and other European countries, through its links with the Council of Europe as well as with places as far away as Australia.[15] The driving force behind the project and its director was John Clark, then Assistant Adviser in Modern Languages for Lothian Region. It was his vision of a better future that inspired teachers in the region to work out for themselves a way to improve the experiences of pupils, not only those in their own classes,[16] but throughout the region.

Background

GLAFFL started in a kitchen, where a very small group of teachers came together with Clark to work out what could be done about the disastrous situation of the subject in many, though not all, of the region's secondary schools, namely the unacceptably high drop-out rate at the end of the second and final compulsory year of language learning. Teachers wanted essentially two changes to take place, the first in terms of pupils' motivation, the second, linked to this, in terms of increasing the ability of learners to actually use the foreign language.[17]

At issue, as the group saw it, was the entire future of Modern Languages teaching.

Scottish languages teaching in the late 1970s was reeling from the findings of the Munn committee, which had excluded Modern Languages from the list of core subjects in the new Scottish curriculum. The committee considered the subject to be elitist; languages teachers, it said, were both unable and unwilling to motivate pupils of medium to low ability. 'The materials and methodology of language teaching for less able pupils have not yet been developed to a point where effective learning can readily take place',[18] the committee reported. The majority of teachers themselves, many of whom were struggling in schools which had once been selective and were now comprehensive, held that many pupils could not benefit from the study over four years of a Modern Language; and 49% of teachers were opposed to the elaboration of a syllabus and certification scheme for 'low achievers', even on an optional basis.[19]

It must be remembered that debate about the common course, mixed-ability classes as opposed to classes 'set' according to ability, raged throughout the 1970s, and that the entire teaching profession was divided, mostly, though not always, on lines determined by length of service and/or political affiliation. Comprehensivisation was accompanied by the raising of the school leaving age from 15 to 16, a move which most teachers supported, while bewailing the fact that there were no materials and no support to help them to cope with a type of pupil they had hitherto not encountered, and one for whom, moreover, there were no 'carrots' in the shape of an examination to keep them occupied at school for a further year.

It was a time when those teachers who believed that pupils of all levels of ability could benefit from and succeed in their subject either had to give up the fight and accept that the subject would remain open only to the few, or take some action in order to change the minds of the powers that be, as well as those of some of their colleagues. It was the campaigning spirit, accompanied by a fervent belief that languages could and should be taught successfully to all pupils, that made GLAFLL, like other Graded Objectives projects in England at the same time, a heady, exciting movement to belong to.

Hope is essential for campaigns, as well as belief in the philosophy of the campaign. Hope was provided by Clark, a known quantity, who had already been Assistant Adviser in the region and who had recently returned there after some years overseas. While Clark was the focus, inspiration and the undoubted leader of the project, a number of teachers were associated closely with it from its inception, so that it would be fair to say that what evolved was a result of common deliberations. It was in no way a preconceived package of panaceas.

'Managing' democracy

The initial 'kitchen' group was small and friendly, an important consideration in the effecting of change. This group, with a few later additions, could be regarded, in terms of military or public health campaigning, as the staff organisation. Personal considerations matter. The creation of sufficient impetus to effect real change in the way people see their role in the classroom is not a matter which can be addressed through the intellect; it requires passion. Like a teacher trying to reinterest disaffected pupils in learning, the effort required demands total engagement. It is for this reason that things external and driven by the needs of institutions and people outside the classroom do not effect real change, however good the pedigree, however convincing the arguments. If individual commitment is not in place, all that will be effected is the cosmetic response – the politely interested faces of people who inside have simply gone to sleep.

But commitment and engagement are not enough. However much groups of teachers and advisers may wish to alter things, a framework is essential if what evolves is to have legitimacy. Curriculum policy in Lothian Region was coordinated at the time by a Regional Consultative Committee on the Curriculum. The support of this key body was essential both to make the case for funding and to ensure the project's legitimacy in the eyes of language teachers in general.

William Gatherer, Lothian Region's Chief Adviser, was the key to obtaining regional support and to ensuring that Lothian's education directorate gave their support and funding to the project. At one stage there was an approach to the SED (Scottish Education Department – later known as Scottish Office Education Department – SOED) for resourcing and support. This was unsuccessful, which in retrospect was certainly to the project's benefit. The SED was then and in my view still is, quite incapable of letting teachers control anything. On the other hand, the region was quick to see the advantages of anything that would involve the teachers in working out their own solutions. Keeping the project a regional, rather than a national effort retained the spirit of a movement taking place outside of 'the system'. In this case, the with-holding of the blessing of the high priests gave a legitimacy much more powerful than SED could have conferred, since it was a legitimacy bestowed by colleagues.

Committees galore

The Regional Study Group in Modern Languages[20] (RSGML) was the natural vehicle for the promotion of the project and its liaison with the Regional Consultative Committee on the Curriculum. For the purposes of implementation, a GLAFLL Co-ordinating Committee was estab-lished, chaired by a Head Teacher who was also a modern linguist. Its membership was the project director and development officer, plus the chairpersons of all subsequent subgroups as and when they emerged. These started out, in response to the initial drive to produce a syllabus, as language groups – French, German, Spanish, Italian and Russian. In French and German they were subdivided into groups whose schools were working on particular coursebooks – Eclair, Longmans, Vorwärts; but as the project entered the realms of assessment and materials, it seemed wasteful to duplicate all these, hence members of the language groups joined other groups according to their individual interests, and reformed themselves as language groups only as and when the need arose – a characteristic of a campaign organisation, as we have already seen.

The ability to change the personnel involved to suit the task, and to allow the tasks to emerge as a result of the internal dynamics, gave the project a flexibility that made for effectiveness. For example, as groups worked on the initial syllabuses and assessment instruments, members perceived the urgent need for materials which would reflect the new approach. Hand in hand with materials, there had to be a consensus as to the type of methodology that would be appropriate. Hence a materi-als group and a methodology group were formed, consisting of people from the original language groups as well as new recruits who had shown an interest. These groups liaised informally through word of mouth and formally through meetings of the Coordinating Committee of which each subgroup leader was a member – a *de facto* 'staff' group. Individual language specific groups (French, German, Spanish, Italian and Russian) decided whether to tackle tasks on their own or as non-language specific groups. There were no rules laid down – each group of people decided on its own way of proceeding.

Servicing and coordinating the working groups and committees was the job of the research and development officer. The nature of these meetings was exploratory. The contributions of all were welcomed. No one was going to rock the boat because it was their boat. No one, including the project leader, thought they had the answers.[21] It was, as he saw it, and indeed as the teachers also saw it, not his role to tell teachers how to teach. This was fundamentally different from the view of training as the following of someone else's 'good practice' or listening to the 'experts'.

Involving everyone

The identification of a group as the 'in' group can be both powerful and dangerous. Powerful because the sense of belonging makes people feel stronger. Dangerous because for those outside the group there will be a feeling of alienation and perhaps jealousy which has to be addressed. The feeling of belonging had to be extended to those teachers in schools, who, while interested, eager and willing enough to change things within their own schools, had been on the periphery in the early days.

One way of attempting this was by means of a structure that allowed teachers to opt in to working groups dealing with their own particular interests. They could be co-opted or co-opt themselves. Whereas prior to GLAFLL there were limits on meetings and a protocol for teachers in school to follow which tended to mean that people were selected to attend, GLAFLL opened up participation to all. Huge numbers of teachers attended after-school meetings at that time. Another way of involving people was through an intentionally light-hearted and 'jokey' newsletter – *GLAFLLnews*, to which teachers contributed. Some groups of teachers held monthly area meetings after school, such as those in East Lothian, to discuss ideas and develop and exchange materials suited to their own needs.

Documentation was important – departments were asked to keep a GLAFLL file for project documents. These ranged from documents essential to the workings of the assessment system to thoughts, long and short, on aspects of theory, syllabus or methodology. Whenever a new issue appeared or a new direction seemed to beckon, the project leader would draft a paper, consult with colleagues, rewrite it and distribute it to schools.

A handful of schools which became involved early on remained at the core, and were always willing to provide advice, practical help and an 'open door' policy to visits from other less advanced schools, and virtually all the region's 50 schools had some staff who were interested.

Sequencing of work

The kind of sequence that some of the work would take is outlined by Clark (1987b: 138–9) as follows:

- A problem was diagnosed and discussed by teachers The project leader produced a starter paper attempting to provide information related to the problem to be resolved.
- Project members read and discussed this, and prepared and examined alternative strategies for resolving the issue.
- Where appropriate, a RSGML subgroup of volunteers was set up, or an existing one asked to work on the production of an appropriate set of guidelines or resources.
- Project teachers experimented using the guidelines or resources produced, and adapted these to their circumstance.
- If there was to be an eventual product, the RSGML subgroup was asked to work on a final version of this. If the product was a set of methodological techniques, a video might be made for observation and discussion purposes. This was available for schools to borrow and was shown at courses and conferences.

Principles of procedure

Clark identifies the following principles of procedure which governed the curriculum renewal process:

- To place the teacher and school department at the centre of all curriculum renewal work.
- To uphold the principle that involvement in the project meant that schools had to develop their *own* version of GLAFLL, rather than adopting a predetermined package, thus involving teachers in discussing, planning, creating instruments, experimenting, obtaining feedback, and evaluating. There were to be no designated pilot schools.
- To ensure an adequate means of involving any teacher or department who might wish to participate in the project at any level of commitment.
- To permit would-be participants to start from whatever curricular entry point they wished (in practice often assessment).

- To create a set of guidelines, instruments, and resources flexible enough to fit a variety of patterns of organization in a variety of different school contexts.
- To promote simultaneous developments in all languages taught in regional schools, and through this to work towards redressing the imbalance in favour of French.
- To provide a framework which might be of use in the development of languages hitherto not taught (for example community languages or other foreign languages of importance).

Using expertise

Outsiders were consulted from time to time, some of whom gave new impetus or understanding to work being done. These were invited because their expertise was needed by the groups, their remit was clear and they were informed about the work in hand. This was as unlike the normal kind of INSET (In-Service Training) as teaching pupils traditionally is from operating a learner-directed model. The result was that a wide selection of teachers had access to the kind of expertise normally available only to a chosen few, and this expertise was perceived as relevant to their work, which now extended beyond their own classrooms and departments. Teachers learnt not to be in awe of experts – and how to use them. Even poor speakers, academics who lectured as if they were thinking aloud and whose OHP (Overhead Projector) overlays were illegible, were found to make a useful contribution because within the context in which they were working, the teachers could see the connection.

It was characteristic of the workings of the project that people did not feel afraid to voice their ignorance, and were keen to find out and engage. Learning was through doing, through experience over months and years. Progress could be seen in terms of tests, materials, videos or In Service Training, but it was the experience in terms of personal development that increased people's satisfaction with their jobs. Self-esteem was enhanced by the fact that people were taken seriously at an intellectual level. Teachers are not parrots mouthing the latest slogans from government reports, nor are they monkeys to ape the 'good practice' of others. We are dealing with people whose initial motivation to study languages had to do with the intellectual satisfaction to be derived from a difficult and broadly based discipline.

The great benefit felt by the participants was the chance to think and to discuss matters of theory within a real task with real outcomes.

Because of the influence of Applied Linguistics, as the discussion over what was and was not 'communicative' advanced, GLAFLL appealed to those teachers who wanted to flex their intellectual and analytical muscles. Those who worked in the assessment group had the opportunity to evaluate together over many meetings hours of recorded cassettes of pupil/pupil and pupil/teacher interaction. Their responsibility was to draw up guidelines for marking that could be easily applied, but which worked on the basis of the meaning of what was being said and heard, not as formerly on the basis of the correctness of what was being said.

For some participants, the feeling of being at bay ensured cohesion and the focus on the task in hand. Through GLAFLL they were dealing with difficult issues and making decisions which are normally made for teachers by outside bodies. Indeed, the maverick nature of the exercise was another strength. Free from external control, acting to its own agenda, with the speed of change determined by the teachers involved, it had its own dynamic. There were periods of consolidation and some great leaps forward. These were, in retrospect, exciting times.

Roles

In order for people to work successfully as a team, it is important that each person is clear in their mind as to the role they have within the team. Clark identifies what he calls the two most important factors in school-focused curriculum renewal as 'the quality of relationships between participants and the sharing of responsibility'. In order to promote these, there needs to be 'a democratic framework of shared responsibilities'. For these to be understood, it is clear that the interpretation of role was of prime importance.

The project leader

It is extremely difficult for an Advisory service to fulfil its remit in terms of curriculum development when at the same time it plays a role in the selection procedures of staff in schools. Advisers in Lothian were one of the team of three responsible for selecting teachers to all promoted posts, and played then, as now, a crucial role in advising Head Teachers about those they might want to call to interview or put on a short-list.

Clark's interpretation of his role, despite his awareness of the possible conflict with that of 'representative of management', was one largely shared by the teachers. It saw him as follows:

- as responsible for establishing the framework for participation;
- as counsellor;
- as facilitator;
- as information-seeker and provider;
- as educator;
- as motivator;
- as coordinator;
- as public spokesman;
- as communications-network organiser.

The research and development officer

In my three years in this role, I learnt a great deal about the problems of being a teacher while not having an actual 9:00 to 4:00 teaching job. Two things were hard: first, to learn to work with and for teachers, with all the privileges of having time out of the classroom, yet remain essentially a teacher oneself. It is all too easy for teachers who leave their classrooms to start seeing themselves as 'different', and they would not be human if they did not relish the increased freedoms that not hearing the bell every 40 minutes brings, and, sadly to my mind, the increase in status which even short-term secondments out of school bring with them. In the transcript of the video on pages 95–103 I can be seen to talk about 'the teachers' as if I were not one myself – a habit I deplore but one which is only too easy to acquire. Secondly, and related to this was the fact that it takes only a few days out of the classroom to forget the realities and limitations of what can and, more importantly, what cannot, be done. It was easy to sit at a desk dreaming up wonderful activities which well-motivated pupils could perform; quite another to take over a group of 12-year-olds and make them work.[22]

In practical terms, the 'development' side of the job brought responsibility in particular for the coordination of materials production, and for the promotion within the schools of innovations arising from the needs of the various working groups. As indicated, this meant many visits to schools to try out and evaluate with the departments different techniques with classes, and the creation of a bank of extensive video material to support In-Service work.

The Advisory Service at the time boasted a magnificent educational technology section which produced high quality videos whose contribution was invaluable to the spread of innovative practices. It was a later victim to the education cuts and a dreadful miss, those who worked in it having developed over the years the ability to pick out what was going on in a classroom and capture on film key moments. It takes time to learn how to work with a film crew, and time to learn about editing. It also takes time for the crew to understand what it is that is wanted; but once an understanding has developed, the results can be worth their weight in gold. In an area the size of Lothian, videos could not be faked. Teachers could see people they knew trying out techniques in their classes, and realise that the methodology which was being discussed at meetings could actually be made to work for them. These videos gave an essential credibility to the work of the project.

It was this experience of working in many different classrooms, with all kinds of teachers, that led me to the view of teacher development as a long-term process engaging teachers as whole beings within a social setting, requiring attention to all aspects of their personality as well as the state of their knowledge, their views and beliefs. It was the demand for theory and discussion, the delight in debate and the stirring arguments that GLAFLL provoked that convinced me that the engaging of the emotions and the provision of intellectual challenge are strong and invaluable forces for the promotion of changes within the classroom.

The group leaders

Responsibility for the final production of syllabus, materials and tests was shared between project leader, development officer and group leaders, the organisation's 'staff', on a purely practical basis. For instance, materials that would be sent out to schools did not require direct involvement of the project leader in their design and selection, which was the task of the whole group. On the other hand, once individual language syllabuses had gone beyond the selection stage (and this was dominated by the members of the groups who, it was felt, were likely to make better judgements as to which item of language was most appropriate to each stage), the task was finished and made ready for eventual publication by the project leader and development officer. In other words, it was the nature of the task that determined who did what. Some group leaders took a more active role than others in shaping the project. Volunteers, not always group leaders, undertook involvement when, for example, Macmillan offered to publish some of the materials.[23] All the Macmillan materials were the result of collaboration and discussion. The finalising of the contents, for example, was mostly done by group agreement.

The class teachers

Characteristic of the project was that 'rank' and teaching experience had no part to play in how people could be useful. Many unpromoted teachers offered their classes to try out activities, either on their own, or in the presence and with the help of the development officer. Some teachers specialised in such things as board games – one particular school ran a lunchtime board games club for pupils at which games were produced and played. These teachers would then be asked to speak at meetings and demonstrate their materials. Sessions were organised whereby departments from individual schools could share their experiences of GLAFLL with other departments. It was fascinating to see how differently each department interpreted the experience, how certain elements were of particular interest in some, and almost totally ignored in others. It was important that GLAFLL was not an ideology where one had to accept all or nothing. Schools and teachers were welcome to select whatever aspect most appealed. Many clearly opted for the tests, since they offered for the first time some certification and motivation to those pupils who opted out of language learning after SII. Others were attracted more by the methodology and did not present their pupils for tests at all.

GLAFLL grew and grew, from an initial 27 out of 49 Lothian schools to virtually every school in the region. Reasons given by teachers who spent hours of their free time in meetings, some of which were nit-picking and frustrating, others of which were richly rewarding in terms of the work executed, had to do as much with the social, enjoyable nature of the meetings as with the sense of achievement in good work done. Years later, teachers would recognise each other as having worked together 'on GLAFLL'.

What is GLAFLL?

Peter Mickan, a visitor from South Australia, who later was to work on the ALL (Australian Language Levels) project, interviewed the GLAFLL team on video in the fifth year of the project. The video, one of the many In-Service Training videos made for the project, is entitled *What is GLAFLL?* The interview gives an idea of the thinking and the concerns of that precise moment:

Mickan: John, I'm interested in finding out more about GLAFLL. How did a programme like GLAFLL come to get started?

Clark: Well, I suppose the main reason why it got started was because of the feelings of lack of success that the pupils got from their normal language lessons, and this was also felt by the teachers who were somewhat frustrated by the fact that there was very little motivation left in modern language learning after about one to two years. The result of it all was that some 65% of the pupils who started out in a language course in the first year gave up at the end of the second year. So we started hoping to improve the level of motivation in the pupils and hoping to make life a bit more enjoyable for the teachers as well.

Mickan: Is that a few years ago when the project started?

Clark: Yes. I think we started in 1977 in a serious way. We were dabbling with it in 1976 and it's taken five years of extremely hard work by teachers to come to terms with what it is they might be doing in the classroom to improve the situation.

Mickan: Can you explain how you went about implementing a project which seems to be quite a major project in language teaching?

Clark: Wow! Well there are various sort of moments that we had to pass through. There was a *syllabus* creation moment, where we had to examine in detail what it was we were leading towards and then create a syllabus of ideas that would help teachers to get there. There was moment when we had to look at the *methodology* and see what kind of learning processes there seemed to be for language learning and set them into motion, and then we had to look at the *resources* to see whether the textbooks included the sort of activities that would best lead to communication, and then we had to look at the *assessment* to see whether the sort of testing that was done in schools was the sort of testing that would most help children come to terms with what they were learning, and then to see whether the tests were genuinely communicative or not; and finally we had to *evaluate* the whole thing. Now I suppose that in an ideal world if you had lots of time you would do each of these exercises in some sort of an order. In the real world where you have to deal with the classroom you've got to keep all these balls in the air at the same time. You can't be doing syllabus only for one year, and not thinking about, well, what are we actually going to do in the classroom? So we've had to keep all the various focuses in mind all at the same time. But we have had a year of syllabus, where the emphasis was mainly on that and at least two or three years on methodology and at least a year of assessment.

Mickan: You talk about the syllabuses being a focus. Syllabuses open up all sorts of possibilities. I wonder what kinds of focuses you put into your syllabuses.

Clark: Well, the main focus of course was how to achieve communication, and for us that meant looking very carefully at the sorts of activities that were normally done in the classroom and trying to see whether they were or were not communicative and whether they could become communicative. The notion of the information gap, the creation of a task in which one pupil has to exchange information with another pupil, seems to us to have been the most important step forward in our understanding of how to get communication going in the classroom

Mickan: I wonder about what sort of topics or themes you have if you are talking about an information gap. Can you explain?

Clark: We don't, I think, really think very much about topics although they do interest us in terms of what pupils might read about or might listen to and thereafter might discuss. We don't think so much in terms of topics as in terms of different types of activity. For that we've drawn up for ourselves a number of what we call communication areas within which activities can take place which demand certain skills and strategies which necessarily imply the building up of a particular language resource to carry out those activities.

Mickan: Could you give me an example of a particular communication area?

Clark: The first communication area and the one that needs no engineering and no syllabus at all is 'the use of the foreign language for all relations, the management between pupils and teachers and teachers and pupils, and pupils and pupils'. So that if you're setting up groupwork, the pupils learn what sort of language they need to use to set up an activity. Now of course teachers find it difficult, it's an act of faith to use the foreign language consistently for classroom management, but those who have tried for about a year find that there is a considerable pay-off. During the first year there may be a good understanding of language used in context, not a great deal will be used by the pupils themselves, but after the second year indeed yes. It seems there's a sort of gestation period that's required. That's one communication area. Another is a communication area which we call 'activities involving

speakers of the foreign language' and you can have face to face communication with foreign assistants or visitors to the school, you can have
penpal correspondence and you can have class links and exchanges
either through class links or through actual bodies being exchanged.
Another communication area we think of is 'activities for pleasure',
reading, listening and viewing television for pleasure And then we have
our three stalwarts which we've put a great deal of time and effort into:
'games', you can have language practice games where you actually
teach bits of language and then practise them in the form of a game you
teach them – you teach the number system and you play bingo, or you
can have more open-ended games where you are saying to the children
not 'use the language I have just taught you', but, 'use whatever
language you've got to do these games and I will listen to you while
you are doing them and I will make a note of whatever weaknesses you
have in your language resource and I will teach them to you afterwards'.

Then there's the other area we call 'simulation' where we are
concerned with fairly large-scale exercises, like making a magazine or
making a television programme demonstrating your school and
sending it to a foreign school on an exchange – something fairly
large-scale, where there are a number of sub-tasks all building up into a
coordinated whole.

And finally, the most popular one of all I would say, is 'communication tasks'. By communication tasks what we mean are small purposeful
exercises in which pupils have to carry out some sort of task which
involves exchanging information and then coming to a conclusion.
These tasks can be the sort of task that a tourist would do, or the sort of
tasks that are done every day by the pupils in their home, like selecting
what television programme to watch that night, or what sort of things
they are going to buy for a picnic. Or you can have things to do with
whatever reading or listening to authentic material you have in the
foreign language, so that they have a menu and have to do something
with it, or they have a magazine article and they have to something
with it. All of these we slot into our communication task areas. That's
them. I've been a bit longwinded, but there are a number of communication areas and they all seem to us to build up an appropriate language
resource and an appropriate number of skills and strategies for the
pupils, and they can either build up the skills and strategies and then do
the activities, or through doing the activities help build up the language
and the skills.

Mickan: What you've just described implies massive changes on the part of teachers and what's happening in the classrooms. I wonder how that's been brought about.

Hamilton: With In-Service Training meetings that we have here. We have various groups. When we started off, we tended, because the emphasis was on the actual materials that were in schools, to form groups using actual courses like the Eclair group, the Longmans group, the Vorwärts group.

Mickan: Was that groups of teachers?

Hamilton: That's right. The ones who were using particular courses felt the need to get together to relate their course to the first syllabus that we drew up. Now that lot has all gone, because that particular bit of work is out of the way and the syllabus has moved on now in any case to a slightly different aspect. We are looking more towards activities than to the actual language that you might teach at any given time, which is how we started off – that is, looking at the actual units of the coursebook and saying 'we'd better put the perfect tense here'. Now the groups have changed from how we started off and we're looking at what kids actually *do* with language in the classroom. So the groups have changed and now we have a very active assessment group, which has just finished revising the tests and a very active resources group which has been doing a lot of work on materials, like penpal letters. We have been collecting original letters and doing things with them, suggesting ways in which teacher might use these materials.

And the other thing is that I go into schools and take classes and do silly things with them. I try to find out for instance whether drama techniques can be used in the language classroom and to what extent – how far along that particular line might one go. I might go in and teach a lesson trying out something new, which the teacher would watch, and then we would discuss it, and usually the teacher will have lots of ideas about how it's gone and whether it's worth using at all.

Mickan: You put quite a lot of emphasis on teacher involvement in developing GLAFLL. Why do you emphasise that?

Hamilton: Well, without it, it would be impossible to run any such project. You can't impose things, it has to be a consensus of people wishing to change the system. You can't change the system by somebody saying: 'Let it be like this!' It doesn't work that way. In fact many of the very best ideas come from the teachers. I think John will agree, that our own wishes are not always fulfilled because the teachers will shoot things down: they will say, 'That isn't going to work, we can't do it like that', and we all learn from each other.[24]

Mickan: I can imagine that somebody trying to adopt a GLAFLL approach to language teaching could face many problems and I think it might be good to anticipate some of the problems that they might face. What sort of problems would an outsider adapting GLAFLL or adopting some aspects of it, run into? I'm thinking of teachers, or I'm thinking of you as people who've been involved in running the project.

Clark: One of the things I would say is that the whole question of which communication areas and how to sort out a framework into stages of language learning at which pupils can perform at different levels of performance, is something that must be different from country to country and maybe even from area to area. Our colleagues in the south of England, for example can put a lot more of their eggs into the tourist basket than we can, since our children will simply not get to France as tourists very frequently. So there are different emphases in the different communication areas. And the different way in which you organise your stages and levels must be entirely up to the constraints of the various institutions and the age levels at which you start and all sort of different factors which will be different. But I think the basic principles of developing communication, the notion of grading, so that each pupil has success at his or her own particular level, the notion of trying to get assessment more tailored towards the pupil's ability to monitor his or her own progress and the criterion-referenced nature of that assessment that tells you what the pupil can do and how well he can do it and draws that into a profile, I think those things are common to whatever moves teachers are making towards a more sane teaching of Modern Languages in schools.

But the actual way in which you organise your syllabus and the actual way in which you produce your own resources and your own tests is very much, I think, local teacher work and can only be done at the level of the classroom teacher coming together with other classroom teachers facing similar problems with similar constraints.

Mickan: We didn't talk much about the main people who are either suffering or benefiting – the students or pupils. What has a syllabus like this and changes in methods meant for students?

Hamilton: One of the big things is that the atmosphere is changing in schools. It has been anyway, I think, schools are more pleasant places, but the idea of negotiation, by teachers with their pupils, of such things as objectives and levels and so on has meant that teachers and pupils know each other better as a result, and have better relationships. And in fact they are also learning all sorts of social skills, the heavy emphasis on teacher/pupils tests, pupil-to-pupil tests and group work, talking, you know, relating through the syllabus, through the activities, means that as a stranger going through schools, I have found over four to five years that pupils actually are better at what you might like to call interview techniques. They are also more sure of what they are doing in the language. If you ask them 'What are you doing?' for instance, they don't say 'We are on page 64' which is what you used to get, they say 'We're learning to … order a meal in a restaurant' or whatever. So they are thinking functionally and they find it very easy to think functionally.

Mickan: The classroom is organised very differently for this type of activity, isn't it?

Hamilton: Yes. A lot of paired and a fair amount of groupwork, much less teacher as the source of all knowledge.

Mickan: I'll ask you a nasty question: does the whole classroom collapse into chaos if you've got students running around doing pairwork?

Hamilton: Sometimes, yes.

Clark: There's a lot of noise which can disturb the classroom next door, but I think the notion of a language classroom which is silent has gone, people are coming to terms with this.

Mickan: Yes. I can see that's important. What techniques have teachers used to structure the classroom, even though you've got students working individually or in pairs?

Hamilton: I've noticed that teachers are more aware of how to teach children to move about classrooms. I mean that it's actually taught, before you teach the language, that you say: 'This is how to move a desk; this is how you go and you pick up a worksheet'. You can in fact have activities going on of a self-access nature and some dialogues, and all the rest of it, and I have seen classes where this is carried out in the most orderly and organised fashion, and I think that's what teachers are learning, that behaviour has to be taught as well. It's not just a question of saying: 'Here it all is, help yourselves', but 'When you are going to get a worksheet do it in this particular way' or whatever. I think that helps.

Mickan: I wonder if you could explain that a little bit more. Before we were talking about pupil access. What do you mean by that? Can you give some examples of pupil access?

Hamilton: Yes, the sort of individualised materials which we have taken from French magazines, where you cut an article out and stick it on a card and put into boxes, either according to topic or according to level, depending on how the teacher wishes to organise it, with answer sheets at the back and the kids come and select something they want to read about, perhaps, and they note down on a grid system what they have in fact read or done with what they have read. This grid gives a sort of profile, or overview. Rather than all the kids in the class doing a certain reading exercise, the notion is that the kids do in fact do more if they can read as much as they like and discard things that they are not interested in, or that are too hard. So nobody is being forced to do a particular exercise. This is happening all the time but that is part of the methodology. Of course, there's every day ordinary teaching going on as well, the grammar, vocabulary and all the exercises that go with it. It's not all one joyous let's all do what we want.

Clark: Yes, that's an important one. People often assume that a communicative approach means that we don't any longer have to deal with grammar, the building up of vocabulary and all the rest of it. Of course we do, we have a very simple way in which we try to encourage people to do that, in which we suggest that the children should them-selves keep a mirror-image of their knowledge, as it were. Now I'm afraid many schools have found this too hard to actually put into prac-tice, but the notion is that they have a blank booklet into which they write, according to a functional category, what language they need in order to do something with. What do I need to ask for information? I need a question form that looks like this. Or a semantic category, what do I need to go fishing with? I need the following implements and we deal with fishing. Or in a grammatical category, how do I express past time? This is how I express past time. So that the pupil have in a sense something with which they are recording. It isn't just language fleeting and passing in the wind. It is also at the same time, we hope, being recorded in a way in which the pupil will learn how the language system works, how it all sticks together, which I hope will help them to memorise it, and will certainly help them to revise it when the time comes. With that and with the progress card, which helps them to see what it is that they are being asked to learn, and that allows them to monitor their progress by ticking off items on the progress card when they complete them, we hope that we've got a much more explicit way of making sure the pupils know what on earth it is that they are learning and supposed to be doing next.

Mickan: Before I came here and before I read about your material, I didn't know the name Lothian at all. Is interest being shown beyond the Lothian Region in GLAFLL, and if so why?

Clark: I think we could say that interest has been shown beyond the Lothian Region. There are a number of schemes in Britain as a whole, also in Ireland and in Northern Ireland as well, so that within the total geographical area there are a lot of schemes going on, some of them are more, some less communicative. All of them are graded, all of them are I think working towards criterion-referencing, and we swap ideas so that we learn from what our colleagues down south are doing and we hope that they can get something from what we are doing. But of course it's a much bigger exercise, because the Council of Europe has started, through their Threshold Level and Niveau Seuil and Kontaktschwelle documents, they have started a deal of activity in a number of countries, and GLAFLL through its contacts has in fact one way or another been in contact with countries as far apart as Austria, Portugal, Finland, I think, that's about all on the European continent – oh, Sweden. We've got a number of contacts with a number of other schemes, and we exchange information and material. We believe that even Australia is getting interested in Graded Objectives, Peter, perhaps you might like to tell us why Australia is interested in Graded Objectives?

Mickan: Well, I think in Australia we've had similar problems to the problems you've had here. We've had inappropriate texts, we've had students who have been bored with the language we've been teaching them, they've dropped out at the very first opportunity they can drop out of language learning, and so by and large we've had bored teachers and bored students.

Clark: It's all very familiar.

Mickan: And clearly the whole thinking in the area of how we learn language is having a marked influence on what we think we ought to be doing in the language classroom. Also in Australia we don't have languages as compulsory, they are not part of the core curriculum and we think that if we want languages to become part of the experience of every child in the school then it's also vital that we provide a very good learning experience in languages, successful in all respects, educational, also in the subject area, in the communicative aspect, that it's necessary for us to have this kind of approach to language teaching and language learning.

What Did GLAFLL Do?

While the above represents a particular moment in the development of the project, after which certain things assumed a much greater importance (the use of the target language, for instance) while others (the strong emphasis on assessment) seemed to moderate, what follows deals in more detail with the changes which took place over several years. Of course the GLAFLL project was not the sole reason for the shifts that took place, but it was responsible for initiating virtually all of the developments that took place in Lothian classrooms, since it was the only vehicle for In-Service in Modern Languages that brought teachers in substantial numbers into the Education Centre.

Changes Within the Classroom

The classroom looked different

At that time it was possible to distinguish the GLAFLL classroom immediately from others in a department by the way it looked. Walls would be covered in posters, notices in the foreign language, lots of examples of pupils' work, charts and graphs indicating successes and work done, national flags and other realia reminiscent of the primary school. The desks, previously in rows, were first arranged in pairs, then in groups.

More talk

The silent language classroom seemed to have become a thing of the past – noise, mostly productive, replaced the occasional sound of turning pages. Later on, teachers were to find ways of allowing for periods of quiet, sustained study as they felt necessary.

High tec

Chalk and teacher talk were replaced by a variety of high tec equipment, the most popular being the PALE (Peripheral Audio-Active Language Equipment) units which allow pairs and groups of pupils or individuals to work on their own on listening or speaking tasks at study points usually round the walls of the classroom. Other equipment includes computers (sometimes used as word processors), video recorders and playback machines. Some schools allowed pupils to use the video cameras.

Increased use of the target language

One of the effects of the debates that took place in the course of the project was the increasing use of the target language. In the early days, a video was made illustrative of a new and exciting technique called the 'simulated novel'. In this a kind of living soap opera took place in the class, with pupils choosing imaginary roles and on a day-to-day basis moving forward the lives of the chosen characters. The resulting film soon became unusable because it sounded 'unnatural' to conduct the activity in a mixture of English and French. Teachers, seeing examples of their colleagues using the target language on video, were quick to discern that here was the logical approach to 'natural language use' as well as making their classrooms 'communicative'. With an increased use of the language, teachers started to look at what they were in fact using the language *for*.[25]

Attitude to error

Discernible in the course of the project was a new approach to learners' errors. Slowly it became accepted that 'errors' could be seen helpfully and developmentally as part of the learning process. Pit Corder's term 'interlanguage'[26] became familiar through sessions with the project director, and teachers realised that certain things which they called 'errors' were an inevitable part of the pupils' learning of a language. Attempts, tentative at first, were made to categorise 'errors' into those that interfered with communication and those that could be regarded as belonging to 'effective but defective' communication.

As the work of the pupils in the various languages became available to the assessment group, certain patterns became evident, such that some practical sessions eventuated in a workable consensus as to what was inevitable and therefore acceptable. A huge amount of experience at analysing pupil performance was acquired by the assessment group. What they eventually arrived at in assessing conversation was a system known inelegantly as 'U/C-ing and LOP-ping': the only criterion for 'passing' a GLAFLL Stage test was whether the pupil or pupils had completed the task. To complete the task, the pupil had to understand and communicate intelligibly – U/C-ing. Thereafter it was a question of LOP – Level of Performance. This took into account fluency, appropriacy, use of strategies, discourse coherence, as well as accuracy, which was not, however, the predominating criterion. Tasks increased in complexity at different levels – so that, for instance, the completion of a Level 3 teacher/pupil conversation task might require the ability to deal with unpredictability. For example, at Stages 1 and 2, if a pupil were asked to buy something in a shop, the goods would be available. If s/he got what was required and hence 'U/C-ed', it was then simply a matter of assessing the LOP. At Stage 3, a pupil helping her or his parents check in to a hotel was likely to find that the hotel was full and had no trace of their booking. A pupil succeeding in getting rooms would 'pass' at Stage 3 as long as s/he could understand the problem and be understood. This way of viewing progression meant that teachers gradually saw grammatical errors as less important in real terms, with the result that pupils who formally had been discouraged from languages now found themselves succeeding.

Changes in Materials

The need for materials which would promote the kind of 'communicative' learning experiences under discussion was felt very early on, as can be imagined. Most schools were using 'Vorwärts' for German and perhaps 'Longmans' for French, with 'Adelante' for Spanish. Russian and Italian teachers tended to rely on a mixture of anything that was available.

In looking closely at existing materials teachers came to understand more about what really was meant by the term 'communicative' and extending it to include not only the material but also the task. This, as well as assessment, was an exercise that produced a real learning experience for those involved. Developing 'communicative' tasks meant developing a new way of thinking about language which took a very long time.

To give an indication of how far people came: to start with it was thought that 'Vorwärts' provided an adequate basis, and that indeed a 'French version' would be all that was required. From there the next step was to hope that the new SED French course, 'Tour de France' would provide the solution. Much of what was understood about it suggested that it would promote all the 'right kind of things'. The group still at this stage thought that the solution to the problems of motivating pupils was to be found in the ideal coursebook. Only one brave school, Lasswade High School, decided to go ahead and write its own 'GLAFLL course'. For the rest it was decided that it was necessary for the time being to produce materials as a group to supplement the out-of-date school texts. Soon teachers found that they were using the out-of-date textbooks less and less, although no one was keen to follow the example of Lasswade (this was in the days when technology made the duplication of materials a matter of banda, roneo and typewriter).

Up to this point the demands of what was or was not communicative had been mostly academic. Now that there had to be a product, it was necessary to arrive at a consensus of just what 'communicative' ought to mean. In the course of the work on materials, much was written, to be used, discussed, refined and perhaps discarded. From the slave to the coursebook many developed not only into adaptors of the same coursebook but into producers of materials in their own right.

Initially seen as a search for authenticity *per se*, (involving teachers in the most hectic scavenging activities when on visits abroad, if not downright larceny), the approach then shifted over the years to authenticity of task or communicative intent and response. In other words, instead of using a text to ask comprehension questions about it, the text would be used in such a way that pupils had to relate to it as the writer may have intended. For example, a text about an issue where the author was clearly proselytising – against pollution, say, or in favour of 50% female representation in government – calls for a response to do with its effect on the opinion of the reader. In such instances, pupils could still demonstrate understanding of the text by, for instance, using the points made in the article to convince a third party of the validity of the argument. Later on, such texts would become part of mixed skill activities and simulations, so that on the basis of what they read, or heard, pupils would make up posters and other material for a campaign, or simulate a radio discussion. Attention was paid to what learners really wanted to read or listen to (this led to pages and pages on 'the pop scene'). Later again, under the influence of ideas about the need to appeal to the learner as a whole person, the materials team started to look at 'needs' in terms not just of practicality or appeal to specific interests, and also at the 'need' to flex the creative muscles that respond to poetry and drama.[27]

While materials were produced, firstly in packs for all Lothian schools and subsequently under an arrangement with Macmillan Education in commercial form, it must be said that it was as creators of materials, rather than as users of materials that teachers derived most benefit. Initially it took a great deal of time to learn even simple things like how to select suitable materials – such basic things as whether a magazine article could photocopy easily, for example, mattered when time was scarce. Devising tasks was hard to begin with, but once groups had the hang of it, they could soon see the potential in all kinds of unlikely sources. This was teacher training by teachers of themselves with a vengeance.

Changes in Attitudes

By working together, teachers adopted a critical attitude not only to what they had used to date, but also to what they were producing themselves. This became a self-sustaining activity, in which it was recognised to what extent the knowledge of 'theory' was important. By designing materials, syllabuses and assessment instruments for general use, and writing guidelines for their use, teachers developed their own capacity to analyse and to communicate in written form to others what they had learnt. In a sense, working on the project was a mini-applied-linguistics course in its own right. Teachers started to read books and articles about language teaching, and to ask for more information on current research. Moreover, it was not only a learning experience but, as already stated a social one, in which the doors of the classroom opened, and after which they never again closed.

Methodology

Slowly the notion of what constituted language practice and some understanding of what was meant by 'communication' became current. That most misused of terms tended as time went on to be replaced by words like 'meaningful', 'language use', 'natural interaction', and terms such as 'discourse coherence' became current as tapes and videos of pupil talk were analysed. Whereas it was common elsewhere at the time to find teachers in other places using 'communication and communicative' where they simply meant 'speaking' or 'spoken', this was less likely in Lothian.[28]

Methodology was comparatively late in becoming addressed by a working group. It was necessary to build up an atmosphere of trust before classroom doors were opened to visits and experimentation. Apart from visits by the Research and Development officer, what tended to happen was that after teachers had chosen to experiment in their classrooms, they would report back on what had happened. As much as possible of what was successful was videoed.

From describing language to pupils, teachers moved to using it themselves, and encouraging pupils to use it 'for real'. Rote-learning and such things as verb paradigms, if used at all, took up less time, although few teachers abandoned the direct teaching of grammar in the traditional way. The emphasis on understanding what was entailed by 'communication', did however, ensure that the kind of virtually scripted 'meaningless' role play that was initially popular, was soon replaced by activities that left the choice of language open to the pupils. Communication tasks, information gap and problem-solving activities became immensely popular. Reading and listening tasks required pupils to interact with the text – and in many classes attempts were made to depart from the constraints of the 'four skills' approach.

Language games and drama techniques appealed to a small minority of teachers as offering opportunities for a quite different way of proceeding. The question had been raised of why it was regarded always as necessary to proceed from presentation of language to practice, then to the exploitation of that language. What if one started with the activity and let the language 'arise' from the needs of the activity? When first mooted in open forum this produced uproar. However, modest beginnings at ways of addressing this were the precursors of what is now if not a common approach, at least one that can be said to characterise that taken nowadays by a fair number of Lothian teachers.

The fact that theory and practice had come to interact in such a way that it was unclear at times whether the need for theory was a result of problems associated with the practice, or whether the chance encounter with the theory actually suggested the practice, meant an increase in interest in the actual processes of learning. These were to remain largely unaddressed at the time. It would be true to say that those few teachers who did grapple with the notion of process made a point of learning how to help their pupils 'learn how to learn'. This was easier in classes which were operating on the basis of self-access materials where the teacher could spend time with individuals.[29]

Teacher/learner Relationships

Although relationships between teacher and learner have altered noticeably over the years, GLAFLL did not seek to transform teachers in terms of their own personalities or the atmosphere and 'ethos' of the classroom. These were still the days of some formidable Principal Teachers, whose pupils – and colleagues, advisers and Head Teachers included, went in considerable awe of them. Some of these were among the most vocal critics of all developments in the direction of increased pupil responsibility, and quite appalled at any notion that pupils would exert any choice in matters of learning. But it must be said, their 'traditional' classes were also among the best and most amenable to work with from the point of view of trying out new techniques.[30] This led me to the view that pupils who are well-taught can be asked to do most things, but pupils who are only well-trained have very little flexibility.

Many teachers did indeed report improved relationships, better motivation and so on. Certainly teachers started to see themselves as being there to help their pupils, as individuals or groups, to guide learners towards selecting what to do. Teachers tried too, to be encouraging and to build confidence, and some aimed at making themselves at times 'dispensable', so as 'not to get in the way of the learning process', to quote Peter Wheeldon, Lothian Region's Modern Languages Adviser.

The pupils

Here the changes were discernible, with reports abounding of increased motivation, willingness to take risks with new language, higher levels of production and greater confidence. Pupils themselves, in their responses to interviews and questionnaires about their learning and their feelings about it, reported on how much they enjoyed the new way of working, and there were few who regretted 'the old way'.

A summary[31] in idealised form of the above changes is contained in Figure 6.1. It is not suggested that all of these were achieved, nor that all teachers would agree that the second column is necessarily desirable, but it indicates the direction of the changes which the project initiated and which can still be said to be the basis for what goes on in classrooms in Lothian Region.

THE CLASSROOM	
From	To
Rows	Groups
Silence	Noise
Chalk	High tec
English spoken	Target Language
Fear of error	We all make mistakes
MATERIALS	
Slave	Critical adaptor
User	Designer
Inauthentic	Authentic
Drills	Context sensitivity
Fixed for ever	Action Research
ATTITUDES	
Unself-critical	Self-critical
Uni-disciplinary	Multi-disciplinary
Behind closed doors	Everyone welcome
'No' to IST	'Yes' to IST
Theory is useless	Theory is necessary
Monolingualism is incurable	Monolingualism is curable
METHODOLOGY	
Product	Process and product
Descriptive	Communicative
Language practice	Language use
Meaningless rote learning	Meaningful utterances
Role-play	Genuine interaction
Teacher talk	Pupil talk
'Learn this'	'Learn how'
Error is BAD	Error is inevitable
TEACHER/LEARNER RELATIONSHIPS	
Authority	Guide
Source of all information	Helper
Confidence	Confidence builder
100% indispensable	Frequently dispensable
Teaching the learner	Learning about learners
THE PUPILS	
Driven	Drivers
Solo workers	Group cooperators
Unmotivated	Motivated
Learning 'things'	Learning HOW
Playing it safe	Taking risks
Unreliable robots	Responsible organisers
'If you don't know it, don't use it	'If you don't know it find it out

Figure 6.1 Changes in the classroom

Things political

I mentioned early in the book the role which politicians and politics can play in the determination of what happens in the classroom, for better or for worse. Lothian Region became embroiled in a conflict with Margaret Thatcher's Conservative government, the immediate result of which for GLAFLL was that, in the course of financial cut-backs imposed by a freeze on central funding, the post of Research and Development officer, along with many other such secondments in the region, was axed.

This in itself did not of course mean the end of the project. Its death-knell was, however, sounded by the prolonged period of industrial action by Scottish teachers in the mid-1980s. Since GLAFLL depended on voluntary, mostly unpaid and unrewarded (but not unrewarding), participation, it was an early casualty. The dispute, the longest-lasting industrial dispute in Britain, put an end to all curriculum development. The eventual agreement makes it highly unlikely that any project on a similar scale could be contemplated given the new teachers' contract and the climate and conditions relating to In-Service work. Here, having fought the battle over conditions of service, the teaching unions may have put a strait-jacket on their members. It is hard to see how an open structure, allowing people to opt in and out of committees and working groups can co-exist with the need to count the minutes worked, decide which travel is refundable and which is not and so on. The needs of a bureaucracy are not conducive to informal organisations such as GLAFLL.

A healthy advisory service makes an ideal campaign headquarters from which to stimulate teacher-based curriculum renewal. It is better placed than, say, a central body, university or other outside institution, by virtue of the fact that it is part of its legitimate role to work along with teachers. It is also the institution most suited to supporting a teacher-driven model along the lines described, where the question of funding and financial accountability cannot be estimated to the nearest penny, and where a region is in a much better position to allocate extra funding and move moneys around in the budget. Flexible financial management is necessary where innovation is concerned. It is almost impossible to cost out in advance something whose outcomes are not predictable, whose groups come and go and whose membership is constantly changing to suit the needs of the moment.

With the likely reform of local government into a one-tier system, due to take place in 1996, which will disband the present 12 Scottish regional councils and 53 district councils in order to set up 28 all-purpose councils, the killing off of the Advisory Services will be complete. In a letter to MP Tom Dalyell, Lord James Douglas Hamilton, the Minister for Education, said that the Scottish Office reckoned much of the Advisory Service's role would become unnecessary once the new curriculum was in place. The letter went on to argue that schools would be able to buy-in services from education colleges, council consortia or the Scottish Consultative Council on the Curriculum. The New Zealand model (see Chapter 3) is but a breath away. Scottish languages teachers are unlikely to feel that the SCCC and SOED, with their history of resistance to any expansion of the subject, are likely to offer any kind of replacement for its progressive advisers. The idea of leadership coming from that direction is nothing short of laughable.

When national groups are formed by SOED they are programmed to last a specific period of time, they rarely bring in new members and people do not move from group to group. Volunteers are never asked for. Clark calls this: 'The pseudo-democratic model employed by the Scottish Education Department, which effectively retains power and carefully selects those with whom it wishes to "consult".'

There is a need, and there should be made a place for teacher-driven curricular renewal movements such as that represented by the Lothian project. Many would argue that it is the only model of curriculum renewal that has a chance of working. All the new examinations and national curricula in the world cannot replace having teachers take a proactive role in their own development.

7 Looking Around: The Bangalore Project

A curriculum development project[32] in India aimed at developing learners' grammatical competence demonstrates the importance of cultural fit and the effects of innovation on the teacher.

The Need for Change

The Bangalore project arose for many of the same reasons as did the Lothian project and at about the same time, as a response to dissatisfaction with the existing approach to the teaching of English based on the 'structural' method as exemplified by S-O-S (Structural Oral Situational) pedagogy. The Bangalore project also started without a fixed position in terms of desired 'outcomes' and, like GLAFLL, it was not intended as an experiment. It was 'a classroom operation for developing a methodology and gaining some understanding of it'. The methodology which evolved has since acquired the name 'task-based teaching', one which is now familiar to many language teachers.

The message

The project shares the overall message of GLAFFL, which is that innovation is about people, not about systems. For this reason I have chosen to include it in this book, despite the fact that I am obliged to use Prahbu's book *Second Language Pedagogy* as the sole source of information on the subject, for want of any personal first-hand experience. The message of Bangalore seems to be that innovation is about people, not about systems because:

(1) Innovation is the product of **analysis** – classroom practice in Bangalore was the product of an 'intuition' about how competence in language develops. This 'intuition' or hypothesis was explored,

113

developed and refined. What happened in Bangalore classrooms evolved on the basis of *a theoretical position about the development of grammatical competence*. This position was based on the creation of *the conditions in which learners engage in an effort to cope with communication*. Part of these conditions depend on the notion of *cultural fit*, in this instance society's definition of the respective roles of teacher and taught.

(2) What matters above all else is a teacher's **pedagogic perception and sense of plausibility**.

A further point arising from the above is that this kind of innovation, which involves simultaneously teacher and curricular development, counteracts dependency and leads to changes which are sustainable as well as cost-effective. The Bangalore model has a great deal to offer developing countries, who are too often led to believe that the only way forward is by the purchase of textbooks in amounts which they simply cannot afford at prices which preclude any other expenditures.

Some facts

The project was conducted from the Regional Institute of English (REI) in Bangalore, southern India (a state institution set up in 1963) by a project team of initially four, ultimately 18 teachers/teacher trainers. The development of the project in the schools was done both through the team of 'specialists' (teacher trainers or specialist teachers of English) and by regular teachers working in schools. Reports and accounts of the progress of the project in Newsletters made considerable impact throughout the country and abroad. The team members shared what Prabhu calls 'a strongly-felt pedagogic intuition that the development of competence in a second language requires ... the creation of conditions in which learners engage in an effort to cope with communication'.

In Chapter 2 Prahbu outlines the history of the project which started in response to dissatisfaction with the existing methodology. Seminars were held throughout the country to discuss some of the new approaches being tried elsewhere, including functional/notional syllabuses, communicative perspectives and language for specific purposes. In January 1978 at the REI, the first of two seminars held there considered functional/notional syllabuses, as proposed in Wilkins (1976)[33] presented at the seminar by Keith Johnson. The second seminar focused on the implications of a discourse view of language, presented by Henry Widdowson.[34]

At the beginning of Part 1 of this book I said that innovation is the product of analysis and hard work. In the case of Bangalore, the analysis of existing approaches which took place (described in some detail by Prahbu) led to a rejection of the functional/notional approach and a rethink of the communicative approach, both of which had been suggested at the seminars.

Operational constraints

Wholesale change in the way things are done is rarely possible, and not perhaps even desirable. The Bangalore project took place bearing in mind several constraints. Firstly there was the fact that in a poor country, the degree of change possible had to take account of both the lack of financial resources and the prevalence of large classes. There was no chance of innovation through technology, no possible influx of funds to provide new coursebooks. All they had were the existing teachers, not all of them very competent in English themselves, large classes, a blackboard, chalk and some paper and pencils.

Secondly, the existing methodology responded to the expectations of local society; to alter it might entail severe problems. The place for the teacher was 'up front' – not only was it a case of what people are used to, here was an instance of role definition by society that would not allow of Western practices such as group work, drama techniques or self-access. Teachers were supposed to act as teachers, learners to act as learners. To innovate in a developing country requires a sensitivity to customs that one might dismiss as immaterial in Britain or the United States, where educational changes are expected by the public as a sign that the schools are responding to social needs. Moreover, in a poor country the only way up (and out) is through the existing school system. To tamper with it is to risk incurring not only the wrath of the parents, but can lead to serious social unrest. The most important subject for advancement is English, hence the way in which the language is taught is of far more moment than it would be in Britain, where the idea of 'language riots' would be inconceivable.

There are other constraints of a social nature which have to do with the way people react to each other. For instance, social distance matters in Indian society in a way that differs considerably from the casual way some other cultures have of relating to each other. Status matters, and the feelings of people in this respect cannot be brushed aside. There are also certain things that cannot be done in certain cultures without giving offence. These naturally also affect decisions about methodology.

The need for legitimacy

Expectations of the institution have then to be considered. School is a place where knowledge is transmitted. It is the place where children are meant to heed the teacher and work hard. If the children fail, it is their fault for not paying attention. It does not matter whether one agrees with this or not, it does not matter how much 'better' the expert knows than the general public, how advanced a teacher's techniques. Without consent, without legitimacy, there can be no possibility of educational reform. Each country, perhaps each locality, has its own tolerances in this respect, and these are all different, particularly with regard to the degree of flexibility permissible.

One of the strengths of the Bangalore project is that it took into account the learners' and teachers' experiences and expectations of each other, using this knowledge to promote the use of techniques and materials best suited to preserve a coherent link with the locality, while striking out into new territory in terms of attempting to find a way of exploiting new knowledge about the mental processes involved in language learning.

The Analysis[35]

Rejecting communicative competence

Prahbu differs from the American/Canadian applied linguists whose work had greatly influenced the thinking behind the Lothian project.[36] He appears virtually to discard as irrelevant Canale and Swain's famous components of communicative competence: linguistic competence, socio-linguistic competence, discourse competence, and strategic competence, concentrating solely on grammatical competence as what really matters. Grammatical competence is characterised by its 'deployability', in the sense that 'it comes into play in direct response to a need to communicate – without any linguistic elicitation and with equal levels of accuracy within and outside the classroom.'

While using much of the thinking behind the 'communicative' approach, Prahbu sees many of its manifestations as irrelevant to the circumstances of the project. What he means by irrelevant seems to have to do with the setting of priorities:

Examples of how grammatically correct sentences could still be socially inappropriate were not very helpful while available forms of pedagogy were found to be inadequate for enabling learners to achieve grammatical correctness itself, and social appropriacy did not seem a particularly pressing objective for second language learners in a formal educational setting.

I may be wrong but I seem to detect a certain dryness to Prahbu's tone, and sense, perhaps incorrectly, the irritation of those who have to work in unsatisfactory environments with inadequate resources, human as well as physical, when dealing with experts, who seem to be at several removes from the reality experienced by those 'on the ground'. There were obviously other considerations at work: '... an internal grammatical competence was still seen by many of the participants in the seminars to be the main objective of language teaching.'

Another reason Prahbu cites against the usefulness in the Bangalore situation of communicative competence is that communicative teaching is aimed at an extension of existing grammatical competence, meant for pupils who already are at an intermediate level in their study of the language. This to a certain extent was true at that particular time.

The main objection to the 'communicative competence' argument lies in the statement: 'The issue of how grammatical competence itself is best developed in learners did not seem to be addressed by the new proposals being examined.' This was the issue which the Bangalore project set out to examine.

Rejecting the defined syllabus

One of the many influences of Prahbu's work has been on the notion of syllabus. Teachers of languages have now become used to operating a version of the functional-notional syllabuses developed in the late 1970s and early 1980s which Prahbu and his team rejected. Many, indeed most of the coursebooks of the eighties depend on these for their structure, which some consider to be as limiting in their way as course books designed to follow a strictly grammatical progression.[37] Indeed, Prahbu is quite scathing on the subject:

> The replacement of one mode of syllabus organisation by another did not entail any major difference, *in terms of classroom activity* (my italics) from S-O-S pedagogy: specific items of language would still

be preselected for any teaching unit and practised in contexts which suited them'.

Thus a defined syllabus is incompatible with the concept of the development of grammatical competence, which develops according to principles which are little understood and which may vary from learner to learner. To ensure the 'deployability' of the learner's language resource, what is needed is an 'operational syllabus', enough for the teacher to plan and to function and for other teachers to benefit. Such an operational syllabus will never be static, since 'language ability develops in direct relation to communicational effort' – and communicational effort is not something which can be programmed, since it belongs to the learner. To this extent, the project can be said to be 'learner-centred', a term which Prahbu tends to reject as culturally alien – perhaps it is better to see it as 'learning centred'.

Where Prahbu does see a role for the defined syllabus is in its capacity to illuminate, *post hoc*, what has been achieved by the operational syllabus. Thus a functional-notional syllabus can provide a check for the teacher against which to assess parts of the operational syllabus. If, however, the defined syllabus drives the teaching, what will eventually emerge is the kind of teaching that arose in the early days of the Lothian project, where teachers were 'teaching' the syllabus as a series of discrete items.

Unfortunately the defined syllabus has a tremendous appeal to policy makers, who feel it allows them to make teachers 'accountable'. The shadow of the defined syllabus haunts the entire 'modular' approach to language teaching and most vocational and specific purposes teaching is heavily dependent on it. This is one of the reasons behind my concern of directions being taken in Australia and New Zealand, as will be seen in the next chapter.

Only the internalisation of a grammar system, however idiosyncratic, can produce a language resource which has deployability. Learners know this instinctively, which is why so many of them give up when taught by teachers who are well-meaning and thorough, but who fail to perceive that a carefully planned and structured lesson may in fact be the last thing the learner needs at that particular moment. Success in terms of the learner has to be the criteria by which we judge our work, not in terms of neat and tidy inputs and outputs. This is conveniently ignored by those who think making teachers answerable means not making them responsible for decisions and choices.

Progress and grading

Levels have remained the defining feature of progress in languages since the 1970s. Prahbu challenges their usefulness and suggests that they in fact impede progress, since they lead teachers to teach in a uniform manner, so that what occurs is that learners are trained to regurgitate fixed patterns. This may impede their capacity to develop grammatical competence which will in turn prevent them from using the language effectively and adaptively. The more levels there are in a syllabus, the more this kind of learning is likely to take place:

> The more behaviour-oriented the teaching and learning are likely to be. This can only result in a gradual reduction of the notion of language to meeting short-term needs, and the activity of language teaching to a matter of equipping learners quickly with linguistic table-manners.[38]

According to Prahbu, what matters is not so much the kind of syllabus or the number of levels, but the teacher's perception of these, since this will affect directly the experience of the learners, which is why the attention to what he calls 'pedagogic perception' (see below) is central to the notion of innovation.

The hard work

In Bangalore the change in the teaching of English would have to take place within the existing constraints (financial, structural, social and in terms of people's expectations of education). The question was how to create conditions for coping with meaning in the classroom so that this grammatical competence could be developed.

What Prabhu and his team developed in a highly pragmatic fashion in the course of their work was the concept of a language 'task' which involved the learners in a reasoning activity. Basically the tasks required pupils to reason out their responses to what were essentially comprehension questions which involved concentrating on 'the truth-value of the utterance'. With the learners' attention on the meaning of what they heard/read, as they negotiated their way through this meaning, they should be developing incrementally generalisations which would become part of an interlingual grammar. Examples of the kind of task and transcriptions of lessons are to be found by those interested in *Second Language Pedagogy* (Prahbu, 1987). The tasks outlined by Prahbu are based on simple realia like school timetables, clock faces, calendars, postal codes and topics such as daily routines, shopping, travelling. The treatment of these represented a complete shift in current practice, and entailed a corresponding shift in the way teachers thought about their interaction with pupils and text in the classroom. As the transcripts show, teachers are concerned with the truth-value of the pupils' responses, not the grammatical correctness of these responses – those teachers who themselves have made such a shift in their methodology know that it requires a considerable amount of effort and constant attention to detail because it is easy to lapse into past patterns of behaviour. It is consequently very hard work.

Pedagogic Perception and Plausibility

While Prahbu has interesting things to say about syllabus[39] and methodology, he also has a view of teacher development which contributes to our understanding of innovation. Prahbu values innovation for its effects on the teacher and the quality of teaching rather than for its importance in terms of the technicalities of any one method of teaching. This is an important point, although a controversial one. It is not one that would be popular with the many people who 'know' how to teach, or who 'know' how others should teach. It does, however, place the teacher firmly at the centre of things, certainly where pupils and parents would tend to place him or her. It is not to minimise the role of an understanding of theory to say that true innovation comes from strength of feeling – 'a strongly-felt pedagogic intuition'. This does seem to suggest that those who would have teachers 'learn and apply' theory, need also to address a teacher's intuition which is somewhat different from a teacher's intellect.

Each teacher has her or his own view of how what they do in the classroom brings about learning in their pupils. The quality of their teaching is dependent on this – Prahbu calls it 'pedagogic perception', a term I have borrowed and used throughout this book. This pedagogic perception has, according to Prahbu, more influence on quality outcomes than the teacher's abilities and the teaching conditions. If that is the case, it has a great deal of relevance to teacher trainers everywhere, and in particular to those working in developing countries. What it suggests is that unless those seeking to improve education become involved with teachers, so as to have a relationship with them in which they can indeed impinge directly on the teacher's perception, there is little likelihood of improvement. It also suggests that teachers need to be made consciously aware of the perceptions on which they are operating, and examine from time to time their source and their relevance.

Prahbu makes another point in relation to the above. It is that only some of a teacher's perceptions acquire 'a sense of plausibility' in the course of a teaching career. Thus while a teacher operates in a variety of ways within a classroom, not all these equally engage this sense of plausibility. Plausibility seems to me to be another, slightly different aspect of ownership, or about what belongs. Some of the things which we do as teachers seem to 'belong' to us more than others. We will readily change certain of our routines when we see a new way of doing things, but may be highly reluctant to give up others. As we adopt new techniques, for instance, our sense of 'what belongs' is strengthened or weakened in the light of experience.

The point about any innovation is that it is likely to disturb or unbalance us, although not necessarily to our detriment. A threat to prevailing routines and to our sense of security is essential if we are not to stagnate. Teachers are no different from the rest of humankind with respect to their ability to operate while holding a variety of different and sometimes contradictory beliefs and intuitions. These are at their most healthy when responding to contact with innovation, which allows teachers to reinterpret what they have been doing. Arguably it is towards that healthy state that teacher trainers and those in charge of curriculum development should be working, rather than towards having all teachers end up with similar, shared, pedagogic perceptions. Stability is seen by Prahbu in much the same unfavourable light as by writers on innovation in other fields. Stability does not in fact promote good classroom practice, but on the contrary weakens it, since it quickly leads to over-routinisation and the weakening of that vital sense of plausibility.

The way Prahbu puts this is as follows:

> The impact of the new perception will ... be probably beneficial in most cases, since even its rejection will have involved a reexamination – hence a heightened awareness – of an existing one ... the impact in all cases is likely to be a modification.

The underlying notions behind this argument seem to me to have in themselves a great deal of plausibility. Most teachers act 'out of character' at times, particularly when they feel obliged to adopt some new, 'approved' method of teaching their pupils. Some seem to repeat the same litany unaltered for years. I have heard myself say things which I know I do not believe, and watched myself do things that I know will make no impact on my pupils. I have also seen teachers, myself included, come to life as they have discovered a new 'way of being' in the classroom, or have produced new materials for use with their pupils. What I think Prahbu is addressing is the importance of belief. Teachers who share materials know that, generally speaking, they feel differently when using those they themselves made up as opposed to those made up by colleagues. For this reason it is important that all teachers in a department are encouraged to make their own contribution to departmental materials. This is one simple way of encouraging innovation at departmental level. Making materials is a way of addressing pedagogic perceptions, since one has constantly to ask the question 'Why am I doing this?' or 'Why am I doing this in this way?'

A teacher's beliefs about teaching are not of quite the same nature as a philosophy, which I understand as something relatively coherent. Teachers are capable of believing a number of contradictory things. Indeed, they may have to, because the whole business of teaching is so complex. Prahbu calls this 'eclecticism' and does not find it in the least unhealthy.

From the point of view of the kind of teacher development described as taking place under the Lothian project, Prahbu's ideas lead us to ask questions about the processes involved when one attempts to make an impact on existing pedagogic perceptions. Looking back at the changes made over the years as depicted in Figure 6.1 in the previous chapter, and trying to see them in terms of individual teachers who, like myself, altered their way of operating, my intuition tells me that these individuals, myself included, were 'disturbed' and to a certain extent unbalanced by GLAFLL, in a way that they were not 'disturbed' by, say, such statutory measures as the new 'Standard Grade' or new 'Higher' examinations. To quote a colleague, 'GLAFLL made you think'. It directly assaulted teachers' pedagogic perceptions, since they had to examine their practices in a new light and had to bring to life their sense of plausibility. This is not something which statutory measures can do, because teachers do not actually make any real decisions, even when they do participate.

Cultural fit

Prahbu is concerned with the nature of the classroom and the nature of formal education in India. Formal education in the Indian context means teaching, and the Bangalore project is to do with teaching, although the book has much to say about learning. The material draws on recognisable features of pupils' experience – number work, the alphabet, train timetables (travelling by train and working out how to get from A to B is, in the context of India, needs related). Prahbu seems to reject what we consider to be the kind of 'learner-centred approach' described in the Primary Pilot in Part 1. On the other hand, when we talk of 'learner-centred', must that not take into account the mainte-nance of comfort? Within a traditional institution there is surely an argument to be made that traditional roles and familiar materials may be more readily conducive to learning than some of us would like to think. Perhaps it is not in fact always necessary for language learning to take place that teachers altogether give up teaching to become purely 'facilitators of learning'. There is another point here which seems worth making, which is that the price of innovation can be a teacher's sense of security. The balance has to be struck between what is perceived as good and beneficial pedagogically and what is good and beneficial in human terms. In Part 3 we will hear from one teacher who puts it thus: 'To suddenly go into a classroom and leave the learning up to the child-ren, it made me feel very insecure, I didn't feel that I was doing my job.'

8 Looking Around: Ideology as Inspiration in New Zealand

In New Zealand sweeping back the power of the state has removed teachers' support systems, while training takes over from education and economics rules the day.

Nowhere more so than in New Zealand have the notions of 'public choice' theories of management had a greater impact on the running of government, the civil service and inevitably the education service.[40] Its case is interesting because the isolation of the schools, which are seen as quasi-independent 'economic units' appears to make lateral spread effectively impossible.

Recent Political History

When the National government came into power in 1987, New Zealand was already engaged in a major political experiment of free market reform begun under the Labour Prime Minister David Lange, whose financial 'guru', Roger Douglas, was the proponent of an economic theory which became famous universally under the name of 'Rogernomics'. New Zealand politics for some nine years was driven by an ideology as totalitarian as that of any communist regime, with a rigid adherence to 'market principles', 'user pays' and 'cutting back the role of the state' which makes Thatcherism by comparison seem distinctly 'wet'. Predictably education, along with health and unemployment, was one of the key issues in the 1993 election.

There had already been enormous cuts in all areas of the welfare state under Lange and the National Government had continued to hack at the public service unmercifully. National won the election by a margin of a single seat. New Zealand's Finance Minister, Ruth Richardson, was the first to lose her job – a sign of softer times to come, perhaps. Because of its rigour in applying economic theory to government, New Zealand has attracted a great deal of attention, and from some quarters admiration. From the point of view of education, and with respect to innovation in education, it raises a whole number of questions, which bear particularly on the issue of central control and reform by diktat.

Driven by a call for decentralisation, accountability and the need to 'downsize' the public service, a massive overhaul of all state agencies was undertaken under Lange. It is indicative of the way ahead that it was the Treasury that fired the first shots, with business and industry joining battle thereafter with recommendations for the restructuring of the education service. Since then talk of 'outputs', 'rates of return', 'the rationalisation of unit costs' (shorthand for increasing the pupil-teacher ratios and making universities earn their own living), became the order of the day, with economists and businessmen recruited to lead the changes, educationists being regarded with suspicion as ideologically unsound and prone to nasty tendencies of a pinkish hue.

Under the guise of 'increased local control' and 'greater parental choice', the public was sold the notion of an education system over which they, the consumers, would have a more direct say. It was argued that the 'market' worked best without government interference and that in order to improve services to the public, government should withdraw altogether from their provision and return them to the private sector. What in fact occurred was an increased amount of central control with, at the same time, the delegation, some say dereliction, by government of their responsibility for the actual running of the service, a positive encouragement to inequality of provision, and the ensuing demoralisation and the potential de-skilling of the teaching force.

Who is in Charge?

The previous Department of Education is no more, and in its place, after massive upheavals, a considerable reduction in staffing and continual changes in job definitions and remits for those remaining, the new slimline Ministry of Education takes responsibility for policy, but not in any way for implementation. It takes nothing to do therefore with the running of individual schools, repairs, staffing or examinations. Controversially, even the management of school land is to become potentially devolved to individual schools (raising the spectre of Maori land rights and opening a whole can of worms for unsuspecting school boards). The government contracts out to consultants, at vast expense, virtually all curricular matters. These consultants – often former employees of the previous Department of Education – hire other consultants, who in their turn hire other consultants. From reliance on a department whose members were themselves mostly former teachers and who had regular contact with schools, there is now reliance on individuals who, even if they were formerly, are now no longer part of a public service institution and who may have never worked in education at all.

To the NZQA (New Zealand Qualifications Authority) government has delegated all responsibility for 15-plus national assessment. This is to be in future on modular lines, more vocationally oriented and much influenced by work in Britain. Its initial modules were all of a vocational nature. It is housed in smart new offices (the inability of government to sell off its unwanted older property is another saga altogether which raises questions about what costs have in fact been saved). NZQA carries out, in addition to its 'in-house' work, lucrative consultancies all over the Pacific, has go-ahead staff and very smart brochures designed to keep the business community and the public happy. It is, in theory, only responsible for the post-15 curriculum. There is, however, no real reason why the assessment instruments it is devising could not be used for school pupils younger than 15, and to say that it has no impact on the school curriculum makes nonsense of the fact that the Ministry curricular teams and the NZQA are being made to work in committee together, despite the reluctance of both sets of people. NZQA represents a very serious rival to those contracted to work on the new curriculum by the Ministry, and as an establishment looks to be capable of, if not already set up for, the taking over of the entire school curricular and assessment package.[41] Yet it is not really clear to many, including large numbers of teachers, what NZQA is. To the question: 'Are these people public servants?', there is an uneasy silence.

In an article in the *New Zealand Herald*, of 9 November 1993,[42] David Hood, chief executive of NZQA, explains the future of learning as envisaged by the Authority. While the article serves as an introduction to the work of the authority, much of which is admirable and in New Zealand's highly elitist system, long overdue, parts of it serve to demonstrate precisely the kind of ideology which can end up determining a teacher's behaviour in her or his classroom:

'The bringing together of secondary, industry and tertiary education into a

single coordinated qualifications system could have more impact on learning than anything since schooling was first made compulsory a century ago ...

The developed world is going through a one in 200 or 300-year change as radical as last century's industrial revolution. New Zealand is not alone in experiencing the trauma this brings.

Nations, enterprises and individuals will need higher and a wider range of skills to succeed in future.

Today's students enter a world where, as President Clinton put it, "everybody's job, directly or indirectly, is threatened by global competition." ....

The head of one of the world's biggest multinationals, Mr Avid de Geus of Royal Dutch Shell, argues that the "ability to learn faster than your competitors may be the only sustainable competitive advantage".

To allow this, the qualifications framework will offer a variety of entry points and pathways for people to gain new skills and qualifications at any age and at any stage in their careers.

All learning is being transformed into unit standards that will be registered on the framework for any accredited provider to offer....

Unit standards set out the knowledge, skills and understandings that learners must have to gain credit or merit for those particular units. Each unit is a building block towards one of three nationally recognised titles for achievement: a national certificate, national diploma or degree...

Australia, Britain, North America and European countries are developing similar qualifications systems. But New Zealand is the first seeking to integrate all learning into one "seamless" system...

Work has now started on transforming existing secondary school subjects into unit standards. This process is driven not by the Qualifications Authority but by advisory groups of educators, including many academics, and industry.

Existing school qualifications will continue next year. National tasks such as written tests and assignments, which are important to ensuring consistency of assessment, will continue.

School certificate and university bursaries/entrance scholarships will remain as optional competitive examinations.

But from mid-1994, accredited schools will start offering the first framework units in conventional subjects.

While this new system will give learners greater choice and flexibility, it also poses challenges to education providers and to traditional practices.

For too long New Zealand has taken the view that "standards" in education are maintained only if there are high rates of failure; that many children are incapable of learning to higher levels; and that all can learn in the same way and at the same pace.

Yet research and experience shows that given the right learning environment, 90 per cent of learners can reach the same academic levels as the traditional successful 30 per cent; that "vocational" experience improves academic attainment; and that the real difference between the able and less able is some learn faster than others.

What we need in New Zealand is a new concept of a quality education system characterised by high success and low failure rates. The qualifications framework has the potential to make that vision a reality.'

What Hood is describing is the utopia envisaged by those with a belief in systems. The world to such people exists in order to be labelled, standardised and controlled: 'All learning is being transformed into unit standards'. This makes chilling reading for anyone who believes that teachers and the quality of their teaching make a difference. Yet increasingly, as Hood says, in country after country, the systems people are taking over.

The approach which was being developed by NZQA at the time of my visit is similar to the work on modules done in Scotland by Scotvec (Scottish Vocational and Educational Initiative). In essence Scotvec has teachers plan their own courses which they then submit to the authority for certification. There is a certain amount of moderation and usually a vast amount of paperwork, but the modules have served a useful purpose in motivating pupils who previously would have had no certification in languages, and they have the advantage that the material can be tailor-made to suit the school and its pupils. The disadvantage is that the input-output model which tends to be demanded by the specifications leads back to the defined syllabus and levels which Prahbu rejected. The pedagogy associated with modules usually has little to do with exploring the development of grammatical competence, while the development of the modules has little to do with involving teachers' pedagogic perceptions, since the exercise is one which involves listing inputs and outcomes, not investigating a methodology. Modules, whatever their advantages in certain circumstances (for instance they can make for a very confident start for some language learners, and offer a very secure basis for uncertain teachers), are the answer of the systems people, the delight of those who want certainty about all else, and because they are relatively cheap to operate, an economist's dream.

Effectively, despite the cosmetics of 'more power to the people', what has happened in New Zealand is that more and more power is exercised by fewer and fewer people, yet as discussed below, these very people are in a position to deny all responsibility for the outcomes of their decisions. The safeguards and constraints offered by a traditional public service (or indeed, as in the case of Britain, a local education authority), have been removed in the overall restructuring of the state, so that the distinction between the roles of Minister and senior civil servants has become fudged. In the absence of local authority responsibility for education and with the constant shuffling around of the remaining experienced civil servants, the question of *quis custodiet* is a highly pertinent one.

Where Can Schools and Teachers Get Advice?

In the absence of any effective local government involvement in education, there is in fact no one who is employed to work on behalf of the teachers and the schools. The ERO (Educational Review Office) which replaces the Inspectorate, is concerned with the schools only insofar as it provides them with a report solely in terms of their performance *vis-à-vis* the aims and objectives of the new school charters. Inspectors do not advise individual teachers, nor do they address curricular matters. Advisers, who are now based at Colleges of Education, are few in number and vastly overworked – one subject adviser may 'service' up to 300 secondary schools. In terms of the prevailing economic trend, one has to wonder at the need for them at all, since they clearly cannot do their previous job effectively. Colleges and universities are struggling to do their own jobs in the face of huge increases in workloads and student-staff ratios and reductions in staff and the funding of courses.

Who is responsible?

By passing the buck to schools and their governing bodies, to outside agencies and consultants, government has virtually abnegated all responsibility for the education service. With the separation of policy from implementation, a move which most countries have found to be a disaster, the Ministry can wash its hands of any defects within the system. Those who remain within the Ministry now have a responsibility only to the Minister, not to the public; they are effectively ministerial servants, not public servants. With a contractual responsibility only for 'outputs', senior Ministry officials cannot be blamed for 'outcomes' – a rare luxury in a public service. Most decisions on matters educational are now taken outside the public gaze, by people who are in no way answerable to the public.

Who Benefits?

The isolation of the teaching profession and the uncertainty regarding their security of employment brought on by the issue of the bulk-funding of schools led to strike action, curricular boycott and working-to-contract at the end of 1992. By the middle of 1993 teacher trainers were suffering staff cuts of around 10%, as government announced a $1.8 million funding cutback. Funds for secondary trainees were effectively reduced by 24%. Typical of teachers' comments on their increasing sense of isolation and frustration was one to the effect that 'It's everyone for himself at the moment – there is no one who cares about how we feel and we now have no one to turn to for professional help and guidance.' It is hard to see how the quality of educational provision can be maintained, let alone improved, in the absence of any institution with both links with schools and responsibility for the ongoing formation of the profession.

The effect of the doctrine of 'user pays', entailing increased charges on parents for such things as art and craft work and sports activities, means huge discrepancies in provision between schools and the denial of access to these activities to some pupils. The hardest hit schools are, predictably, those in areas with a high percentage of parents who are unemployed, and/or of New Zealand Maori or Pacific Island origin. The encouragement to use the school's economic position to attract the best staff means that what are already different educational experiences become vastly different educational opportunities.

The argument that economically the education service will be in better shape as a result of the reforms does not stand up. There is no hard evidence to show that the private sector can deliver the same level of service as before. The cost of new agencies, redundancy payments, building maintenance, the head-hunting of high-flyers, the hiring of consultants is carefully hidden within the Budget, but has been estimated over all government departments as up to four times the previous cost.

The loss of the notion of public service in education, the loss of expertise earned from a long apprenticeship in schools and subsequently in the education department, means that the agenda to which individuals are now working is not necessarily how best to serve the schools and the teachers, nor indeed is it meant to be. 'Getting the job done' is the new concern. People hired to 'do the job' are not meant to have a long-term interest in or commitment to the system as a whole. In public choice jargon, disinterested behaviour does not exist.

The real cost

When any institution is disbanded, it is not only people that disappear. Traditions of service built up over years, links forged with those served by the institution, stability, attitudes to work, the willingness to undertake tasks not strictly within the remit of an individual but which contribute to the general good, the abnegation of self, the ability to see oneself as member of a team, the appreciation of experience, so that individual and one-off performance is not viewed as the sole criteria for advancement, all these go too. Worse, once gone, an institution is gone forever, it cannot be remade in the way that 'targets', 'outputs' and 'policy' can be remade to suit the trend of the moment. The replacement, on behalf of an unproven ideology, of a department set up to serve, by *ad hoc* groups whose interests must, perforce and indeed per intention, lie elsewhere, may make the New Zealand experiment a very costly one indeed in terms of its educational provision.[43]

9 Pause for Thought: Discouraging Dependency

Dependency is created by handing out aid and eroding people's capacity to think and plan for themselves. A sustained campaigning mode is one way of counteracting the dependency habit.

Spot au four

The problem with statutory reform is that in general little account is taken of differences of outlook, location and background, and hence of cultural fit. Only relatively recently, for instance, have teachers started to complain about the problem of course writers and examination boards using the nuclear family as the norm in a day and age where this is often the least common domestic arrangement. The situation of teachers in poor countries, stuck with English texts of the 1960s and earlier, is even worse. On a visit to the tiny, isolated Polynesian atoll of Rakahanga (population 250), after a perilous sea journey of five hours in a open aluminium boat, I discovered the pupils in the senior class working with 'Janet and John'[44] readers, and a textbook extolling the wonders of the British Raj, which must have been more than a little puzzling. As for 'Spot, the dog', most of the pupils had never seen a dog – and if they had heard of such creatures, it would be in the context of a favourite dish on the main island, Rarotonga – dog stew!

Creating Dependency

The way in which teaching is viewed in rich countries percolates through time to the developing countries, not always to their advantage. If in rich countries the way ahead is through the textbook, developing countries will concentrate on obtaining aid money to buy new ones for themselves, rather than on working within their resources and training their teachers. This in fact suits the international donor community very well. Money loaned or 'given' returns to the donor countries almost 100%.[45]

The teaching profession has also over the years become the recipient of aid, in the form of statutory provision – from coursebooks to testing packages and new, national curricula. All the thinking has already been done. All the packaging is done. Simply administer. The parallel between encouraging dependency in poor countries and encouraging dependency in teachers makes itself.

Teachers in rich countries have become used to a level of materials provision which has made them careless about selection. Years ago they had to be more provident, and also more self-reliant. Teaching can benefit when teachers are thrown onto their own resources. In far-off Rakahanga one of the teachers was using stories written by the senior class to teach the young ones reading. This is something to which teachers in better-off countries have come with the sense of starting something really innovative! The lack of resources which drives one teacher to improvise and innovate becomes, in another situation, a different kind of motivation altogether – the need to have pupils consider the audience for whom they are writing, for example.

There is every reason to worry about the resources that are being put into educational reforms such as we saw in New Zealand. It is not the case that the question of creating dependency has not been taken into account, dependency is actively encouraged in the belief that teachers cannot be trusted, but systems can. It is in essence no different from the international aid business, where the provision of all kinds of technical assistance to poor countries ends up by undermining these countries' ability to do things for themselves. The Chinese[46] saying about teaching a man to fish is often used in this context – the fact that it is easier to give the fish than to spend one's time giving fishing lessons is not limited to the area of international aid.

It was quite the opposite in the GLAFLL project. Many teachers experimented with new methodologies long before the introduction of new technology or materials to their departments. Those who improvised tended to find that they preferred the new way of doing, even when it was not easy. The teachers decided to embark on innovation irrespective of their degree of comfort. Many put up with the shifting of unwieldy furniture rather than wait for the installation of new tables, and, wonder of wonders, carpets. That is however not to minimise the importance of those aids to teaching that make certain ways of behaving in the classroom easier to put into effect. Teachers' morale is at all times an important factor in their professional development – and the provision of the appropriate technology is one way in which an education authority or school board can and should legitimise innovations.

Legitimacy alone is not enough

There is a tendency, however, for legitimacy to lead first to respectability, then to the routine, the regular and indeed the regulation, driven by the requirements of a statutory assessment system or national curriculum. At this point the teacher ceases to feel any sense of commitment. This is where the notion of a permanent campaigning capacity can ensure that innovation becomes something sustainable. The formative nature of campaign work ensures that people do not stop developing once they have found a few routines which work.

The danger is that materials, systems and machines start to become the focus of classroom activity, so that the teacher thinks first: 'How can I make use of the Pale units and minimise the size of the groups?'; 'Time for group work'; or 'I must get that good reading exercise done today', rather than what would make for effective learning.

Key Figures

The funding of the development of a few, carefully selected individuals for study in a field which encourages analytical thinking and discussion should perhaps again be considered before moves are made towards the construction of more educational monoliths such as Staff Colleges, to mention just one idea that is mooted, attractive as the idea may seem initially. To return to the military metaphor, the Prussian General Staff consisted of only about 300 people at the time of the Prussian army's greatest success. Education does not really require masses of people all to go through courses aimed at groups large enough to meet the criteria of 'value for money'. Less expensive and less potentially wasteful would be just the kind of training that the Education Department of Edinburgh District Council once offered in conjunction with the Applied Linguistics Department of Edinburgh University. It was an excellent investment. People of good sense can pick out those teachers who have intelligence and leadership qualities early on, and an idea of their long-term suitability as 'investments' can be gained from the nature of the service to their institution rather than to self. The training they receive can be tailor-made, rather than something 'off the rack' and packaged for a mass market.

I would like to say a further word on the idea of Staff Colleges. The origin of the Staff College lies with the Prussian General Staff. Its role in the training of officers in the forces of most countries is well established, and a number of civil services in different countries have used Staff Colleges to train their senior executive staff. The idea is not without appeal for education. Some of the problems which have arisen in civil service experience are, however, worth considering. The most serious seems to be that like many teacher training colleges, there is a danger of remoteness. College staff rapidly become out-of-touch, and spend more and more time emulating colleagues in university departments, caught up with their own academic achievements, publications, consultancies and so forth. The studies which can be done at one remove from actual work experience are not the kind likely to produce sustained self-directed development in the way we have been considering in this book. Indeed, the kind of further education or training of an academic nature which teachers might need and want could probably be supplied far more cheaply by university departments of education and psychology, by management institutes and other such.

Teachers who are regarded as likely to benefit from this kind of training would profit from a more flexible and eclectic approach rather than what would have to be, on grounds of cost, fairly standard fare across the board. Perhaps a more efficient way of tackling the training of senior teaching staff would be some kind of small-scale career consultancy service, offering information and advice about how selected teachers might plan their own development. This would have the merit of fitting in with the spirit of the times at present, in terms of teacher appraisal as well as moves towards privatisation and consultancies. Costs could be met out of a school's staff training budget, for instance. A more radical solution would see a 'training incentive scheme' whereby teachers would be entitled, after a number of years, to a sum to be spent by them in ways they determine towards their own professional development – a scheme similar to that used for foreign language training in industry, where company employees have sums at their disposal to spend however they want as long as it helps them to learn a language.

Needing to innovate

When the common course was introduced into Scottish schools in 1976[47] and language learning became compulsory for the first two years of secondary education, only the innovative teacher stood a chance of survival. Many who had been regarded as good or excellent teachers in the selective system found the experience they had acquired over the years had totally failed to provide them with the flexibility to deal with the new situation. Earlier on I said that a good, or even an excellent teacher was not necessarily an innovative teacher. This was demonstrated graphically in the mid-1970s. Some up until then excellent teachers gave up after a few years and left the profession disillusioned, others struggled to find ways of teaching mixed ability classes in the absence of any suitable textbooks, and learned a great deal along the way.

A little learning and some amateur economics

Everyone is an expert on education, and it is always enlightening to see what experts in other fields make of what we teachers try to do. In the following instance, the management specialist, Drucker, gives a view of teaching which one hopes, few teachers would seriously endorse:

> What really made universal schooling possible – more so than the popular commitment to the value of education, the systematic training of teachers in schools of education, or pedagogic theory – was that lowly innovation, the textbook... The textbook was probably the invention of the great Czech educational reformer Johann Amos Comenius, who designed and used the first Latin primers in the mid-seventeenth century ... Without the textbook, even a very good teacher cannot teach more than one or two children at a time; with it, even a pretty poor teacher can get a little learning into the heads of thirty or thirty-five students.

Drucker is clearly on the side of giving the man the fish – this is what happens when economists make the decisions. He would be very much at home in the international donor community. Of course, we note that Drucker is not using the term 'education', but the term 'universal schooling'. We have returned here to the distinction between well-educated and well-trained – the well-educated being the offspring of the 'selected few'. One would like to think that nowadays teachers are doing more than getting 'a little learning into the heads of thirty or thirty-five students'. If that is what management specialists believe, then with the kind of technology available today, they will soon be arguing that there is in fact no need for teachers at all, when with a good satellite TV system you could 'get a little learning into the heads' of the whole world, no doubt!

Notes to Part 2

1. I am endebted to Glynn Cochrane for access to his work in draft on the subject of campaigning within the context of the international civil service.
2. General Bronsart von Schellendorf (1905) *The Duties of the General Staff* (4th edn). London, HMSO (pp. 566–7)
3. For some elaboration on what is meant by 'public choice' see Appendix 1.
4. See note 1.
5. ALL (Association for Language Learning) in response to Sir Ron Dearing's interim report on the National Curriculum and its assessment suggested that the graded objectives style of assessment would lead to more coherent testing of a range of skills in languages. It also supported Dearing's statement that more trust should be placed in teacher assessment (a hallmark of GOML) and that the role of national tests be played down.
6. Few Head Teachers nowadays inspire staff to the extent that they refuse to look for jobs in other schools, although it does still happen. One teacher, working in an area of considerable deprivation from which one might have thought he would be glad to escape, but whose legendary Head Teacher, Hugh MacKenzie of Craigroyston High School in Edinburgh, mentioned in Part 4, inspired exceptional loyalty, quoted to me 'I really cannot imagine working for someone else after working with Hugh'.
7. See note 1.
8. '… innovative companies are especially adroit at continually responding to change of any sort in their environments.' *In Search of Excellence*, Peters, T.J. and Waterman, R.H.
9. Burns, T. and Stalker, G.M. (1961) *The Management of Innovation*. London, Tavistock (p. 120).
10. *Projects and movements*. In education we often use the term 'project' to describe all kinds of developments. The term, however, has connotations of something pre-planned, short term, and applies better to a top-down, management-inspired model for effecting change. Since what I am intent on describing are the kinds of ongoing teacher development aimed at substantially extending the competencies and enhancing the job satisfaction of teachers, I prefer the term 'movement'. The two 'projects' which this section of the book describes fit better the definition of 'movement' as explained below: projects, by their nature, tend to be of fixed duration (which is how they get funding), goal-oriented, resource-bound, having clear objectives, and determined outputs. They tend to have 'directors' or 'managers'. Different from a project is a movement, which is characterised by a groundswell of strong feeling in reaction to something, in which it is unclear to start off how things ought to develop, and where directions are determined only

once the movement gets under way. In a project there is a problem, a prescription and the medicine. Movements have leaders. Projects rely on conscripts, movements have volunteers. Idealism, an unfashionable word, is the driving force. Developments in both Bangalore and Lothian were always referred to as 'projects' and I have therefore continued this practice.

11. Lothian Region was not in existence at the time when the Applied Linguistics course was being offered to languages teachers. It is to the Department of Education of the former Edinburgh District Council that credit is due for this far-sighted move.

12. The World Bank invested US\$2.3 billion in diversification and vocationalisation programmes in education worldwide between 1970 and 1980 in order to persuade developing countries to promote scientific and technological education. For a variety of reasons, including the inability of poor countries to continue to equip, staff and maintain the institutions constructed under the programme, the 'irrationality' of students who opted, despite the vocational training which they had received, for white-collar jobs, the programme was a disaster. According to Cooksey and Ishumi 'D and V can be written off as a 2.3 billion experiment which failed.' Cooksey, Brian and Ishumi, Abel (1986) *A Critical Review of Policy and Practice in Tanzanian Secondary Education Since 1967* (p. 12).

13. Rubagumya, C.M. (ed.). (1989) *Language in Education in Africa, Tanzanian Perspectives*. Multilingual Matters; Rubagumya, C.M. (ed.) (1994) *Teaching and Researching Language in African Classrooms*. Multilingual Matters; Criper, C. and Dodds, W.A. (1984) *Report on the Teaching of English Language and its use as a Medium in Education in Tanzania*. Dar es Salaam: British Council.

14. For a detailed account of the project see Clark, J.L. (1987) *Curriculum Renewal in School Foreign Language Learning*. Oxford: Oxford University Press.

15. John Clark, Director of the GLAFLL project, was seconded to Australia to work on the ALL project referred to in Part 1.

16. Quite a number of those most closely involved in GLAFLL could be said to be succeeding in conventional terms perfectly well. However, they had in common what may best be described by the phrase used by Stewart, a 'divine discontent' about the *status quo*, and a passionate desire to improve things for all, not just for their own pupils.

17. The term 'communicative' with all its potential for misunderstanding was just entering common parlance among teachers at that time.

18. SED (1977) *The Structure of the Curriculum in the Third and Fourth Years of the Scottish Secondary School*.

19. Scottish Central Committee on Modern Languages (1978) Survey of Scottish teacher opinion on the Munn and Dunning reports. *Modern Languages in Scotland* (16, pp. 22–33).

20. The RCCC 'takes a global view of all curricular matters ... For every specialist area of the curriculum we have Regional Study Groups. These, consisting of specialist teachers and normally chaired by a head teacher, take responsibility for guidance on their specialist area. A Regional Study Group may set up working parties and may conduct surveys for research and development projects. At any time it may seek the Regional Consultative Committee's support for a major change in the Authority's policy. While its status must remain an advisory one, it is nonetheless a potent influence in the region....'

from W. Gatherer, Foreword to Clark and Hamilton (1984).

21. It was still possible at that time to see the Adviser primarily as consultant, doing what is best in the interests of the teachers, pupils and schools and at the same time representing the management position. However Clark (1987) points to a concern that the two roles 'are unfortunately becoming less and less synonymous as Directorates become more and more obsessed with economic cuts and quantitative accountability exercises, and less and less concerned with the quality of education'. While individuals may attempt to do what they can to overcome this, it has become increasingly clear that authorities throughout Scotland, if they have Advisers at all, have increasingly seen them as part of a controlling mechanism over teachers. There is no real prospect of the Adviser taking a substantial role in curriculum renewal for the present. To quote one Adviser: 'my job is to get my teachers to adopt the department's policies'.

22. I nearly always overestimated what could be done, and in fact without the help of colleagues who gave their opinions quite frankly about the more esoteric of my suggestions, and who put their classes at my constant disposal, I would have lived in cloud-cuckoo land even more than I did at the beginning.

23. *The Lothian Series* Cumming, M., (1986) *Hear Say: Listening Tasks for French, German and Spanish*; Hamilton, J. (1984) *Corresponding with a French Penfriend*; Hamilton, J. (1984) *Corresponding with a German Penfriend*; Hamilton, J. and Cumming, M. (1984) *Corresponding with a Spanish Penfriend*; Hamilton, J. Harris, M., Jardine, K. and Meldrum, D. (1985) *French for Real*; Hamilton, J. Priester, J., Watkins, S. and Wheeldon, P. (1985) *German for Real*; Hamilton, J.and Clearie, J. (1985) *Take your Partners, French Pairwork Exercises*; Hamilton, J. and Wheeldon, P. (1985) *Take your Partners, German Pairwork Exercises*; Hamilton, J. and Cumming, M. (1985) *Take your Partners, Pictorial Pairwork Exercises*; Hamilton, J. and Wheeldon, P. (1986) *The French Writing Folio*; Hamilton, J. and Wheeldon, P. (1986) *The German Writing Folio*; Hamilton, J. Cumming, M. and Wheeldon, P. (1988) *The Spanish Writing Folio*; Hamilton, J. and Wheeldon, P. (1989) *Italian for Real*.

24. A highlight of many meetings, especially at the beginning, was the arguments. These would be sparked off by some idea or suggestion of Clark's which to practising teachers simply seemed impractical. Someone would explode with cries of 'pie in the sky', 'totally unsuitable'. Someone else would say 'well, I don't know – what if we did this...' One example of an idea that was initially rejected by virtually all principal teachers was that of using authentic foreign handwriting in the tests. The first time this was suggested provoked a mass outcry of 'unfair to pupils'. The discussion then ranged over the meaning of authenticity: if one of the most likely things for pupils to read in the foreign language was letters from penfriends, these would have to be deciphered. A search went on in schools for examples of such letters, and teachers were surprised to find how many pupils already had them. Many teachers started encouraging their classes to write, *en masse*, to classes in France, Germany, Spain, Italy or the Soviet Union. It was clear that having a foreign penfriend meant learning to read their handwriting. As for the test materials, it was decided that pupils could ask for help with deciphering the writing during the tests. This was no national examination – the 'authentic' thing to do with difficult handwriting is to ask for

help. In fact this was a very useful instance of demonstrating an approach to testing that concentrated on having the pupils tackle something real, and showed its lack of concern at what used to be regarded as hallowed testing behaviour, such as 'no talking, no help from the teacher', which let the pupils see the teacher in a somewhat different light, as essentially being on their side.

25. When teachers use the target language mainly for language practice revolving round exercises designed to increase accuracy, and do not engage their pupils directly in real conversation, such as they would in chatting in English, it is sometimes the case that these pupils find it almost impossible to relate to another teacher or a visitor who uses it 'for real'. I have visited several schools where the target language is used nearly 100% in class, but where it is extremely difficult to hold a conversation with the pupils as one would in the mother tongue. Such pupils seem to be constantly on their guard, expecting their language, which they 'offer' as if handing in an exercise, to be assessed or corrected. They also tend not to take risks with it, limiting themselves to what they know how to say. Where so much emphasis has been on accuracy activities, there is a need for more fluency activities. I have noticed occasionally that once the emphasis on accuracy has been laid down, it can be virtually impossible for some pupils to make the transition. Mind set is an extremely strong force, and their mind set tells them that language is about getting it right, not about 'getting it out'.

26. Corder, S.P. (1981) *Error Analysis and Interlanguage*. Oxford: Oxford University Press.

27. 'Saying what children need is only a cloaked way of saying what we judge they ought to have'. Hirst, P. (1974) *Knowledge and the Curriculum* (p. 17).

28. The point here is not a purist argument that deplores loose terminology as such, but to say that an understanding reached in common through participating in common tasks where such an understanding was crucial is far more important than whether the judgement reached about the meaning of a particular terms meets the approved definition. There is no merit in being correct if one is the only member of a team to be so. In a team, it is the consensus that matters. GLAFLL was not for individual players.

29. Work on process went on later at Balerno High School (see Part 3) where teachers found that the way in which pupils used the dictionary often indicated what was going on inside their heads.

30. Two departments in particular, James Gillespie's and Broughton, run by PTs who were pleased to call themselves 'traditional', were among the most successful at producing pupils who were able in a communicative setting such as a communication task or a simulation, to use language naturally and communicatively despite (?) a grammar-based approach as rigid as any anywhere. These departments were ones used extensively for the GLAFLL collection of videos, since the pupils had a wide enough language resource to deploy to all kinds of situations.

31. Hamilton, J. (1987) The changing role of the classroom teacher. JCLA Conference paper.

32. A full account of this can be found in Prahbu, N.S. (1987) *Second Language Pedagogy*. Oxford: Oxford University Press.

33. Wilkins, D.A. (1976) *Notional Syllabuses*. Oxford: Oxford University Press.

34. Widdowson, H.G. (1978) *Teaching Language as Communication*. Oxford:

Oxford University Press.

35 Prahbu gives a detailed account of the thinking behind the choices made by the project at the beginning of the book.

36. See Canale, M. and Swain M. (1980) Theoretical bases of communicative approaches to second language teaching and testing. *Applied Linguistics* (pp. 1–47).

37. It is a very real problem for publishers that they have to consider the 'flavour of the month' so much before committing themselves to the expense of commissioning a new course. While the profits can be considerable, the risks are too. The words 'functional/notional' and 'communicative' were for a while the sure way to mark a new course as ideologically correct.

38. Levels were certainly important in GLAFLL, and of central importance initially. The new graded tests (there were eventually to be two sets – the second set much more 'communicative' than the first), attracted many teachers to the project. Some indeed really only became involved because of the 'carrot' of certification, which was one way of motivating disaffected second year pupils. However, as GLAFLL progressed, it would be true to say that teachers found the syllabus levels and tests less and less necessary, and motivation continued to improve, according to teachers' reports and the rising take-up rates, long after most teachers had ceased to use them to concentrate on matters of methodology.

39. The Lothian GLAFLL project was one where, as a result of dissatisfaction with strictly functional-notional syllabuses, the concept of a procedural syllabus along the lines described by Prahbu had considerable impact, leading to the development of Part 3 of the GLAFLL syllabus guidelines, with its emphasis on communicative activities. As time passed and the attention of the GLAFLL team was turned from the selection of language for learners to use towards the creation of opportunities for learners to communicate, the early functional-notional syllabus became what Prahbu would call an 'illuminative' syllabus', serving teachers as a check that the communicative activities engaged in during the course of their teaching covered the functions and notions regarded at that time as appropriate for different stages of learning. Later work would lead some to a rejection of even this tentative link, and to a rejection of that kind of notion of progress to one more in sympathy with that of Prahbu. One of the strengths as well as the frustrations of the GLAFLL project was that there were three separate syllabus models, all of which, including the final one published by CILT, were subject to criticism and rejection as those in the project formed their own conclusions about what was most applicable. Unfortunately in some ways, the final CILT syllabus, since it was the only commercially published one, became one of the models for much of the work on the Scottish Standard Grade examination.

40. See Appendix 1 for a discussion of public choice in more detail.

41. One science teacher's response to the new and controversial science modular approach was to say that 'the pupils gain an enhanced confidence in their ability to answer scientific questions. They know that windmills are the answer to New Zealand's power problems (without doing a cost analysis); they know that radio transmitters give off the nuclear radiation that causes cancer and that high-tension wires give off nuclear radiation (all

radiation is the same). The only problem with all that confidence is that they are wrong. And to my mind to be wrong but confident is much worse that not to know and admit it.' (Dr Lydia Austin in an article in the *New Zealand Herald*, 'Science curriculum, Science catastrophe', 8 September 1993).

42. Hood, David, Qualifications by the unit, *New Zealand Herald*, 9 November, 1993.

43. Most of this material was gleaned over the course of a study visit to the country and discussions with civil servants, officials from the Ministry of Education and of NZQA, educational advisers and consultants to whom I am indebted for their time. I am particularly grateful to Dr Roger Peddie of Auckland University, who was the source of a great deal of useful information on the impact of the reforms.

44. Janet and John are boring middle class English children, the subject of Ladybird books from which many children learnt to read in times past. They spent a great deal of their time in the garden, where John climbed trees and Janet read a book, accompanied by their dog, Spot, while mother was in the kitchen and father mended the car.

45. See Hancock, G. (1987) *Lords of Poverty*. New York: The Atlantic Monthly Press.

46. If you give a man a fish, you feed him for one day. If you teach him how to fish, you feed him for a lifetime: Confucius.

47. Until 1976 state schools streamed pupils on entry according to test scores. Only the most academically able qualified to be taught a foreign language. The common course caused havoc among language teachers who were quite untrained to deal with non-academic pupils. My own teaching career in languages started at the deep end with an appointment as a 'remedial teacher of French and German'. At one point I was in such despair that I spent an entire lesson hiding in a cupboard while the pupils rampaged round the classroom.

Part 3
Social Organisation for Innovation

10 Inspiration

Innovators need an ideal, something to aim at, some vision of what might be possible. A visit to an experiential school in Canada provided all these.

Terry had popped into school on the morning of my visit to check with Don and to ask if she could use his phone. While Don and I carried on our conversation, I could hear Terry in the background phoning some firms in a rundown area of Toronto. She wanted to find out how long the place had been in business, who had worked there longest and, if possible, to make appointments to see shopkeepers who had been in the area for some time. She had brought Don a questionnaire which she had drawn up, designed to get the desired information from the shopkeepers when she went to meet them. Listening to her on the phone, one would have taken her for a university undergraduate doing social science research for some thesis or other. Actually she was 15 and had a history of aggressive and sometimes violent behaviour that had made her 'unsuitable' for normal schooling.

She called Don by his first name, but otherwise her relationship with him was respectful and polite, as was his to her. Here was a partnership, where each partner had rights, each partner took the other seriously, although it was never lost sight of that Don was the one calling the shots – his requirements would have to be met – and these were extremely high. In fact, in the short time I spent in the school, I was astounded by the standard of work expected, and achieved.

Joanne came in later to see Don to propose a new project. He seemed to me to give her a really hard time. She had found a diary, held in the family for many years, written by her mother's uncle who had fought in France in World War II, and Joanne proposed doing a project on the war, seen through the eyes of this young Canadian. Far from sounding encouraging, Don posed a series of tricky questions, expressed doubts that the subject would be treated with sufficient rigour, and sent Joanne off to present, as he put it, a more thoroughly thought-out proposal. This to a 14-year-old!

'I learn what I do' is the starting point for a method of education called 'experiential education' that I was fortunate to see on a visit to Toronto in the 1970s. With so many school visits over many years, some events still return with almost perfect recall, and this was one that I have never forgotten. In essence, the experiential schools offered a way of catering for 'difficult' adolescents, those who had rejected the normal school situation or who had been rejected by it. Some of these pupils were as traumatised as any I have ever encountered, with some individuals having broken down to the extent that they had even lost control of their bodily functions. School, for some was an impossibility, a physical impossibility, not just a place they disliked. School phobia, often not recognised in Britain, had led to violent behaviour, catatonic states, as well as to the milder symptom of persistent truancy. These were not all youngsters characterised by low ability, or those with 'difficult backgrounds', although some could be reckoned slow learners and they had their fair share of society's problem families amongst the parents. One former pupil, whom I later met socially, had taken a degree in languages, having been, as she put it, 'rescued' by the school, and was now herself training as a languages teacher.

The school worked on the basis of contracts, whereby the pupils were free to negotiate their curriculum, their goals and even their actual attendance, as long as they managed to reach an agreement with the members of staff responsible for overseeing their work. It was almost as if each pupil was on a post-graduate programme, with regular consultation about the progress of each person's work being the order of the day. Research methods formed the basis of work done, so that pupils would have to set up their own hypotheses or their own subject for investigation, and then track down the evidence or investigate the topic 'on the hoof'. While many university students are hard pressed if asked to come up with a topic of their own for their thesis, these young people were learning to think for themselves, organise their time, accept responsibility, set targets and produce work of good to high standard.

Don and I discussed the way in which the school operated and in particular the type of teacher that worked there. I have never forgotten what he told me: 'To be selected to teach here, you have to be a good, traditional teacher. You have to be a real stickler for things like punctuality, the presentation of work, good manners. Many people think that you'd need to be a really liberal thinker, someone who thinks the kids should be allowed to do much as they please. On the contrary, all of us here are what you would call traditional teachers "of the old school".

What these kids need are people who are consistent, who set high but realistic goals for them as individuals and who are not sloppy or sentimental. You have above all to be strict but fair.'

Choice, responsibility, the support for creativity with an insistence on high standards, within a framework which offered consistency and an unsentimental approach to learners – these became the ideals which were to lie behind the work subsequently undertaken by the Modern Languages department at Balerno High School.

11 Built for Innovation: Balerno Community High School

Balerno Community High School was built for innovation. This chapter attempts to give the reader glimpses of what it was like to work and to learn there.

It is extremely hard to write about how teachers work, and to try to do justice to the work of a department over some seven years is quite beyond the scope of this chapter. Moreover, it is tempting *post hoc* to tidy up loose ends and sequence events, as if things were part of some neat and tidy preconceived masterplan. It is also tempting to manipulate facts to make them fit a particular thesis.

All those who write about teaching seem to start by saying how difficult it is. There are so many variables which affect what teachers do. Apart from the things one can actually observe, even the things one can deduce, there are the invisibles – like the invisible presence in the room of the parents who complained last week that their child was not getting enough attention, or the invisible external examiner, who will eventually decide the fates of the pupils, and sometimes also the reputation of the teacher.

What I shall attempt to do in this chapter is to convey to the reader an impression of a department as it evolved and developed. I have adopted in this section of the book a technique borrowed from anthropologists, who, while living among a group of people, use what they see, and particularly what they hear, as the evidence for their analysis about how a society functions. Anthropologists have some claim, of course, to the attention of languages teachers. Those pioneers who worked in remote areas had to be the most efficient and daring of language learners, starting as they did with the needs of the learner to get to know a whole community, whose language had perhaps never had a written version. Using their ears, their eyes, their own previous knowledge of what language is about, as well as all the contextual clues from around them, noting down in their own individual system what they thought they heard, even when they did not understand it, and immersing themselves totally in the foreign-language speaking environment, they had a great deal to teach language teachers of the period, had any of them cared to listen.

The functioning of Balerno's department will be presented in a roughly chronological manner, by a variety of means including transcripts of what people said in interviews and on video, as well as some recent contributions from individuals in response to questions raised while this book was being written. It is hoped that the structuring of the account in this way will give the reader a sense of the dynamic nature of departmental developments and some kind of 'feel' for the department and what it was like to work there.

I have called the sections written in the first person by the name of 'témoignages', a word suggested by the editor. When people wrote or said what they did, they were not of course doing it with this book in mind. I cannot therefore offer sections neatly under headings to fit the quotes. I have not edited, except occasionally to cut somewhat, what people said. This is a record of people's thoughts and feelings about their work at different stages over a longish period of time. To facilitate the task of the reader, the 'témoignages' are interspersed with comments about the decisions and changes made and the directions taken within the department. The work of the department attracted a great deal of interest and was the basis for several articles and conference workshops, as well as three videos. Some of the material used in this chapter is taken from these sources, it is hoped thus offering a kind of 'freeze frame' of certain stages of development.

What I hope to show is by what means and for what reasons changes were made and decisions arrived at; the influence of individuals, and more or less chance encounters, which led to reassessments of what had been achieved. It is a well-known feature of innovation that it can lead to stagnation as things become systematised, and it is depressingly common in education. I hope to show how the momentum of the initial action research approach in the department was maintained and how a self-renewing process came about as a result of which teachers were continually developing new approaches, attitudes and perspectives.

The GLAFLL project was the basis, as the Toronto experience was the inspiration, for the way in which work in the department began. What this meant was a deliberate attempt to use as a starting point in terms of practicalities, those methodological shifts illustrated in Figure 6.1 in Chapter 6, trying to take a position as far to the right as was feasible. While the interpretation of this methodological shift was to develop and vary over the years, in terms of an ideal to aim for, the Canadian experiential experience was to remain for me the guiding vision.

One of the themes of this book is that organisations which mirror society seem best able to serve that society. The example which follows may give some idea of what this meant in the practical context of a school foreign visit.

A School Visit with a Difference

Any school is a social institution and a 'community' school all the more so. It has to take account of its surrounding area and the aspirations of the local people. To innovate successfully a school needs the support of the community and any opportunity to work with known community leaders is a useful one. Balerno Community High School was fortunate in having an extensive and popular programme of language classes for the local community which many local parents attended, either in the course of the school day or in the evenings. Some parents and local adults chose to attend classes alongside the pupils. Lesley MacIver came from attending a community class to running one such class on a mutual self-help basis. As a parent active on the Parent-Staff Association and future chairperson of that Association, she took a prominent role in school-community links. Through her involvement in both these activities, she was an obvious person to accompany pupils and teachers on visits to France, which she did on three separate occasions.

The pupils involved on foreign visits were mostly in their third year of language learning – aged around 14 to 15. Parents were involved closely, but the actual planning of what to do once abroad was a matter for the pupils themselves. There were compulsory meetings after school hours at which the pupils worked in groups with the parents who were to accompany their group, planning in detail how each day would be spent. Prior to this, the groups would have carried out on their own research about places which they might want to visit, having sent off themselves for the information they needed. They then drew up their own agenda for the time abroad and were responsible for working out such things as the best means of transport, how to obtain group reductions, what they could afford within their group's budget – all the things teachers usually do for them. Communication with parents and teachers in the planning stage and once abroad was carried out in the main through the target language. Pupils knew from the beginning that they would be responsible for the success, or failure, of their own outings. They were not 'made' to go anywhere. Since the groups all went off on their separate pre-planned ways for most of the day, they would meet up in the evening with lots to tell each other. The parents, who had experience of the other kind of school visit where groups of reluctant pupils were bussed as one huge group from one cultural experience to another, found the difference refreshing.

Témoignage 1: Lesley MacIver, Parent

'The involvement of parents makes sense from several points of view: one important factor is that the school resources are not depleted any further than they have to be. A disadvantage from the child's point of view is the inhibiting factor of a parent being present all the time. This can be avoided by placing the child and parent in different groups if they wish. My daughter enjoyed seeing Paris for the first time with me, but my son preferred to be more detached. Involvement with the groups prior to leaving was very useful, as we got to know each other and learned to work together. Small worries would come out in conversation, which would not have emerged in a large briefing session.

The children had all been accustomed, from their first French class in their first week of secondary school, to hearing French spoken all the time, and could respond to it, but only in a school context. It came as a shock to some of them that those of us among the parents who were fluent in French would actually use it as a modus operandi, but this helped them to realise that French (or any other foreign language) was not just for classroom use, to be discarded after exams – here were perfectly ordinary 'Mums' (ie not teachers) conversing fluently. Many of them had been on holiday in France, but this was their first opportunity of total immersion – or as near as we could provide.

They mostly knew the major landmarks of Paris, and responded well to suggestions to find other things to do and see. This resulted in our group deciding one afternoon to visit 'les égouts' – the sewers ... I have to confess that I opted for the Musée Rodin, as I simply couldn't face the prospect, and other adults in the group didn't mind. The children's reactions were mixed ... they reported that it was interesting but they didn't think they would do it again!

My daughter still remembers it vividly. A group of art-lovers were stunned by the Monets at the Musée Marmottan, which is off the beaten track normally. There was a visit to the Marché des Puces at the Porte de Clignancourt, impromptu jazz in the Latin Quarter, visits to FNAC (...'and find out what it stands for!'), the Renault showroom café, Parc Astérix. Not just Versailles, but Chantilly as well. Saddest of all was a visit to the memorial for the deportation, in the little garden beside Notre Dame, which a group of boys found very moving.

What did they remember most? Probably Parc Astérix ... or the fracas caused by Dutch teenagers, when Emily fell downstairs, or the time when Mme. Hamilton tugged the doorhandle and it came off in her hand, leaving her marooned with the girls and having to yell out of the window for help; and of course the Turkish grocer who chased Mme. H. round his shop. Some of them remember taking the wrong route on the Metro and having to find their own way back. They remember the funny hotel, and walking up to Montmartre in the rain with Miss Murray at night. Mike Linn remembers ordering a fish in a restaurant, and it arrived 'alive' – well, with its eyes still in, anyway. When I asked son Angus what he remembered, he immediately said 'La Sainte Chapelle and riding on the Carousel under the Eiffel Tower'. They learned to accept the strange characters who seem peculiar to Paris.

Of course there wasn't time for everything. Even when you think you have planned your day and evening, something else crops up and it takes longer. My son is still trying, after several visits to Paris, to find time for St. Julien le Pauvre, which he painstakingly researched. But there always has to be something to go back for.'

A Community School – an Innovation in Itself

Balerno Community High School, in Lothian Region, Scotland, was the result of a politician's dream. We have already seen the influence of politicians at work in this book. To George Foulkes, Labour Member of Parliament for South Ayrshire, erstwhile Chairman of the Education Committee, goes the credit for the creation of Lothian Region's community schools. The fact that Balerno is a Community School made possible certain things that would not be possible in a normal High School.[1] It also meant that as an innovative concept in schooling itself (there are fewer than a dozen Community Schools among Lothian's 53 state secondaries), it was expected that innovative teaching would take place there. For one thing teachers were expected to agree to the presence of local adults in their classes, and Principal Teachers (Heads of

Departments), were expected to oversee the provision of evening classes in their subjects. In some schools, but not Balerno, an alternative contract was worked, with enhanced salary and time off in lieu of classes taken in the evening.

The school is open to the community every day of the week including Sundays, from early morning until the evening, for adult education classes and community affairs and meetings. It has a custom-built area designed to offer high quality sports and recreational facilities to the community, including a creche for the children of local people attending classes in the school, a swimming pool and a coffee bar. The school is equipped and staffed to a high standard. From the point of view of the Modern Languages Department, there were two key factors in favour of the kind of teaching developed there: one, the well-equipped and spacious Print Room which offered an excellent service for the composing and duplicating of in-house materials; two, the contract of the Principal Teacher of Drama, appointed two years after the school opened, which stated that part of her remit was to work in and with other departments.

Intake

Balerno is a predominantly middle-class suburb of Edinburgh and the majority of pupils come from relatively prosperous families. The neighbouring Dean Park Primary (see Part 1) accounts for the majority of the school's intake. The outlying villages of Ratho and Kirknewton give the school a much needed social mix.

Staffing

The key to the success of any enterprise is the quality of those who work there. Management experts are now discarding their long-held belief in the value of systems to return to a belief in the value of that unattractive term they like to use 'human resources'. Staffing was undoubtedly the key to the ability of Balerno's Modern Language Department to develop its own informal action research approach to teaching. Those coming to work there came, for the most part, by choice. The initial staff of Principal Teacher (PT) and two assistant teachers expanded to seven when the Primary Pilot came on line. There were also, each year, part-time foreign conversation assistants for French and German.

Rooming

The department had three classrooms, one of which, having been designed as a language laboratory, was very large. It had been decided, between the Adviser, the Principal Teacher and the Divisional Education Officer responsible, prior to the school's opening, not to equip it as a language laboratory, but to install PALE[2] units on shelves round the walls of each room. This made it the first school in Lothian Region thus equipped on a custom-built basis. It was to be a critical decision in terms of facilitating an activity-based methodology. The layout made the two classrooms appreciably smaller, but left plenty of room in the larger one for games, drama and other activities. Without tables and chairs, it could hold two classes if necessary, and was used both as an assembly point and as an activity room. In addition, just outside the department was the vast concreted 'Concourse' area, similar to the interior of an aircraft hangar – however unfortunate its appearance, it offered a huge space for all kinds of movement activities of a not too boisterous nature.

Languages offered

Both French and German were offered, year about. Later Spanish and some Italian and a little Latin were offered to senior pupils, mostly on a supported self-study basis. The school was effectively too small, it was felt, to offer a choice of languages to an incoming year group. The study of a second foreign language was offered in the third year to all pupils, regardless of ability.

Pedagogy: Involving the learners

Two aspects of pedagogy in Balerno's Modern Languages Department attracted considerable attention and were the focus of several articles and In-Service Training sessions throughout Britain and indeed overseas. These were the use of the target language and the department's attempts at developing pupil responsibility through involving them in their learning. The department was initially greatly influenced by the GLAFLL project – indeed, the first assistant teacher to be hired, Anne McLeod,[3] recalled how in her interview she was warned that teaching at Balerno would be 'like GLAFLL, only more extreme'.

The first attempt to involve the pupils was, along the lines of GLAFLL, by negotiating with them the items on their progress cards.

This proved to be unsatisfactory and came to be seen as a device which only *seemed* to involve the learners. It had its parallel in the kind of 'negotiation' with which teachers are themselves only too familiar, where the outcomes are predictable in advance, because those in authority have already set out the ground rules.

As a result of general dissatisfaction and still within the first year of the school's opening, the teachers decided to consult the pupils on a wider range of issues to do with *how* they were learning and how they felt about it. This was carried out initially through group and individual interviews and then through questionnaires regarding what was taking place in their language course, with particular emphasis on the use of the target language by the teachers, which was proving problematic with all but the first year and the third year 'non-certificate' classes. Details of what occurred were published in *Modern Languages in Scotland*, under the title of 'A hornet's nest: consultation and negotiation in the classroom'.

The article stressed the intention of altering the balance in the teacher/pupil relationship:

> Above and beyond changes in methodology, we were also intent on bringing about a complete shift in normal teacher/pupil relationships. What we intended was to offer pupils a partnership in learning in which their wishes would be taken into account and acted upon. (There is no point in consultation if the power to alter things only belongs to one party.) Our hope was that a mutually critical relationship would develop within which pupils would understand what it was we were trying to create and hence cooperate in making it happen.

The article shows how by two years after the school opened, there had been some movement towards this, as teachers responded to pupils' answers in the questionnaires. Gradually there were fewer mentions of frustrations in foreign language learning and the vast majority seemed to be experiencing success. Questionnaires and interviews, while useful at establishing what was regarded by the pupils as important, could at best only bring about a change in attitude, they could not provoke a change in behaviour. The ideal of experiential learning of the kind described in Chapter 10, with well-motivated, responsible pupils making intelligent choices to help them learn better, remained the guiding vision for the Balerno department, but it was to seem on occasion very distant. The nature of negotiation in the Canadian establishment was that it was initiated as much by the pupils as by the teachers, and it was of an individual nature, which offered real choice which affected what pupils *did* both inside and outside the school, not just what they learnt or even how they *learnt* it. While in Balerno the attempts at consultation by means of questionnaires and individual interviews did let pupils see that teachers were prepared to make changes on their behalf, this came nowhere near offering pupils the amount of freedom available to them within the Canadian system. It was also still a case of seeing pupils as a group and, perhaps more fundamentally, it did not demand anything in return from the pupils. You cannot of course negotiate effectively if one side is not in a position to offer something.

Before looking at this issue through the eyes of a number of people, it seems appropriate to dwell for a moment or two on the nature of the relationships between staff within the department.

Témoignage 2: The Principal Teacher

Flashback: Speaking personally

I was fortunate in that I had two shots at running a department. Like a former pupil of mine who, aged 14, informed me with great seriousness that he intended to get married twice, once 'for practice', I got the practice first time round and made all the classic mistakes. Unlike the modern marriage, a teaching career does not offer everyone the second chance.

My first shot 'for practice' is one I shudder to recall. I was the embodiment of the one-person band keen to demonstrate that my appointment was justified, despite my, what at that time were tender years for such a position. Lacking confidence, I hid behind the rank of Principal Teacher, and set out to reform things overnight and make visible progress to impress the Head Teacher. Classically, I stayed only two years, and fortunately got the chance to try again, after a spell in the Advisory Service where I had to learn to work with, not against, people, and during which time I had the opportunity to visit many establishments, including the one in Canada mentioned earlier.

In my first PT appointment, when I arrived, equipped with new broom, the department had happily managed to conduct its business over a cup of coffee in the staffroom. I was determined to exercise my authority and control by holding the meeting in the staff base – a much more workmanlike atmosphere, I recall thinking – with no such unnecessary luxuries as coffee. I cannot imagine that my long-suffering colleagues enjoyed these sessions any more than I did. Obsessed with what was 'good theory and good practice', I subordinated departmental well-being to notions of efficiency at great cost. Team-teaching, new books, new homework and correction arrangements, new assessment procedures, new methodologies were all introduced without consultation. The teachers in that department, willing to please, adopted my ways 'cosmetically', to use Prahbu's term, while not really believing in them, nor feeling 'at home' with them. I doubt if they derived much benefit from the experience. My own feeling has always been that the two years in that particular job were not a success. The experience certainly caused me to change my ways drastically.

In contrast, in my second 'shot' at Balerno, departmental meetings were characterised not only by a decent cup of real coffee, but also by a variety of 'goodies' in the shape of biscuits and sometimes homemade cakes, as well as by the consumption of other substances in keeping with a European, rather than a British tradition. Though often extremely productive, this was not so much a case of what got done during, *but for what happened* after *the meetings, as people went off in small teams to carry out various commonly agreed tasks. Meetings were a chance to relax as well as to plan.*

Trying to Build a Democratic Structure

I have talked about the kind of negotiation with which teachers are only too familiar, and it would be inconsistent to attempt to involve pupils in decision-making while expecting colleagues to toe a particular predetermined line. Most language teachers are familiar with the German collegiate system whereby a department consists of people of the same rank, who reach common decisions by consensus. Tasks such as the ordering of books for which some extra money may be earned are allocated, usually by vote, to a member of the department, who is, however, only seen to be carrying out the wishes of the rest. This can mean in practice a certain amount of frustration for those who would see the department move in particular directions at particular times, sometimes an absence of the leadership which seems to play a part in most innovations. There is, however, much to be said for working in a democratic organisation. Teachers in Germany are treated like grown-ups. Too often nowadays in British schools, the opposite applies, as more and more decisions are taken not *by* the teachers but *for* the teachers.

It is virtually impossible to set up a non-hierarchical structure within a British state school, given the system of promoted posts. In Balerno this meant in effect that certain decisions, such as committing the department to making and using its own materials as much as possible, were made in the term before the school opened. Attempts were nevertheless subsequently made, as will be seen, to devolve responsibilities and operational decisions to non-promoted members of staff.

Trying to develop a consensus approach

The tiny original staff of 2.4 allowed for informal, word-of-mouth handling of all matters. However, it was felt important to record developing modes of operating and policies in a departmental handbook, to be added to each year by teachers in the department as decisions were taken and changes made. There were two practical reasons for this: firstly there would be new staff arriving almost every year; and secondly it was hoped that the school's foreign conversation assistants would take an active role in the department, developing and contributing to the methodology and materials, as well as to the evening class and day-time adult education programme. To complement the growing handbook, a small library of videos about methodology was set aside, including the GLAFLL videos, to introduce newcomers to practices which the department was keen to follow. A library of books on pedagogy was established, containing such practical classics as Penny Ur's *Discussions that Work*, and *Drama Techniques in Language Teaching* by Maley and Duff,[4] as well as many books on Applied Linguistics and approaches to learning in general. The ground was laid for involving everyone in discussions of how best to approach methodology.

The way in which the handbook developed depended on the focuses of each year and the new people who joined the team. Depending on needs, interests, strengths (and weaknesses),[5] people would write short papers for discussion at departmental meetings. These were to form the basis for work on policy, methodology, materials and syllabus as time went by. Anything which represented a shift in the way of doing things or thinking about things would be written up as a short paper and added to each member of staff's individual folder. It is important to note that the Principal Teacher was by no means the sole source of papers – all teachers contributed.

Responsibility

The issue of pupil responsibility, which grew out of attempts at both negotiation and consultation, was an area which highlights the importance of Prahbu's notion of real, as opposed to *cosmetic* change, which is at the heart of teacher development. What follows is an attempt to show how different perceptions of learner responsibility can underlie practices that, viewed from the surface, can look very much alike.

Responsibility is of course an attitude of mind not a matter of materials, systems and procedures. It is not 'self-access' nor is it 'supported self-study', although it may involve these. Even in the absence of banks of self-access materials, pupils can be made responsible for their work and their behaviour, while all the self-access materials in the world will not on their own make for responsible pupils.

Responsibility also applies to our treatment of each other as much as to our treatment of our pupils.

There was a considerable amount of muddled thinking about this over the entire time of the Balerno experience which in itself would provide enough material for a book. I think it would be true to say that the initial perception within the department was of responsibility training as a kind of methodology, akin to self-access procedures and group-work. Indeed the way in which teachers tried to arrive at encouraging pupils to take responsibility for their own learning was through designing all departmental material in such a way that these could be used independently by the pupils. The shift in terms of the kinds of materials produced was in fact mainly to do with the department's increasing interest in the potential of language acquisition as opposed to simply language learning. Hence from making materials designed for supported self-study in terms of language to be *learnt*, the team moved to making those which would encourage initiative and creativity through suggesting ways in which language could be *used*. At no point do I recall our debating the entire issue of whether giving pupils choice in terms of materials to use and activities to do would in itself be enough to produce responsible pupils. At the time this seemed to be largely taken for granted.

Before looking at how a different view of responsibility came to develop, we should first look at the kind of materials made and the criteria for their production. These criteria did not of course appear fully formed at the outset, but developed over time and with experience. Those who joined the department later were able to fit in quickly to the 'rules' below, but those who had gone through the experience of making mistakes undoubtedly learnt more.

Criteria for materials production

Materials had to:

- be in the target language;
- provide a wide range of things to do, activities for groups as well as for individuals;
- have provision for self-correction;
- have provision for self-evaluation;
- provide material for all levels but encourage pupils to stretch themselves;
- give a sense of achievement.

Written booklets had to:

- contain a progress card for pupil and teacher use;
- and an activity sheet to help pupils select what to do.

These latter two were the key to the way in which pupils were supposed to operate. The progress card mapped out both what learners were able to do, and what they knew about the language they were learning – with some core and some optional items. The activity sheet provided the structure for the planning of learning and showed what was on offer in terms of skills, tasks, materials, games and drama techniques. Together they formed a learner syllabus, and provided for work at home as well as in class. What pupils selected was up to them – inevitably the ambitious took on everything on offer. Others were content to limit themselves to what appealed. In the last analysis there was some control, because no new workbook would be given to pupils who had not done themselves justice. It was normal for pupils in a class to be working from up to three different workbooks, as, unlike in a lock-step course, the faster workers did not have to wait for the rest to catch up.

The following gives an idea of the kinds of materials which were built up over the years and how they were used to train pupils to take responsibility for their own learning. This sets the scene for the 'témoinages' of experienced teachers new to the department about how they felt on working there and including their attitude to the notion of responsibility.

Materials: each pupil had:

Workbook   Need for self-access material to be easy to control
                         – motivation for pupils in moving on to next

'book'. Covers of workbooks often designed by pupils themselves, as part of their contribution. These were regularly revised according to experience, e.g. instructions first given in English were later translated into the target languages.

Dictionary

Essential for independent work – basic tool for learning how to learn. Providing a dictionary of their own meant pupils had to 'do' something themselves towards learning a language. In rare cases teachers would help out those pupils whose home circumstances made this hard for them.

Cassette

Needed for 'comprehensible input' as homework and for self-study. These were invaluable for beginner learners. Pupils were expected to provide their own blank cassettes onto which teachers copied the material.

Some pupils had:

Diaries

Needed for accountability, to focus learners' attention on planning and recording what had been learnt.

'THWIK' books

'This is What I Know'. This was a spin-off from the GLAFLL project. THWIK enabled pupils to fill in under a number of headings, which were taken from the original GLAFLL syllabus, chunks of language that would enable them to perform various functions (see Chapter 6, p.101). They were meant as an aid to effective studying to help keep track of what had been learnt over a couple of years and to enable pupils to put what they learnt into useful categories for reference. It was stressed that these books should only contain what pupils could do with ease in the language. Thus they could be seen as a concrete example of a procedural syllabus, containing examples of what might reasonably be expected from the individual pupil in terms of performance.

All classrooms had:

Reading materials	These were mostly graded to give a wide choice and encourage sensible selection. Interestingly, material graded in the 'almost impossible' category was extremely popular, such is human nature!
Cassettes	The same applies to these. Pupils would often work in pairs on listening tasks. Mixed-skill activities involving 'detective-work' and jigsaw listening were very popular.
Large dictionaries for self-help	
Blank cassettes	For recordings of communication exercises to be corrected as well as for the making of broadcasts and recording of plays.
The Lothian Series[6]	These were referred to in pupils' Activities Sheets and workbooks and provided a variety of tasks of a 'communicative' nature.

Classroom materials judged worth the effort and capable of becoming self-correcting eventually did so as a result of cooperation among the staff. Making these materials was a learning experience for everyone, and the discussions and team-work involved were invaluable in creating a climate of investigation and research, as materials were defined, refined or discarded. But, and a very large 'but' it is, the product came dangerously close to a 'system'. In truth, the materials were only different from a coursebook because they were written for a specific purpose by their users who consequently had a commitment to them. If those who wrote the materials all left the school, what remained would in fact be none other than a course. At which point, supposing these teachers had hit on the ideal course for this institution, what happens next to teacher development? A kind of creeping institutionalisation or fossilisation seemed to be happening as a result of the emphasis on materials, which could in itself end up as a strait-jacket. It is indeed the classic dilemma of the innovator, and it requires some kind of catalyst to break it up and start the renewal process all over again. And, as we have seen each time with innovation, the catalyst came in human shape.

Before looking at two human catalysts, namely former Balerno teacher Brigitta Murray and internationally recognised teacher trainer,

Leni Dam, we should cast a quick glance at classroom practices in Balerno at the time. Hand-in-hand with the materials-making, and more fundamental in terms of innovation, teachers were engaged in an ongoing assessment of how their classroom style reflected their stated aim of creating an atmosphere in which pupils could be trusted to work responsibly, and how their reactions to the normal irritations of the job – pupils chatting, interruptions, bad moods – could be made consistent with the creation of such an atmosphere. For each teacher it was a case of learning to behave in a certain manner. For some it came much more easily than for others, but the pay-off, if and when it came, was rewarding.

First steps

In setting the scene for readiness for learning, certain strategies were adopted by the staff. Pupils were told, from their first day in the department, that they must always be working (or looking as if they were working) when the teacher came into the classroom. Whether the teacher was in the room or not, they had to get down to choosing what to do and get under way. After a week of this, the teacher would then arrive deliberately late for a class. Naturally, up to half the class would not be working. The teacher would show signs of disappointment and request cooperation. A few days later the teacher would be late again. This time a different teacher would enter the class. Her reaction would be one of extreme displeasure – and culprits would be dealt with. The advantages were that the class learnt early on that all teachers here had the same expectations. (Similarly, classes who were working well could expect other teachers to 'visit' and praise them.) From the pupils' point of view, it made sense for them to work in the languages class, there was no focus for disruptive behaviour, no place for class heroes to 'take on the teacher', since she was in any case most of the time not holding centre stage. This does not, of course mean that she was not in charge. It is important to note that a sense of security depends on known roles being performed. This was no free-for-all.

While most lessons (unless they were drama lessons – see later on in this chapter) would see the teacher moving round the classroom, there were times when it was judged important to sit back and simply observe the pupils at work. Notes were made about how individuals conducted themselves, how things could be made more efficient, noise levels could be monitored. This had the added advantage that in the absence of their normal languages teacher, the pupils were used to continuing with work themselves, making the department very popular for 'please takes'.

A brief word about discipline

Discipline was not a problem in the school as a whole, although, as everywhere, incidents could and did arise, and some teachers found some classes easier to handle than others. Departmental policy was clear: discipline was everyone's responsibility – if any class or pupil disturbed the work of others nearby, whoever heard it went immediately to investigate. This was vital, as teachers might often be out of their rooms, setting up a video camera recording with a small group in the audio-visual studio, helping a group in a computer room and such like. It would have been quite impossible to operate the responsibility element without each teacher taking responsibility outside his or her own classroom. Since the PT's classes were just as likely to fall from grace as anyone's, and since all classes did, occasionally, need a sharp word, there was no stigma attached to having another teacher enter the classroom and administer a reprimand. Communal standards agreed by the teachers also ensured that the high standards of behaviour needed to operate such a system were generally adhered to. Sanctions were withdrawal of privilege: having to work on one's own, not being allowed to participate in drama or group activities.

The very few serious lapses were dealt with by the appearance of a punishment folder. After whatever event had provoked its appearance, and in the privacy of an empty room, the principal teacher would write an account of the incident as she understood it, and invite the pupil to sign it, or else to write their own account. There was never any objection to this on the part of the pupils, but perhaps because it was used very rarely, it seemed to produce the desired effect, and apologies were usually soon forthcoming. Its use dropped off, as with time it was not needed.

Snapshot: Brigitta Murray

Years: 2 – 6

Materials help, as does a common approach, but it is a bonus when a member of the team develops a particular skill. The department was fortunate in its staffing, in that the strengths of the teachers seemed to lie in diverse areas and complemented each other. One member of the department in particular developed a special ability for work on responsibility: Brigitta Murray's classes were outstanding in their sense of pride in their work and the trust they could be given to get on with things without direction or the constant recourse to the teacher that some find accompanies much that is called self-directed learning or pupil autonomy. This sense of responsibility has to be taught and worked at. It has to do with *being*, not only with *doing*.

As a student teacher Murray had seen on video some of the work done in the GLAFLL project presented by John Clark. At the end of the session she asked him where she might see this in practice and he suggested Balerno. She then persuaded her training college to send her there on teaching practice. Murray was not initially planning to enter teaching directly after training. She had such a successful teaching prac-tice however, that the department, having a vacancy, was extremely keen to retain her services. In particular she had shown herself to be an innovative producer of materials. More crucially for the department, she was also a perfectionist, who having decided that something was a good idea, would approach it in the way of a terrier. If something that appeared good did not appear to work, then a way had to be found to make it work. Second best would not do.

Such an attitude can be a disadvantage for a teacher – not many pupils and increasingly few colleagues seem to share this belief. Murray's first year of teaching was characterised by a refusal to compromise on the standards of behaviour which she set her pupils. The rest of the department, no mean sticklers for discipline themselves, watched in amazement as Murray tried every device in the book to make her classes not merely well-behaved and hard-working, but entirely trustworthy, extremely well-mannered and quiet. High stan-dards of homework and class work were insisted on – even pupils with reading and writing difficulties found that they could not hide behind this – Murray would enlist the help of the Learning Support Teacher, find out the best work that pupil had done for her, and insist that she expected the same – every time. It worked.

For a beginning teacher, such is usually not expected, and pupils are quick to look for weaknesses. It cannot have been an easy year, but by the end of it 'Miss Murray' had earned herself quite a reputation. Inter-estingly, Murray was not interested in discipline in the narrow sense of having quiet and docile classes. What she concentrated on was attitude. What she highlighted for others was that some of our classes, while superficially well-behaved and hard-working, were failing to bring anything, for want of a better expression, to the negotiating table. She was no bully, though she could be tough, nor did she have an excessive need to control. On the contrary, because she expected pupils to make a contribution, she always gave her classes ample rein to carry out all kinds of adventurous activities. Her classes, like others in the department, organised excursions, had class picnics, made videos (one even made their own hilarious version of 'Blind Date'). There was a great deal of fun – and the occasional mammoth disaster.

I showed extracts of an in-house video of Balerno classes at the first CILT 'autonomy' conference. Videos of classes in Balerno were common-place and the camera made no perceivable difference to the behaviour of pupils. Murray's class had been filmed the last two periods on a Friday afternoon preceding the Easter break. It was hard to believe this. Groups organised themselves with materials and machines, Murray was engaged in correcting spoken work done on tape in one corner of the room while the class worked independently and with consideration for each other; the noise level was, in comparison to that of my own classes, positively hushed.

There is a difference between being able to control a class and getting individuals to take control of themselves. It was this insight which Murray brought to the department. Most of us, particularly when we start teaching, are only too relieved if we can do the former. Murray, in the two promoted posts she has had since leaving Balerno, has never settled for anything but the latter. One Balerno parent commented: 'Miss Murray's classes can do anything.'

Témoignage 3: Being a 'Real Teacher'

Period: Year 5 – a settled department

Most teachers have a particular settled mode of operating in which they feel more at ease than in any other. Some teachers have a settled mode in which they are clearly not at ease, but which they have adopted because it is their perception of what is expected of them. Not all teachers by any means find a mode in which they do feel comfortable and complete as people. To illustrate what I mean by this I have transcribed in full an extract from a video made by Moray House Institute of Education entitled 'Monolingualism is Curable' – the motto of the department. This was borrowed as a motto from GLAFLL, which in turn 'borrowed' it from the South Australian ALL project. Anne McDonald is now Principal Teacher of Modern Languages in Castlebrae High School where 'learning how to learn' is part of a whole-school approach. She talks of how this aspect of the work at Balerno made her feel, as she puts it, 'a real teacher'.

'I started teaching 18 years ago and I have been in quite a number of schools with a lot of different methodologies.... I found Balerno challenging, I found it hard work, I found it stimulating and for the first time in teaching I felt that I was in control of what I was doing, that I wasn't acting out what someone else had written down: I was making real decisions in cooperation with children and I was really helping them to learn, I wasn't just using a coursebook. Other schools I have taught in I have found to be very coursebook linked and it was very difficult to get children away from the book because of that. I enjoy that because it means that I am really doing a job that is worthwhile.

The methodology here is just totally liberating, you are free to do whatever you want and I think that the proof of the pudding maybe is in the results that we get, the motivation, the keenness to learn of children. The uptake is very high, they want to learn languages. Other schools I've been in, by Christmas in second year they don't want to know. They are totally demotivated, and drop French or drop German and this is because they are not learning them in a meaningful way, they are hidebound by what's in the coursebook.

The teacher's role I think has become much more important than it ever was. I can remember days as a teacher when I sat behind the desk and I disciplined pupils who opened their mouths and I had very often very reluctant pupils in my classroom.... But I think that I have got high skills, I've got high skills in languages, I also, I think, have pedagogical skills and I have a good knowledge of psychology, and I am constantly using these in Balerno. I am not suggesting that other teachers in other schools aren't using them, but here I am liberated to use them in a way that I haven't been anywhere else.

I have the knowledge of resources, I have the knowledge of pedagogy to help children to set their own limits, because very often they don't know where they want to go, or they don't know how to get there. So for me I am a real teacher here as I have never been before.

Assessment isn't really a problem because it's ongoing. It isn't really a question of saying 'This group are going to do speaking tests today'. Pupils come to you when they are ready to be tested or you would monitor them simply by being in the group and seeing what's happening. They have progress cards, they have activity sheets and by keeping an eye on what's happening you can very soon see if anyone isn't keeping up to what they want to do.

I think that the methodology here requires a great deal of self-discipline on the part of the teacher. First of all they need to be quite clear about what they are setting out to do. Once they have decided what they are setting out to do, then you begin to devise ways of doing it. I would say that the vast majority of my work is done outside the classroom – a massive change in the distribution of what I do – I would say that 90% of what I do is preparation, probably about 5% is about assessment and 5% is what goes on in the classroom, that's the frightening bit. I enjoy that, I really enjoy it because, when it works – and it doesn't always work – but when I've got it right in the classroom, I've got happy motivated kids that are really working hard and that's why I am a teacher.

I think in this school it has been particularly easy because the whole department works together and I think for a probationer teacher, it would be very difficult to do this in a department where there was not a lot of support. We support each other all the time, in every way and we make up for each other's deficiencies and I think that's the way it has to work.'

It is clearly easier to accept help from one's peers, to whom one can offer help in return, than to have to ask for help from a senior member of staff. Beginner teachers usually feel understandably hesitant about consulting their Heads of Departments about problems in case they seem to be incompetent. Heads of Departments often feel reluctant to interfere in case such interference diminishes the new teacher in the eyes of the pupils.

The notion of mutual support was raised spontaneously on the video by every member of the department. Somehow a collegial approach to individual problems became the norm. This atmosphere was not the plan or the creation of any one individual, it was a feature of the nature and type of relationships existing between individuals, a feature of the social organisation of the department. One example of what developed was the informal use of 'Mental health days'. (I say 'informal' because the school and regional authorities were kept totally in the dark about this – you might call it a 'creative' way of getting round the rules.) This was 'borrowed' from the system in Canada where a colleague had worked. In essence, it was an informal agreement that when stress levels became high, or when people were simply very tired, the person concerned would inform colleagues that, if it was all right with them, she or he would phone in 'sick' the next day. Plans were made for internal class cover and work would be left in the same way as when a colleague was going on a course. This was something which I encouraged as PT, and which I did not hesitate to do myself, since otherwise the rest of the department would naturally not have adopted it. It was also known for me to inform colleagues who looked tired that I did not expect to see them the following day. I consider it an excellent scheme and until the authorities come round to this enlightened way of thinking, thoroughly recommend it to colleagues as a way of avoiding prolonged and costly absences.

A research role

The department moved over the years from using the GLAFLL syllabus as a guide to input, designing workbooks round the functions, notions and topics therein, to an approach more akin to that of Prahbu's procedural syllabus, where the actual written syllabus was only occasionally referred to as a check to see that nothing vital was being missed out in terms of the learners' experience. The main investigative focus of the department became with time the extent to which a 'process' approach could be successfully applied in a 'normal' foreign language teaching setting. This meant that teachers and foreign conversation assistants needed to work together to find ways of building up a capacity to learn in pupils rather than designing materials aimed at output or product. This was illustrated in a communication from Anne McLeod, Principal Teacher at Queensferry High School, formerly a probationer teacher in the department when it first opened, who, after 10 years of working along these lines writes: 'It hardly matters what the content is – it's how you deal with it, the type of activity you involve the pupils in, and the use of the target language that matters more.'

There was little to guide the department about how precisely a process approach might be implemented. The work of Stenhouse[7] provided a starting point. His 'principals of procedure' had been used by Clark to illustrate the kind of processes in which teachers might involve their pupils. These were such things as inquiry, discussion, the creation of hypotheses, making choices, taking risks, working together and applying what they were already able to do to new challenges and circumstances. Most teachers will accept that ideally, this is what should take place; the department at Balerno made it a major aim to work out how it could be *made* to take place.

Opinions and practice varied as teachers worked out their own approach in the classroom. A focus on learning processes clearly meant that the role of teacher as facilitator would extend to that of teacher as 'mind-reader', if she was to help pupils make and explore their own hypotheses. From the practical point of view, time for this had to be created, and from an early concentration on working with groups a shift was made to working with individuals. Sometimes a teacher might in fact spend an entire lesson concentrating on one particular pupil. This had more in terms of 'pay-off' than might immediately seem possible. It was found that once pupils had come to terms with certain ways of operating, they were as effective, if not more effective with their peers than was the teacher. Investigative learning, while it took time to instigate initially, once established, did mean that pupils could be relied on to be actively involved with the task in hand.

It was hard for newcomers who were used to the notion of teacher as the source of all knowledge to understand what was going on when teachers did not *offer* explanations to pupils but rather tried to get them to work out their own, often partial, explanations and rules. It meant, for instance, having to accept that some pupils were operating the 'wrong' rules – or indeed the right rules at the wrong time. It also meant that teachers had to keep some kind of notes in order to keep track of the stages through which pupils were going. Only later did the notion of pupil and teacher diaries go some way to solving this problem.

It was initially the idea that pupils should build up their own understanding of how the foreign language operated by using the 'THWIK' books to help them note in their own words what they hypothesised about grammar and language functions, e.g. – 'I know how to ask for permission', 'I know how to get things done' and 'I know this about verbs/nouns'. This possibly helped teachers more than it did learners – enabling them as it did to see what the pupils thought they had learnt. Attempts at systematising what they had written were made, as well as assumptions about what seemed to come with ease and what seemed hard on the basis of the pupils' freely chosen selection of 'what I know'. Various models of the THWIK books were tried out. A small, thin version with fewer things to fill in seemed to work much better than the original 'fat' model. Not all teachers and classes used them – but they did serve to inculcate good study habits in pupils, and were useful for revision and written work.

As a result of these and the fact that teachers gradually became adept at knowing what language pupils seemed to find easiest, certain structures were identified which could be used consciously by teachers on a regular basis and repeated in workbooks.[8] The idea was that all learners acquire language in much the same way, and what worked for one class or year group should continue to work. This conscious selection of language which experience had showed us was 'early acquired' achieved a compromise between those who wanted a more strongly acquisition-based approach and those who wanted something more structured. The structures which featured in the classroom materials reflected those which had emerged over the years as the most frequently used by those teachers operating the 'acquisition is IT' model. Thus the demands of consistency could be achieved, to facilitate the practical needs of pupils moving from teacher to teacher in the course of four to six years in school. The actual themes or topics varied, however, and pupils seemed to manage to start learning a language with practically any topic that interested them – although the least successful one was the personal language area, for reasons I elaborate on in a later note.

It is important, because of what will later be said about the nature of organisations which promote innovation, to stress that teachers mattered more than theories about language learning. While there was continuous discussion of how effective or not certain methodologies might be, and while teachers all had their own strongly held opinions, account had to be taken of the opinions of others and accommodation reached. The direct teaching of grammar was a case in point. Some teachers after the first few years did not teach grammar at all 'as such' to their classes, but gave explanations where those were sought. Most never taught verb paradigms. New or part-time staff of course took time to adapt. Self-access materials or sometimes workbooks offered partial explanations, for pupils to consult if they wanted. Senior pupils sitting traditional examinations would complain about 'all this grammar', but in fact they were spared much more than most.

I regret to have to admit, since I incline to the 'acquisition is IT' way of thinking, that it made no difference to examination results how the grammar had been taught, or learnt, or not taught as such; pupils seemed to cope equally well in conversation tests, translation, comprehension and written tests no matter who taught them what in terms of grammar. Results were always extremely good no matter who had taught the pupils, which bears out my instinctive feeling that the technical aspects of teaching and methodology make little difference, it is the attitudes and perceptions of the teachers and their relationship with the pupils and each other. I do not mean this in a woolly liberal way – I mean that well-motivated teachers who are rigorous with themselves and adopt an enquiry approach to their teaching and set high standards for their pupils get results. Where I think an acquisition-based method did make a difference was at the beginning of learning, where all teachers conformed to teaching only what was necessary to enable pupils to make meanings and understand what they met.

Témoignage 4: A Convert and a Caveat

Wendy Brown: Principal Teacher of Guidance, part-time department member

Guidance teaching has much to do with getting people to talk. It is essential to be a sympathetic listener. Not surprisingly, Wendy Brown, Principal Teacher of Guidance at Balerno, interviewed on video, emphasises the aspects of the change in her Modern Language teaching methodology which most closely mirror those things which are similar to her practice as a guidance teacher:

'I started teaching about 18 years ago and I have taught in two other schools before coming to Balerno High School. Initially I taught in a fairly traditional school in the time of the raising of the school-leaving age which was causing some problems. After two years I decided that my main interest was in Guidance, and moved in that direction while continuing some modern language teaching. The school I went to is situated in the north side of Edinburgh where there are substantial amounts of social and economic difficulties, which create at times severe discipline problems. In consideration of the problems, the methodology at that time was for pupils to sit in rows, the teacher at the front spouting forth, children repeating. The only conversation that really went on was between teacher and one pupil at a time, not always particularly meaningful at that, while the rest of the class simply listened. This meant they really weren't getting very much practice. The methods we use here involve the pupils conversing most of the time with others, either in groups or in pairs recorded on tape which means that for the vast majority of time that they are in the language classroom, they actually are using the language themselves – much better.

It is of course unfair to compare the two schools because of the difference in the richness of the environment. The facilities of this school and this department are far superior to those of my previous school.

Another difference in method approach is that we, like other departments, are trying to encourage pupils to take more responsibility for their own learning. Using a lot of self-access materials increases this responsibility and the success of the approach can be seen particularly in the run-up to exam times. We have just been doing the Standard Grade final proficiency tests,[9] and it was very obvious to me how much work they have been doing at home – with guidance of course – in preparation.

When I first arrived it was a total and utter shock! Speaking only the foreign language constantly in the classroom was a nightmare, to begin with, just a nightmare, though not so much in French which is my stronger language. It was very interesting for me because it enabled me to relate more easily to the problems encountered by the first-year pupils in their new 'language situation', to help them get over their nervousness and persuade them that perfection was not required and that understanding every word wasn't necessary, but to look and listen to what THEY needed was what it was all about.

It took me a long time to get used to the system, but now I can't see me ever going back to the old methods. It's so much more enjoyable for the teacher, and the students themselves find it much more rewarding once they get used to the way of working. But as I said, the change in methodology was quite a shock to me and I think anybody coming new to the system from any other school would say the same. I have had to 'unlearn' a lot of previous practice. For instance, the ignoring of errors if they did not interfere with the communication process did not come easy! But having got into it and having received a lot of encouragement from the Head of Department and other members of staff and having watched their good example, I wouldn't dream of teaching any other way.'

Wendy Brown's reaction to the new ways is that of the convert. She had been some years in the school before these comments were made. The 'shock' she recalls with typical honesty was in a way probably greater for her than for others who joined the department because her departmental role had for some years taken second place to her role in guidance, which is where her professional development and In-Service Training efforts had been concentrated. Because her strengths lay in the guidance area, and in dealing with pupils as whole beings, not as disembodied intellects, this probably made it easy for her to take to the notion of pupil responsibility. The use of drama, which she does not in fact mention, was another feature of the methodology with which she, as a guidance teacher, readily identified.

It is interesting to find in the videod material that Brown is talking about a 'system', because in fact when the department had been in operation for this amount of time, this is what had indeed happened. From the vidoes and from articles and conference notes of mine dating from that period, it looks as if certain patterns were becoming set, consensus had been achieved and complacency was just waiting round the corner.

A key conference

Fortunately this was made plain as a result of an encounter with another catalyst. CILT had organised two conferences on 'autonomy', which I attended. Conferences are now a more common feature of the life of teachers, and although those who attend them attest to their reinvigorating effects, it is hard sometimes to produce evidence that they can be instrumental in bringing about real change. Here, however, is one example of this. Leni Dam, from Denmark, has perhaps the most extreme version of 'autonomy' going. Her pupils are allowed to learn in any way they choose, as long as they adhere to certain simple rules.[10] The quality of work produced by her pupils and the atmosphere prevailing in her classroom as seen on the video produced by CILT following the first 'Autonomy conference' gave teachers at Balerno something to think about and something to aim for, while discussions with Dam forced me to make a re-evaluation of the direction in which we were heading.

I seem to recall my own sessions at the first conference as suggesting that the successes in terms of pupils' behaviour and performance at Balerno were due mostly to the operational structures and materials in place there. While these may indeed have played a role, one cannot explain something as complex as pupils' and teachers' behaviour as if all that was needed was a set of rules and a bundle of materials. I consider now that the changes in attitudes that took place were of far greater importance; but these are of course virtually impossible to measure.

What Leni Dam's approach to responsibility entails is something quite different to the 'recipe book' or 'system'. Those interested in this area are advised to take any opportunity to become familiar with the work of this champion of individual, experiential learning, which I consider in terms of Modern Language teaching to be much more akin to what happened in the Toronto school example given earlier than the consensus arrived at in Balerno. Having said that, it would, I think, be true to say, that Dam's way of functioning is less of a departmental than an individual approach. Some of Balerno's classes did indeed operate more closely to that ideal than others. The conferences and the video produced by CILT made for some reassessment and a great deal of discussion. I did and still do consider that transferring all-out responsibility to learners in the way Dam does might prove inappropriate, even potentially damaging, for certain teachers. I wish, however, that all teachers could have the chance to encounter Dam in person, who is one of the most inspirational of teacher educators it has been my privilege to meet. But just as Prahbu suggests that teachers in Bangalore wanted to continue to behave *as teachers*, so the following case from Balerno, recorded at the same time as the two previous examples, illustrates how being asked to 'leave the learning up to the pupils' can be to ask too much.

Témoignage 5: Mary Anderson

Period: Year 6 – The sceptical returnee

Those who had no experience of operating a 'system' which placed so much responsibility on the pupils found it hard at first, and it took time for new teachers to settle in. This process forced those used to 'the system' to rethink some of the assumptions under which they were operating. It also made them consider how this 'system' appeared to outsiders, and forced them to justify what they were doing. If one accepts that some extremely fine teachers are nevertheless by temperament and training unlikely to embrace whole-heartedly the notion that pupils can be trusted to take responsibility, some kind of accommodation has to be reached if a department is to continue to function as a team.[11] All Principal Teachers, probably all Head Teachers, have sometimes to decide to rein in the horses in the interests of the stability and overall well-being of the passengers. I recall how infuriated I was when first presented by a Head Teacher with this point of view. It is nevertheless a question of balance – since one can rarely ensure continuity of classes with a particular teacher, it makes no sense to have repeatedly to 'rein in' groups of pupils.[12] As the next 'témoin' indicates, following a teacher whose class was used to a particular approach could be an unsettling experience. Being 'unsettled' is certainly one way in which teachers come to alter their pedagogic perceptions; there is a fine line to be drawn, however, between being unsettled and being undermined, which those responsible for others have to bear in mind.

Mary Anderson had been out of teaching for some time to have a family and was initially most reluctant to embrace the notion of 'learner responsibility' which had grown up within the department.

'I really wasn't very confident that this type of language teaching would be

successful. I had heard about the methodology which allowed the learner more responsibility for his or her own learning and had been keen to visit the school for some time. Having discovered that a shift in methodology was taking place generally, I decided that rather than wait until my own children started school themselves, I would return to teaching sooner than I originally intended for fear of being left behind. I wanted to see for myself, so I came to the school for a visit initially.

I had, in fact, been very sceptical before I came to the school, having had it impressed on me during my own training that the most important thing in going to teach a class was being thoroughly prepared, to have a very structured lesson and to have your objectives very clearly stated. To suddenly go into the classroom and leave the learning up to the children made me feel very insecure indeed. I didn't feel that I was doing my job and I found myself having to unlearn many things which had become instinctive. I found it very difficult, I must say, and very worrying.

But having started with a fresh first-year class of my own[13] this year, for whom German was a completely new subject, I have tried to adopt and adapt to the notion that the learner is indeed capable of taking more responsibility. I am now using the self-access materials, organising drama activities and thoroughly enjoying myself. I cannot believe how much the children can understand at this stage. Their spoken German is very good but their comprehension is absolutely incredible. However, despite my gradual acceptance of the methodology, and my admiration for those teachers in the department whose commitment to the system has ensured its success, I do find it much more difficult to manage. Having taught in a fairly traditional manner previously, where the attention of the whole class was focused on one child offering a response, I now find that lots of activities are taking place at any one time. I am still trying to adjust to the new level of noise created as a result of this activity and freedom of movement. Like a lot of teachers, I am allergic to noise, particularly at the end of the day. What I try to do is zoom in on a certain pairs or groups doing work and try to shut myself off from the rest. That I find difficult.

The main advantage is, I think, that the children are much more highly motivated, and that's a very good start to learning anything. It's much easier to learn something if you are actually enjoying it. I've even seen second-year pupils smile during a German lesson and that's something I don't think I ever experienced before.

Having watched my colleagues and seen how they manage, I feel less insecure now and I panic less. I still do feel a little insecure because I am not in control of what everyone in the class is supposed to be learning and I do think this type of teaching can be stressful. I've discovered, for example, that I have to be well prepared not only for the next lesson, or set of lessons, but for a whole unit of work. The content of this unit can involve a vast range of activities and I have to be able to give help and guidance when required and to answer any questions that may come. If there are five or six activities going on at any one time, you can have 10 children standing in a queue waiting to ask you five different questions and that is very draining and time-consuming. If I find that happens, I now tend to stop the group doing that activity and clear up the problem with the whole group. It can also be quite a strain having to organise different activities at once. Although the setting up of a unit of work and organising the activities demands a lot of the teacher, we are not left on our own because the whole department contributes, so it's not all left up to you, and there's tremendous cooperation between members of staff in the department and people are always ready to help. I just feel that I always seem to be asking for it.

I think there are always a few children who are unable to work on their own and I find that I give these children a lot more attention than they would otherwise get, but most of the class do more work than you would expect them to do, considering that they are not closely supervised at all times. Although this type of teaching does create organisational difficulties, I do think that in the end it's worth it, it's worth the extra work to see them making so much progress and to see that most of them actually enjoy it.'

The above example is an extremely useful one and I am grateful to Mary Anderson for allowing me to use her frankly expressed doubts. It illustrates graphically a shifting, even a vacillating pedagogic perception, and clearly demonstrates the kinds of accommodations that she is having to make and the kinds of resistance which she feels she ought to overcome within herself. A highly organised person who operates well and comfortably in one system needs time to come to terms with what is new and what seems uncontrolled and uncontrollable. It seems to me that the definition of 'prepared' is the crux of the matter. It has a different meaning in different contexts: in primary schools the way in which young children run and direct their own learning is a source of mystery to most secondary teachers, yet teachers there have to be more thoroughly prepared than most secondary teachers in order that the pupils can work independently on a wide variety of different activities and topics.

Some four years later Mary Anderson was asked whether indeed her experience of teaching in Balerno's feeder primary schools had altered her perception. This is what she said:

*'I felt much more comfortable with this kind of teaching in the secure envi-
ronment of the primary school, where the class is already a homogeneous
group, used to working like this, and I did not have to worry about things like
creating a particular atmosphere or making sure they all got on together. Now
we start in the primary at P6, and I find I take about six months of preparatory
work before we start integrating the teaching of subjects* – (the kind of integrated project work described in Part 1, Chapter 3). *By the time the
children are in P7, they are able to do this kind of work in German with a
minimum of instruction and they can work on their own.*

*What was a bit of a disappointment was that when the primary pupils came
to the secondary school, they were of course no longer in the same classes, and
in addition there were newcomers to the school, some of whom might not have
had any German. We do have a 'catch up' course for these pupils, but it is quite
hard to get your class all working together when they come from very different
backgrounds.[14] I think I am perhaps still reluctant to "let them go" in
secondary, because I don't quite feel the same security as in the primary
schools, where the children themselves have confidence and feel secure.*

*When I start a lesson in primary, everyone is ready, the classroom belongs to
the children, and everything I need is there. In primary I can allow myself the
luxury of taking my time, and feel much more comfortable. There is time to
experiment and to do the things I want to do. I have certainly benefited from
my experience there and the help of my primary colleagues – watching how
they operate has taught me a great deal. I do think my own classes have benefited – and I know I have.'*

Comment

The attitude to the child who clearly had no intention of working
unless pushed was one which I once described as benign neglect. That
is, that unless the child was seeking to disrupt the class, they should be
left to choose to do something, or to do nothing. No one likes doing
nothing. In my own class, the real crunch always came when the rest of
the pupils were getting new workbooks, or when some pupils were able
to go to the library, or could be given the use of cassette recorders to
record plays in another room – all these privileges of course were
unavailable. Soon an attempt would be made to negotiate, demands
would have to be met, help to catch up would be required too.

This is an extreme position. It was akin to that of Dam, who quoted a
telling example of a pupil of hers who chose to spend his entire English
lessons for weeks playing dominoes. Each day Dam would read in his

diary 'Played dominoes', and wonder when this would run its natural course. Days, weeks went by. It became increasingly hard to bear, but finally the day came when she read: 'Played dominoes. Dominoes is boring'.

Such an approach takes patience, it takes a belief in the pressures that will eventually make a pupil want to belong.[15] But it also necessitates a long-term relationship with a pupil. It is not something to be done as a 'one-off', since it is important that this 'benign neglect' should not appear as a punishment inflicted *on* the pupil by the teacher, but should be the direct result of a decision taken *by* the pupil, to be altered at the pupil's instigation.

Avoiding 'systems'

The classic dilemma which attends innovation is, as we have noted, our propensity to systematise and simplify. To a certain extent this is inevitable, and routines themselves are a necessary part of teaching and learning. Uncritical acceptance of established ways of doing things quickly becomes complacency, however. Innovation at Balerno did not in fact become altogether 'routinised' and materials governed. This was in part due to the constant arrival of new people both on the staff and as visitors. The opportunities departmental members had to attend and to speak at teachers' meetings and conferences also meant a fairly constant influx of new ideas.

Moreover, the issue of pupil responsibility, as we have seen, evoked different responses from each departmental member, and this served to keep it alive. Newcomers' doubts helped in this, as those who arrived required practical assistance with class organisation. The practical advice given depended on which camp the people asked fell into – there were those who clearly liked to organise their classes (i.e. at the beginning of a lesson, offering a variety of activities) and those who held that pupils should learn to organise themselves. One of the questions raised by the arrival of new members of staff was whether you could in fact progress from one to the other, or whether by organising groups to carry out certain activities, you changed the nature of the relationship by limiting choice. Everyone had to clarify their ideas – which encouraged debate, and a certain creative tension. Differences of opinion were welcomed, and were probably quite helpful to newcomers who did not feel obliged immediately to adopt any one position, although as is clear from the *témoignage* of Mary Anderson, it was an area about which people had to do quite a lot of thinking.

One matter about which teachers reached a quick consensus was drama techniques. Balerno High School was fortunate in that its structure allowed for teachers to train in drama techniques by working collaboratively with Sandra Reid, Principal Teacher of drama. Her remit included the requirement to work with teachers in other departments, team-teaching their classes for which she provided materials that would support the class teachers' own teaching aims. Team-teaching was thus a legitimate school practice. It was another example of how the way in which school management draws up its organisational structures can actually foster innovative practices – the breaking down of subject boundaries by offering timetabling support for cross-curricular work is one way in which doors can be opened to a whole variety of new methods of helping pupils learn.

In the course of a long and happy collaboration between drama and Modern Languages, teachers learnt new skills, reviewed standard practices and produced a great deal of material.[16] There was no standard pattern to how a unit of work might be planned, or how drama might be incorporated into an existing unit, but drama was perceived by all the languages staff as having the potential to solve a variety of problems from the pedagogical to the social. Sometimes it was obvious that certain skills possessed by Reid were required by the languages staff – for instance, how to get pupils to mime effectively. At other times, a problem with a particular class or even individual would be discussed at a departmental meeting, (these were attended by Reid from time to time, both on an *ad hoc* basis and on invitation) and Reid would suggest techniques from her field that could be of help. Teachers would select those with which they felt comfortable, and where uncertain, would request Reid to co-teach a lesson so that they could see exactly what was involved, and then adapt the techniques to suit themselves. It is a considerable tribute to Reid that all those teachers who subsequently left Balerno, as well as those still there, have continued to use, in their everyday work, techniques first developed with her there. One of these which fundamentally altered the ways used to encourage pupils to speak voluntarily, is the warm-up.

Témoignage 6: Solving Problems Through Drama

One of the commonest problems besetting language teachers is the basic one of getting the pupils to speak. It becomes more, not less difficult, when the target language is used exclusively by the teacher, (because you cannot cue speech in English) and when there is pupil choice as to what activities to undertake. Promoting extended speaking of a communicative nature required the help of an expert. One of the gaps which became immediately apparent to Reid when she observed departmental practice was the absence of any warm-up activities.

To quote Reid:

'*The warm-up is preparation for later activities. The components of drama, or indeed communication skills, are language and movement. It's my belief that movement precedes speech, and that speech may result from physical activity. People move first. They move the moment they are born. They make noise when they are born. It takes some time to develop speech and language skills. So we start with the basics – the familiar – movement and noise.*

The warm-up is designed to get the muscles moving, to create noise and chaos, so that a cover-up, a kind of anonymity for the student is created. It should make the student feel relaxed and unobserved. It should always be enjoyable. They should feel they are in a comfortable and safe environment, one in which they can afford to take risks. Instead of self-consciously having to speak 'cold', the noise, the bustle, the apparent chaos of the warm-up will allow the student to express freely her/himself without fear of making a mistake. It may look and sound like mayhem at times, but if there are very clear definitions of the task and its rules, it will not degenerate into indiscipline.

Children are far more willing to talk in this situation. You are giving them an environment where there is enough noise, enough activity for someone who would normally choose to keep a low profile in a classroom to still feel "hidden". Because they feel unobserved, they might just say: "well right, let's go for it and see how it goes". I think that there is an enormous number of children who will choose to speak in this kind of situation who would not choose to speak in a more formal and in their eyes a far more risky situation. I think it's far more valid that the choice is made by the student and not by the teacher and it's far more likely to produce continued development. If the teacher pinpoints somebody, they will speak back, but they will sweat buckets, they will feel uncomfortable and they will hate it. I think that no child is going to do something that they absolutely deplore, whereas if they are comfortable with it, they are relaxed and they are having fun, they are far more willing to give, and the more they give the more they are learning.'

A selection of accounts of some activities arising from collaboration in the field of drama teaching follows. Each was undertaken as a result of a need perceived by teachers and discussed with Reid at departmental meetings which she attended.

Need 1: The pupils who would not talk

When a senior class presents a problem, it can be of far greater worry than anything a rowdy second year can come up with. In this instance, a class of 16–18 years olds, all bright pupils, doing well enough in their written work to pass the then traditional Scottish Higher examination, simply failed to gel. They didn't exactly seem to dislike each other, they just didn't want to talk to each other. They also did not socialise in English and appeared to have little in common. The most intelligent of all was going through a prolonged period of almost clinical withdrawal, and spoke to practically no-one, not even her closest friends.

The class teacher, Richard Easton, had two options – leave well alone and spend the better part of a year in a class where he felt he was somehow failing to get across, or get help – which he did. Reid's cure was radical and only the bravest of teachers, having heard the prescription, would have agreed to it. It worked, however. This is what happened.

Pupils were asked to leave their books behind for a week and to come to school wearing loose clothing as they were going to be spending some time on drama activities. They already had experience of working with Reid, both from the normal drama lessons and in French, so although they may not have seen an immediate relevance, they were generally in favour of the idea. Reid decided to use what are called 'trust techniques' with the group.

Reid, a natural communicator, can make her foreign language skills stretch to huge proportions, and is an ideal model for pupils to see how to make a little language go a long way. Through French, using the teacher as dictionary when necessary, she conducted a series of exercises, which involved pleasant experiences connected with trusting oneself to others. For example, with eyes closed or blindfolded, the subject would stand between two others, facing one and with her back to the other. She would then allow herself to lean gently forward – to be caught and held by the person in front. After a moment that person would slowly push her a short distance in the opposite direction, where she would then be caught by the shoulders by the person behind. All of this repeated, very slowly, with a maximum of concentration. (I remember the first time I read an account of such an activity – sceptical was an understatement, but in the right hands it not only works, it is, for the person in the middle a most pleasant experience – but you have to try it to believe it).

Through such exercises the group learnt that they would not be 'let down' by anyone in the group, that they were safe. Not being 'let down', in point of fact, was extremely important to the teacher, who at one point joined the class, who had already performed the activity, and in a gesture of faith, entrusted his not inconsiderable frame to the group. This involved his lying on the floor, eyes closed. The pupils and Reid slipped their hands underneath his back and legs, and with one pupil in charge of keeping his head even, they raised him into the air, and then rocked him backwards and forwards before lowering him to the ground again. However bizarre it may sound, this was an activity that contributed to a change in the classroom atmosphere – after all, here was something you simply had to talk about!

The final exercises were concerned with getting the pupils to do all the talking and involved the use of blindfolds. Essentially it was a case of having one person take charge of a blindfolded person and move them from A to B. For the grand finale the school minibus took the entire group up into the hills, where natural obstacles like muddy puddles, rocks, narrow paths with marshes at the side, bridges and stiles would present a real challenge. By the time they returned they were glowing, not just with fresh air, but with a task success-fully accomplished. Even the pupil who had been having such severe communication problems in general had managed to guide her partner round the hill without damage – just as well, since her blindfolded partner was the teacher!

Need 2 : To encourage creativity

Improvisation, as distinct from role-play, requires the investment of the pupils' imaginations from the outstart. The collaboration of Reid was requested to enable teachers to find ways of getting pupils away from the set pieces of cafes and robberies. Moreover, teachers had found that however motivating it was for pupils to rough out these kinds of scenes, and however well they acted in them, the language element was, as far as they were concerned, the one that received the least atten-tion. If one considers it from their point of view, this is logical – there are so many things to think about in a 'performance' – props, cues, costumes, movements – all require attention, and the words you actu-ally need and can remember can become reduced to 'Hände hoch, Geld her!' and 'Schnell, schnell!!'.

Moreover, teachers wanted to get away from set phrases and the rehearsal of language – to find a way of putting pupils in situations where language arose to fit the situation, as it were. One might say that, ambitiously, teachers wanted to allow for the production of natural language, under circumstances that would, teachers hoped, mitigate against the set phrase or the cliché. This meant the need for an immediacy of response with no time for 'scripting' even in the head.

With a combined class of some 40 pupils, in the largest of the languages classrooms, Reid undertook some rapid warm-ups with a language basis – 'Bonjour' – where pupils had one minute to run round shaking as many hands as possible saying 'bonjour', a mime, a word association, then a 'Paul Jones', where two circles of pupils facing each other would go round in opposite directions until stopped, and told to talk to the person facing them on a topic called out by the teacher.

From there the pupils moved into groups. They were asked to brainstorm sentences in which the sentence itself would let a hearer know all that was necessary about:

who was speaking
where they were speaking
the situation
what was happening/had happened

The example Reid gave was 'Vos billets, s'il vous plaît'. A very short time was given and groups called out samples of sentences. One was notable for two reasons: firstly it was volunteered by a boy who was not normally keen to speak out in class, secondly, it produced a French word that he hadn't met before. What he said was 'Passez-moi le scalpel!'.

Teachers speculated afterwards where this language had come from and why he had produced it. 'Passez-moi' is something that teachers say a great deal – pupils do not usually say it to teachers, and it was unlikely that he had used it before. He might certainly have said 'passe-moi' to a classmate, since the class had got to the stage of communicating with each other a fair bit through French, certainly when the teacher was around. Alternatively he may have been using the infinitive 'passer' – there is no way of knowing, though on either hypothesis he was using it in a new way. 'Le scalpel', produced with a vaguely French accent was clearly an offering awaiting acceptance by the teacher, as it was said with a slightly questioning intonation. This at least was a strategy that had been taught. A look at any page of a French dictionary shows pupils what a vast number of words are the same or very similar in the two languages. The problem with French is the sound. 'Teaching' pupils to guess, particularly in certain categories of words, means that they have a reasonable certainty of being right most of the time.[17] Good linguists do it all the time. Teachers were pleased in this case because they had made a habit of encouraging the strategy, giving pupils practice at it in class, so that they could see for themselves that it often worked, and in what circumstances it worked best. This was a classic example – and it had served well someone who needed his confidence boosted.

The rest of the group rallied round, and produced the following in rapid fire:

Teacher: Qui?
Pupil A: Le docteur.
Teacher: Très bien … pause – plutôt chirurgien, répète – chirurgien.
Pupil A: Chirurgien.
Teacher: OK, où?
Pupil B: L'hôpital.
Teacher: La situation?
Pupil C: Une … opération?
Teacher: Très bien … oui. Et qu'est-ce qui s'est passé?
Pupil D: Il y a eu un accident.
Teachers: Bravo!

The teachers were both astounded and delighted, because none of this was in any way prepared or rehearsed, there had been no time for consulting dictionaries or asking for help – and the situation was not one they had 'covered' previously. It had, it was thought, been selected because Ian, the one who started the ball rolling, wanted to study medicine. The sentence 'Il y a eu un accident' had indeed been met, if only briefly, in a reading booklet in the pupils' possession and on their homework cassettes. Its emergence at this point was, however, totally unexpected.

From this promising beginning through the 'freeze-frame' technique to which Reid introduced them, teachers built up the picture of who was being operated on, how the accident had happened, what the outcome was, how the relatives reacted and what appeared on the evening news. Other groups were working on developing their own situations which were on all kinds of different subjects, although these did include the inevitable robbery: 'Votre porte-monnaie – vite!'. Sports matches and a trip to the moon also appeared, and a vast amount of 'new' language was produced, and most importantly pupils could see the rewards of doing this. All this was timed, so that there was a degree of urgency to have their improvisations completed. Giving a time limit to such activities is as important as the rule of stopping any activity while it is still enjoyable with the pupils wanting more. Drama work should not drag on trying to extract the maximum from everything and everyone.

Need 3 : To extend skills

For some time, as already indicated, teachers had been trying to get round the rehearsed dialogues and, in the course of a series of meetings with Reid, developed a plethora of materials designed to overcome their limitations. These were mixed skill materials, which also combined the information gap with the role-play, so that pupils 'in role' as robbers, teachers and so on, were forced to stretch their language resource to communicate necessary, but not shared information. These materials coincided with the time at the beginning of second year of language learning when teachers were trying to have the pupils use the target language themselves in the language class. Teachers had, therefore, need of material that could show them that they could, in fact, do this.

In the 'Staff Outing', for instance, the scene was set with a mime – pupils had to move like teachers entering the staffroom first thing in the morning. This had, like all other drama lessons, been preceded by a warm-up – in this case miming walking on various surfaces – hot stones, stinging insects, mud, ice, for example. Reid pointed out to pupils that teachers did not, as the pupils had done in their first attempt, bounce into the staff room filled with enthusiasm for the new teaching day! They were not always polite to each other and some, at least, were likely to be late. This produced a most imaginative perfor-mance from a newcomer to the class, who had, until then, loathed French: 'I hate it – it's nothing but verbs', he told the year head before he came to the department on his first day in school.

'I think you may find it a little different here', was the answer. Chris gave a superb mime of a teacher, late for work, panicking, dropping things, forgetting things, spilling other people's coffee as he dashed towards the door on hearing the bell.

Pupils then worked in groups of six and were told that they were members of the school social committee. Their task was to organise a farewell dinner for a colleague who was retiring. They were issued with information gap cards, giving their name and their teaching timetable on one side, and on the other side some appointments they had to keep. They had first of all to consult their timetables to find a time when they were all free to meet and plan the dinner. Having done that, they had then to work out when to hold the dinner according to a variety of constraints, and what restaurant to go to, with the help of suitable restaurant adverts showing days closed, numbers, prices, menus. Having made the decision, they had to 'phone' the restaurant and make the booking. Finally they 'acted out' the retiral dinner.

This 'scenario' and others of a similar nature (bank robberies involving complicated information to be collected and exchanged before the robbery could take place; kidnappings with built-in dynamics as the teacher distributed new information to the group; spy games with secret codes and bizarre meetings) took up several teaching periods. These had the advantage of almost completely freeing the teacher once she had distributed the cards, to monitor groups in whatever way she deemed necessary. The tasks gave the teacher the opportunity for plenty of discussion with the pupils about the 'here and now', and it did sometimes seem as if they barely noticed that they were talking nearly all the time in French or German (there were dual language versions of all these activities).

Other devices to encourage pupils to use the target language were the planning and organisation of class picnics, treasure hunts, and a 'Wandertag' for all German learners in second year, who set off into the Pentland hills behind the school accompanied by as many German-speaking adults from the community and from among the friends of the foreign assistants as possible.[18]

Need 4 : To improve discussion skills

Teachers of senior classes were concerned that pupils had a very limited idea of what it was to discuss something properly. This was true for work in other subjects as well as in foreign languages, it must be said. There was a clear lack of experience among pupils of how to debate, how to make points, listen to each other and follow up ideas.

Reid's solution was the use of a mystery-solving exercise, designed specifically to improve discussion skills. The technique consists of issuing to the whole class (up to 30) a series of (mostly one-line) clues, ideally one per participant, from which all the details of a crime can be worked out. The pupils sit in a circle, and the only way to solve the mystery is for them to talk to each other – and listen to each other. The first time they do it is a learning experience, for them as well as for the teacher, who must at all costs avoid being involved at all. Her job is to watch how the pupils go about things, in order to help them work out afterwards what they might have done in order to improve their chances of finding the solution quickly. There were several of these mysteries, and they became very popular.

What tends to happen the first time is:

- initial silence and confusion;
- appeals to teacher;
- someone plucks up the courage and reads aloud their clue;
- others try to read their neighbour's clue;
- teacher intervenes to remind them this is not allowed;
- more people read their clues out;
- since this is at random, more confusion arises;
- someone works out that all those with clues relating to one person, or object, should read them out;
- people start to talk all at once;
- certain pupils will say nothing;
- one pupil will take the role as leader;
- a certain line of inquiry will open up, leading to a partial solution
- it will dawn on some that their neighbour has not read out their clue;
- they will work out some way of ensuring that everyone contributes;
- someone will offer a solution;
- this will be modified/altered and offered to the teacher.

The teacher will then ask how they felt while doing the exercise and pupils will almost inevitably express their frustration. The teacher will aim at making them understand why they must be 'on their own' and show that they did, after all, find the right answer. They will then be asked to draw up their own rules for future discussions, so that the next time, should they wish to repeat the exercise, they will be better able to do so. Classes were in fact always keen to repeat the experience.

Two things, however, need to be said about the nature of relationships with respect to this exercise: first, there needs to be a good rapport with the teacher – the exercise must not look like a test, or as if it is intended to put pupils at a disadvantage, secondly, pupils must not 'put each other down' – the job of the group is to ensure that everyone contributes willingly. While this exercise can promote a great deal of language, as well as be very enjoyable, it does depend greatly on the establishment of a relaxed atmosphere. (I once saw a student teacher conduct it as if the group were 'on trial' – it was a most unpleasant experience.)

Lessons from the drama experiences

Drama enabled teachers to get to know the pupils in ways normally not available to language teachers. Teachers discovered unexpected abilities – the good mimer like Chris, who could find a role for himself in future as a model for the others to copy, the logical brain who could work out the solution to the mystery quickly. They learnt the importance of creating the right atmosphere with warm-ups – the difference between the activity 'cold' and after even a short warm-up convinced teachers that this was time well spent. Teachers learnt to build on the inventiveness of pupils with language, and to keep note of how new structures were being acquired and by whom. They asked the pupils to note in their diaries those expressions they felt most comfortable with. Sometimes what happened in a drama session would result in teachers producing materials designed to expand on what had happened, for example, reading and listening material on a topic that had been popular, or materials designed to stimulate writing.

Collaboration elsewhere

Collaboration is fun, and it is infectious. Teachers were at the same time working with the computing, music and PE departments. The computing department worked with modern languages pupils who were engaged in producing the school foreign language magazine, OINK, which won several prizes in national competitions. Pupils were chosen by their classmates to work on the magazine and excused class for whatever time they felt they needed to produce it.

From the video, Anne McDonald recounts:

'The school has had a Modern Language magazine since it first opened. It was called OINK to illustrate graphically the need for learning foreign languages. The first magazine had a pig on the front communicating with a snake, and the idea was that anyone can learn to communicate in a foreign language. The slogan is 'Monolingualism is Curable' and that's one of the department aims. I was given responsibility for getting it out when I came to the school last June. Much of it was already ready but the pupils who had been involved wanted much more 'green' input – they felt that the magazine was out of date and they wanted a "Grüne Oink". Much of the work, most of the work was done by them and I really just gave them advice on layout. It was an integral part of their coursework.

They are very motivated to help in this kind of project. They are willing to give up not just school time, because they are allowed time in the department to do it, but also they come in at weekends to help out. And it's not just the high-fliers that help out – right across the board, practically all of the present third year have a contribution in this magazine.'

With the music and PE departments collaboration took the form of preparing for performances. Parents also made a contribution to these, not just in terms of costumes and lighting, but in aspects of the production itself: an army drill sergeant was 'recruited' by his son in first year to tidy up the marching of the 'angels' in Hansel and Gretel (these 'angels' were cast from among the toughest boys in the year group, dressed in black and silver, forming a guard round the sleeping children). Also for 'Hansel and Gretel', Principal Teacher of Music, James Wilkinson, transposed the score into easier keys and even wrote extra solos for those children who volunteered but were not chosen for major parts. The entire first year would spend several weeks working on the opera, which was performed for primary pupils as well as at the school's 'Midsummer Music Festival'. The Festival also provided the focus for the primary classes to put on performances of their own, such as a puppet play of 'Theseus and the Minotaur', by Kirknewton's Primary 7 class, for which Wilkinson composed music for the recorder players in the class, himself visiting the school to rehearse in his non-teaching time. There was also an unforgettable and slick 'cancan' from Dean Park, choreographed by the pupils themselves, where half-way through some of the boys in wigs, make-up and magnificent dresses joined in with the girls.

The fact that Balerno was a community school made these things possible, since the school was open all hours and at weekends, and since parents used the building and its facilities in the same way as any community resource. Because parents were frequently on the school premises, they knew what was going on in departments and there was never any problem getting volunteers to help teachers who were short-handed. This underlines the point made earlier about the school's being itself an innovation.

Postscript

I have referred elsewhere in this book to lessons from various management studies on the nature and occurrence of innovations. These have mostly had to do with internal organisational arrangements and structures. I now want to look at some of the external factors which might account for the presence or absence of innovative practices. I have already pointed out in the case of Balerno's Modern Languages Department how certain external conditions contributed to the nature of developments there. I would like here to relate the Balerno experience to a study made in New Zealand which seems relevant. This is the influential 'Porter report'[19] in which Professor Michael Porter of the Harvard Business School and others, in an analysis of the New Zealand economy, identifies four broad determinants of national competitive advantage which shape the industrial environment to the benefit or hindrance of a nation's firms. These determinants '... are the forces within a nation that provide firms with the pressures, incentives and capabilities to undertake (such) improvement and innovation.' What follows is a very brief description of the four conditions identified in the report:

(1) Factor conditions

These are the resources, human and otherwise – in teaching they would include the level of qualification and competence within the teachers, the available funding, etc.

(2) Demand conditions

Home demand is identified as meaning to what extent the domestic market insists on high-quality goods and services. The example is given by Porter of the problem of New Zealand cheese exports. New Zealanders, unlike the French, are not fussy about the cheeses they buy, nor do they look for much beyond a kind of 'composite cheddar'. Although manufacturers *could* produce wonderful cheeses in New Zealand, they fail to do so. Lacking a discerning public, unlike the French, they have failed to take advantage of gaps in the export market which they could otherwise fill. On the other hand, they are world leaders in electric fences, for which there is a high and discriminating demand since in New Zealand the inhabitants are vastly outnumbered by the sheep. (To be fair to New Zealand cheese-makers, quality has improved somewhat in recent years. It is even possible that the Porter report itself was a kind of 'demand condition'.)

Increasing parental choice[20] is meant to create 'demand conditions' in education. In terms of foreign language teaching, home demand has already produced an increase in the teaching of Modern Languages in the primary school to younger age groups.

(3) Related and supporting developments

In industry, the presence of developments in other fields provides a stimulus for innovation: one motor manufacturer's new car will stimulate the production of a whole new range of accessories. Applied linguistics and other research, technological innovations, even architectural design can contribute to educational innovation.

(4) Firm strategy, structure, rivalry

This fourth broad class of determinants encompasses the goals of a firm, the social norms within the country, as well as how matters are managed and organised. As Porter says: 'No one strategy, structure or managerial system is universally appropriate.' Since Porter *et al.* are firm believers in market forces, it is not surprising to find them saying that: 'Government policies that succeed are those that create an environment in which companies can gain competitive advantage rather than those that involve government directly in the process. It is an indirect, rather than a direct role.'

As far as education is concerned, I find myself at variance with Porter here. This is the doctrine which has schools competing for pupils, charging parents the 'going rate' for materials for art and science classes, and creating huge gulfs between the educational experiences of the 'haves' and the 'have nots'. Like most teachers I am reluctant to accept that competition should play a role here. Similarly, I dislike school management techniques which deliberately invite departments to compete for resources (funding, timetabling and staffing advantages, attracting pupils, etc.) – these may encourage departmental advancement, but at the price of collegiality and cohesion.

Here is how the Porter model would account for the success of the use of drama in language teaching in Balerno High School:

(1) Factor conditions

- Human resources – a PT Drama and a Modern Languages department who wanted to work together.
- Remit of PT drama designed by management for just such work.
- Previous experience of PT languages in this area.
- Availability of literature on the subject.
- Physical resources – a school designed for an open approach to

learning – both in terms of the building itself and the 'mind set' of the staff.
- A department keen to try out new techniques.
- Timetabling resources – the PT Drama was timetabled to work with other departments.

(2) Demand conditions

- Pupils in Balerno come from a mainly middle class environment and they have high expectations of the school and of themselves.
- Teachers are 'stretched' to provide what the 'consumer' wants – the parents see to that.
- Parents not only support innovations of which they approve, some of them suggest ways in which the school ought to be developing.

(3) Related and supporting developments

- The 'market', which could be defined as the environment of the new community school, lent itself to innovative teaching.
- Both the local authority adviser in Drama and the adviser in Modern Languages were keen to promote the work through In-Service training sessions based on work in the school.
- A contract for the publication of a book on drama techniques in Modern Languages[21] could certainly also be construed as an incentive to both PTs to refine and develop materials and techniques.

(4) Firm strategy, structure and rivalry

- The goals of the innovation were coherent with the goals of the department.
- Drama enhanced the status of language learning in the eyes of the 'consumers'.
- The encouragement to cross-curricular work inherent in the nature of the school as a centre for community education, together with the job descriptions which promoted interdepartmental work, also provided the necessary legitimacy.

The problem with innovating at departmental level is that spread can be slow and uneven, and it depends on outsiders and chance encounters for its proliferation elsewhere. Through Lothian Region's advisory service, the work at Balerno was well known and Balerno's drama PT and modern languages staff were frequently invited to speak at teachers' meetings and conferences in Scotland and elsewhere in Britain. Many teachers from other schools visited the department. Student teachers from St Martin's College, Lancaster, accompanied by their tutor James Burch, even hired a minibus in order to spend a day there and practice their own techniques on pupils who were only too keen to be 'guinea pigs'. This was the first example I had encountered how much schools could benefit from a relationship with an innovative teacher training establishment, and it was one that inspired later collaboration in teacher pre-service training between Lothian Region and the local teacher training institution.

Another way in which spread is achieved in teaching is through promotion: four members of the department teaching at Balerno as unpromoted members of staff went to PT posts elsewhere in the region, where they have continued to innovate. This is one by-product of innovation which ought to encourage authorities to offer additional support to those departments which do innovate. Viewing departments as bona fide training institutions in their own right and making it possible for them to carry out this role effectively in itself offers a far more cost-effective means of teacher development than some other approaches to In-Service Training, while having the additional benefit that theory never risks becoming divorced from practice.

12 Looking Around: By Limo to the Bronx

An institution devoted to innovation sounds like a dream come true. This American dream was based in the solid reality of the slums of Harlem and the Bronx.

52 Vanderbilt Avenue is an unlikely address for an institution devoted to the slum schools of Harlem and the Bronx. By Grand Central Station, with gilded, immaculate glass-domed awning, one would imagine that such a building would be home to some slick corporation, or perhaps even a fashion house. Yet here are to be found a small group of the most down-to-earth of former school teachers imaginable. Friends from 'way back', they have been selected to form the task force of a privately funded bid to end the inequalities, the appalling waste of public education in New York's most problematic districts. Horror stories about the New York public school system abound and tales of armed students and terrified staff are no exaggeration. Stories of waste, corruption and inefficiency are numerous as well. Despite a budget of $7.4 billion[22] to cover 1 million pupils in 1000 schools, the 4000 bureaucrats employed by the city's school board manage to get less than 50 cents per dollar devoted to education to actually reach the classroom in the form of spending on materials, surroundings or staff.

By limo to the Bronx gives one a strange feeling. But it does enable conversation. Over to our left is a huge appartment block overlooking the river. The apartments have been recently cleaned up, and the school below, which Medina points out, while old and somewhat jaded from the outside, does not look in too bad shape.

We go in first with the elementary school. You know how elementary teachers are great at having the kids' work all over the walls, colors, plants, that kind of thing. It's no use asking high school teachers to do it – you look at any high school classroom and see what I mean – maybe just the odd poster or two. Of course, by the time you get to college, there's nothing there at all. No, we get the elementary teachers to set the scene – get things going, and then we bring in the intermediate kids – that's 10 to 14. The teachers kind of pick up on what is already going on, the kids are used to it – and the way the place looks has already been set.

Carlos Medina believes in keeping schools small – '800 is as big as any school should get'. He is almost obsessive about the appearance of a school, too, and will pick up the litter himself if no one else looks as if they are going to. A background in the toughest of schools in the toughest of areas, with the influential post of superintendent of schools behind him, Medina knows the ropes. He does not believe in hanging around waiting for bureaucracy to give the okay either. 'Do you know, there are over 800 bureaucrats sitting in offices dealing with education – no wonder it's a mess.' One imagines the average bureaucrat faced with a determined Medina in full swing and sees immediately that the battle will be over before it starts.

'We call it "creative non-compliance"', he says. The 'we' Medina is referring to are the four directors of the Center for Educational Innovation, located in the Manhattan Institute for Policy Studies and funded mainly by one of those philanthropists that American society throws up in such quantities and that disappeared from Britain with the welfare state. Its task is to do what it takes to get public education going again. With metal detectors at many school gates and tales of knifings and shootings commonplace, it is a tall order.

One of the team's characteristics is that theirs is no doctrinaire approach. Medina continues as we cruise by burnt-out cars over streets pitted with holes, while I reflect that Manhattan's poshest streets are but some 20 minutes away: 'There is no one best way, all kids are different. Why create similar schools for everyone? What leads to effectiveness is a good match between school, staff and child. That means we will be happy to support the most traditional of schools as well.'

What we are discussing is not, however, a kind of privatisation by the back door. These are believers in state education, even if they are prepared to take many lessons from those that run New York's parochial schools (mainly RC), particularly when it comes to such things as the proper behaviour – for teachers as well as pupils. No woolly-minded liberals these. With 88% of American children in state schools, and with the challenge to the American economy from the infinitely better-schooled Japanese, one can easily see the need for a turn-around. Excellence, not mere tinkering with the system, is the ultimate aim.

Obviously it helps to start anew.

> You have to begin with the small kids. Clear out the school, teachers, kids, the lot, clean the place up and start again, with the right teachers, the kindergarten kids and plenty support. Then you start slowly to build up the rest of the school til you have elementary, intermediate and high school in the one building with the one way of doing things.

Medina does not use words like 'ethos', although it is on my lips. Indeed, Medina is, refreshingly for a gifted educationalist, a highly pragmatic person. But he is not prepared to wait for the unions to show willingness to negotiate nor to let bureaucrats drag their heels. If necessary you alter the rules so that the new establishment has built into the teachers' contracts clauses that go right to the heart of the matter as he sees it:

> Education is about kids. If it's not about kids, what on earth are we doing? And I say if it's in the kids' interests, do it – our job is to find the way. We have all worked in the system for years, and we have gotten round the red tape in our time – it can be done, believe me.

I have no problem believing him.

Talking later to the principal of Community School 214, Montrose Spencer, I began to understand how it is done. Spencer is instantly recognisable as the kind of effective, inspiring leader capable of getting the best out of a mostly young, inexperienced staff; her conversation was full of words like 'growth', 'challenge' and 'learning'. When School 214, re-opened, cleared of previous teachers and kids alike, 'it had nothing but nice clean walls – there was absolutely nothing here'. But Spencer turned this into a learning opportunity: 'It gave us a chance to plan – and by teaching with little, we were able to see what in fact was really needed. Teaching for me is all about learning. When you get too comfortable, then you're in trouble.'

The hooter for lunch let me see how effective the juxtaposition of elementary and intermediate pupils had been. The 14-year-olds were noisy, as would be expected, but polite, careful of the smaller ones, who gave no sign of being ill at ease with such large, energetic creatures.

This mixing of sizes gave the school the impression of being an extension of the family or tribe. But then there were no large amounts of kids anywhere, no jam-packed corridors. 'There are high schools of 5000', Medina told me. 'Crazy!'

Lack of hierarchy dominates operations. Encounters with teachers and administrators show Medina to have the necessary 'street cred.' to be accepted – they know he has done it himself, as superintendent of Community School District Four in East Harlem, where he developed an extensive alternative school system which gained international recognition for its success in educating inner-city children. He may now have offices in the smart part of town, but he inhabits no ivory tower. Moreover, the CEI goes only where it is wanted – and can get things for teachers that do not involve the completion of page after page of forms. If the case can be made verbally for particular resources by a teacher, although this is only a small part of the work of the Center, these will appear within the minimum delay. Having a rich benefactor means that funding is only a phone call away.

How can four people possibly change the face of public education in such a huge and depressed area as the Bronx? This is where newly elected or about-to-be elected Presidents of the US are filmed with their promises of a better future – though there is little evidence of it, despite some attempts at renovation and the addition of some low-cost private housing. Part of the answer is that these four have already done it in District Four, which in the 1970s ranked 32nd of the city's 32 districts on standardised reading and maths tests. By 1987 the district lay 15th, and was competing with richer, predominantly white areas. Yet this was not due to the pouring in of additional sums of money, but rather to the risk-taking and dedication of a group of East Harlem's teachers who, starting small, set up schools where teachers were in control – much to the fury of New York's Board of Education.[23] 'Knowing the red-tape meant we knew how to get round it too.'

Another part of the answer is that the effectiveness of these four people is multiplied many times over by the contacts they have with former colleagues on the ground. In the office collegiality rules – none of the less-than-subtle British distinctions of rank here: 'Maybe Sy is the most famous of us – he has done a lot of writing' – but no one has a higher status or salary, a bigger desk or more potted plants.

The 'Sy' referred to is Seymour Fliegel, co-author of the book *Miracle in East Harlem*,[24] who became, to quote the *New York Times*, famous as a 'school Serpico', when, with concealed microphone he set about uncovering corruption among school board members who were recorded speaking about 'doling out jobs to their friends and political supporters'.

Now the work of the Center is extending to many other areas of New York and interest is flooding in from all over the States. Thirty-six more high schools set up on the model were due to be opened in the city starting in 1993. There are, all stress, no golden rules as to how reform should be carried out, or indeed which reforms should take place. There is no ideology: the prescription only goes as far as to recommend small schools, greater parental choice and involvement, starting from scratch and with a recognisable theme.

13 Pause for Thought: Organising for Innovation

Informal organisation allows for flexibility and brings out the best in people. Modern Language departments run on such lines should be able to take control of their own professional development in conjunction with the development of their own curriculum.

The way in which a commercial enterprise is structured, management writers tell us, can determine the extent to which that enterprise promotes innovation,[25] and innovative capacity is one of the factors which is held to be central to the profitability of an enterprise. Is there perhaps a lesson here for educational management as well? To return to the Burns and Stalker analysis of the success and failure of small firms in Scotland, already mentioned in the Introduction to Part 2, the researchers list six characteristics of informal organisation which they consider as the key to success. It seems plausible that the internal arrangements which they identify also apply in the case of innovative examples of Modern Language teaching already given in this book. This is not to generalise altogether from a few examples, but to suggest that those interested in promoting innovative practices might well start by considering to what extent existing structural arrangements favour such practices or not.

The Adjustment and Continual Redefinition of Individual Tasks with Others

In informal organisations tasks are to be shared; the task *per se* is not seen as paramount; nor is it necessarily beneficial to have one particular outcome in mind when embarking on a piece of work. 'Normal' practice in education is that a group is given a clearly defined task to which they must adhere. There is no scope for altering the remit, which is almost always predetermined. In other words, the task is not set by the doers of it, and the outcomes are not in their hands. 'Ownership', to use a popular term, lies elsewhere. (I dislike the term 'ownership' though I concede it can serve a purpose. My experience of it is that 'ownership' is mostly used when people in authority are trying to make others do something which the authorities have decided is a good idea and what they really mean is 'responsibility for implementation', not ownership at all.)

The sharing of tasks may not always seem to be the most efficient or the most rational way of going about their performance, not the fastest and simplest way to get results – not the most efficient or profit-oriented approach. Rationality would suggest that an expert be brought in to 'get on with it'. Rationality, cost-effectiveness, would of course, in education terms, suggest the central syllabus, the coursebook and the national examination as the way ahead. But what is indicated by Burns and Stalker is that efficiency is not the driving force of success which the rational model would suggest, that there is something more important at stake – something in the nature of a process.

In the Lothian Region GLAFLL project it was the group that decided which tasks were to be performed, and these tasks evolved in the course of events. No one was excluded from making a contribution. Efficiency was not the aim – nor indeed was task completion the driving force. GLAFLL was about teacher development, not materials development.

In Balerno, tasks such as materials preparation were always a shared matter. Those who taught the year group would agree whose turn it was to produce something, and the work would be open to addition and criticism from the rest of the department. Within the groundrules for workbooks, decisions about content or themes rested with those in charge of production. They were also liable to alteration as new ideas circulated. Few workbooks remained unaltered for use with subsequent year groups, however good they appeared, they would have items removed, new items added, the wording changed.

The same could be said as regards both Primary Pilots described in Part 1, where a huge amount of time was spent by teachers getting to know each other, learning how each other operated and adapting their behaviour to the given norms socially as well as professionally. In fact Balerno and Dumfries and Galloway were by far the slowest of the pilot schools to 'get off the ground'. Efficiency thinking would regard all this as a complete waste of valuable teaching time.

Problems may be Posted Upwards, Downwards or Sideways as Being Someone Else's Responsibility

A situation in which each member of the team can be relied upon to act in the communal interest promotes responsibility: but to end up with such a situation demands time and training, and more importantly a sense of mutual dependence, where the group is more powerful than the individual. We have seen the teachers at Balerno comment on the amount of support they had from colleagues. In Dumfries and Galloway, a similarly flexible attitude to problems was taken. The absence of hierarchy, the easy relations between those involved has already been commented on in the section on GLAFLL – collegiality was the order of the day. In all the examples given, problems were dealt with on an *ad hoc* basis.

The Spread of Commitment to the Firm Beyond any Technical Difficulties

Commitment to the firm is another way of saying 'sense of service', which, if we are to believe the managerialists, does not in fact exist, since people are only motivated by self-interest. Self-interest flourishes within a hierarchical structure, where individuals have to compete against each other for monetary and other rewards. The more differences of rank that exist, the greater the encouragement to self-interested behaviour.

Teachers have traditionally demonstrated a strong sense of service, which many believe has been eroded over the years. The willingness by teachers to give of their free time in the Lothian project is one example. It was also present to a remarkable extent in Dumfries and Galloway, where teachers spent a large amount of time after hours learning German and making materials for their classes. Some even financed their own visits to Germany. It is noteworthy that both GLAFLL and the Dumfries and Galloway pilot produced a very strong 'in-group' feeling, with an accompanying identification of the self with the group. People in Lothian thought of themselves as 'GLAFLL teachers', and even developed a common vocabulary with which they identified.

Technical difficulties in Modern Language teaching terms might be stretched to include things such as different levels of competence in any one language. Taking the primary pilots as examples, the 'technical difficulties' encountered by primary teachers with languages in which they were not, for the most part qualified, were set aside because of their commitment to helping their pupils. There probably is some justification for union worries that with the extension of primary languages to all schools, more than a little advantage of the nature of the relationship of primary teachers to their pupils will be taken by the powers that be.

Knowledge about the Technical and Commercial Nature of the Here and Now Task may be Located Anywhere in the Network, This Location Being the *ad hoc* Centre of Control, Authority and Communication

Control centres in education are to be found at the top of the hierarchical pyramid. Control and power mostly rest with the location of the money, not with the knowledge. To what extent in the examples given was knowledge equated with control?

Budgeting in the primary pilots depended only partly on SOED approval. What happened in terms of finance in both pilots described was that regional funding was much more readily accessible than national funding, since it demanded less form-filling, less justification on paper. Usually a phone call would suffice to get things moving. On the other hand, things of which SOED might not totally approve or the necessity for which they might not understand, could take weeks if not months to clear. In other parts of Scotland where regional funding was less generous, or where regional authorities were less inclined to take a stand, much more use was made of courses of which SED approved.

As far as the Lothian project was concerned, a fairly generous budget was set for the project; teachers requiring financial assistance to implement GLAFLL-related activities would apply to Clark, who tended to meet all reasonable requests in full, and even those which appeared unreasonable in part. The removal of a proper budget from advisers was undoubtedly the key to rendering them less effective.

In Balerno most decisions about resources were taken by those who had to use them. The disbursement of the departmental per capita was a common decision. Requisition forms could be completed by any department member. Requests for Print Room services were similarly uncensored, at least until the money ran out.

A Lateral Rather than a Vertical Direction of Communication Through the Organisation; Communication Between People of Different Rank, also, Resembling Consultation Rather than Command

A lateral direction of communication means, to put it in simple terms, 'treating people like grown-ups'. The more marked differences of rank are, the less 'grown-up' are those at the bottom of the pyramid. Of course in education people are not so foolish as to deal in actual commands, but the effect of some of the so-called 'consultation' is in essence no different. Yet innovation is clearly a task for 'grown-ups'.

On the small Pacific atoll of Pukapuka, which until 1994 had no air or regular phone link with the rest of the Cook Islands and to which a boat with supplies comes roughly once every two months, the worst punishment which can take place is to lose one's status as an adult. It is the custom to treat those members of the community who offend against accepted norms of behaviour by designating them to be a child: offending adults lose all adult privileges: they cannot vote, they cannot join in discussions, they have to eat what they are given, go to bed when told, and lose all 'rights' to participate in the normal shared social activities. It is in fact a fearsome and much feared punishment. It is no coincidence that adults everywhere resent instances where they feel they are being treated in this way. In Pukapuka, there used to be only one punishment worse than this – when the offender is given a canoe and a few coconuts and sent on their way into the vastness of the Pacific ocean. Death is seen there as the only thing worse than being treated like a child.

To return to questions of efficiency and effectiveness of the kind which has led to the present reforms in New Zealand, consultation is not of itself efficient. It is quicker by far to issue edicts, invent a new system which you control, write some memos and then require people to fit in than to go the other way round.

A Content of Communication which Consists of Information and Advice rather than Instructions and Decisions

This makes much the same point as those already made. In terms of teacher development, what is often most lacking is the information on which teachers can base their judgements. The point is made in Part 4 about the necessity for greater contact between teachers and researchers and for the need for researchers to take on a proactive role as 'information brokers'.

It was noted in Part 1 how teacher training for the Dumfries and Galloway pilot started off with the innovative 'Pilgrims' team and their use of drama techniques, none of which was at all familiar to the teachers. This set a tone of enquiry in which everyone was a learner. We saw very much the same thing within the GLAFLL project, where guest experts would be invited to talk on all kinds of subjects, about the relevance of which teachers could make their own decisions.

Teachers are highly social beings – there are few 'loners' in any staffroom. It is said in terms of industry that inventors tend to work best on their own, while innovators work best with other people. If that is indeed the case, the quality of personal relationships must also be of critical importance. It would be interesting to examine in close-up those teachers whom their colleagues judge to be innovative, to see whether they are also rated high on sociability.

Teacher Development as Departmental Development

In Parts 1 and 2 we saw examples of curriculum development in action as teacher development. Teacher training, in other words, was on-the-job training. Everyone knows that when training is not related to daily experience it can fail to take effect, just as when teaching a subject is not related somehow to the actual experience of pupils they may fail to learn.

For this reason it makes sense to have teachers extend their competencies within the social framework in which they normally operate, and have individual departments take a far more active role in planning the development of individuals in the interests of all. Devolving responsibility in general to teachers within departments for this would seem to be a sensible starting point. Creating time for planning departmental and teacher development tied to curriculum development ought to be a management priority.

There is room, too, for a revision of normal departmental practices. As long as non-promoted members of a department have no real power, there is (apart of course from the good fortune that some people may well enjoy working with each other) little incentive for them to participate in task-sharing. Real executive power means deciding how money is spent, who teaches which class, what in fact is taught as well as how it should be taught.

This begs the question as to what Principal Teachers are for. As I suggested earlier, might it not be more effective to see their role more in the light of facilitators of teacher development and less in the role as managers of money and materials? It is to diminish them to suggest that they are merely instruments for the implementation of school, or education department policies, although it is by no means uncommon nowadays to hear such a view expressed. I would like to see all Principal Teachers take a much more pro-active role in the area of teacher development. Those who do, probably have far greater prospects of job satisfaction than those who spend their time filling in forms and dreaming up better and more streamlined systems for the control of files and school and departmental property. A great deal of the administrative burden at present placed on PTs can just as well be undertaken on a shared basis with the entire department.

Traditionally the mysteries of timetabling and requisitioning have been the domain of the PT, and many a newly promoted PT has wished they had had more experience of both. It seems to me that in order to participate fully in departmental work, all teachers should feel that they are able, as well as entitled, to do these things. This is not a question of consultation – of asking people what classes they would like to teach. What is being suggested is that all teachers are given the whole timetabling picture, instructed in how to work out the 'blocks' and asked, if they wish to, to make out their ideal timetable for the whole department.[26] Just as when a department has to work together to decide how to spend the per capita there soon develops an understanding of why certain things cannot be done, so also in terms of timetabling a corresponding sensitivity to the common good rather than individual wishes can be seen to arise over time.

When it comes to the upgrading of skills, whether they be language, pedagogical or organisational skills, it would seem to be a logical conclusion for departmental members to take joint responsibility for their own development and to plan their own training as a department, plugging gaps on a departmental rather than only on a personal basis. Since training is a highly time-consuming activity, some things might be regarded as achievable in the long term, others in the short term.

Funding would come into play, too, since training is expensive. Yet if education is to be more cost-effective (surely that is what the reforms are all about?), then perhaps training based on school departments is one, at least, of the possible answers. Perhaps it is time to think of making individual departments responsible for the administration of their own training budget. Alternatively, as in some commercial firms, individuals might be offered a 'training allowance' to be spent at their own discretion on approved training schemes – this is one of the ways in which British industry, for instance is tackling the language training of its managers.

Learning processes for teachers

There is another dimension to teacher training which can only take place within departments. The right of learners to make mistakes is generally accepted, but this right is rarely extended to the teaching profession. Of the many 'mistakes' which teachers make, the most serious belong not to the technical side of the job, but to the social. 'Teaching' something wrong such as some incorrect grammatical rule, not correcting someone's homework, or forgetting to cover part of the examination syllabus, unless these are repeated mistakes, are soon forgiven and forgotten by pupils and parents who are otherwise content. Treating someone the wrong way is not. People are not born with a talent for treating others properly. This has to be learnt, and it takes a great deal of time; most people make mistakes and continue to make mistakes. It cannot be learnt at training colleges. It has to be experienced to be learnt. It does not get 'learnt' on a management course, but as a result of sustained contact with other people who have made it their priority.

What this part of the book highlights is the social learning model as inspiration for innovation. Take the Toronto experiential school, for example. The description given is of a social system in the same way as what Firth describes in Tikopia was a social system. What has happened to education in many developing countries is the construction of institutions at total variance to the social system. Schools are artificial, alien places, where bizarre rituals and rules are encountered which are largely unknown to the society as a whole and often largely incomprehensible to the children, the more so in countries where the medium of instruction bears no relation to the language the children use at home.

What appears to work is that where people get on well with each other, an environment is created where they can do their best work. So-called 'primitive' societies instinctively understood this. Pacific Island culture still lays great stress on people coming together in shared tasks, such as fishing, sewing bees, singing in the church choir, organising 'morning teas' and 'umukais' (feasts – the 'umu' is an underground oven) dancing competitions, funerals, the unveiling of headstones. The entire energy of the community is directed to the social side rather than to the professional or money-making side of life, which is seen as a tedious sideline to the main business of living and which hence receives scant attention. This makes for a highly sophisticated and extremely pleasant existence, where public arguments and raised voices are rare and family and group activities take priority. Cook Islanders have social skills of the highest order – the notion of anyone needing to be 'socialised' in school would be greeted with complete incomprehension.

Community schooling is a way of reproducing, or sometimes reinvigorating, the social system of a local area, which is why it is so often successful. The experiential school in Toronto and the languages department in Balerno High School were both social systems. Perhaps the lesson is that if you organise within education in the way people organise naturally within society, a climate can be created in which learning can flourish and innovation may take place. On the other hand, where schools are cut off artificially from society, and where artificial restrictions and hierarchical constraints abound, things tend not to work so well. Alternatively put, perhaps if teachers behave like human beings, so will pupils.

Notes to Part 3

1. High School in Scotland means a secondary school, taking in all pupils from the area whatever their ability from the age of 11 to 18. There are no selective state schools in Scotland and while there is a small private sector, the majority of pupils attend local state schools, sometimes known for reasons of tradition as 'Grammar' schools or 'Academies'.
2. PALE (Peripheral Audio-Active Language Equipment) consists of wall- or desk-mounted cassette recorders with two headsets, allowing pupils to work in pairs, individually, or in group mode, at the teacher's discretion. It can operate from a console in the same way as a traditional language laboratory, but is infinitely more flexible, as each machine can be self-standing. Pupils who wanted to make their own recordings, or listen to a cassette, simply moved to the machines and got on with their work on their own.
3. Ferguson, A. Don't smile til Easter, a probationer's frantic reflections. Published in the sadly now defunct and much missed *Modern Languages in Scotland*.
4. Maley and Duff (1978) *Drama Techniques in Language Teaching*. Cambridge University Press; Ur, P. (1981) *Discussions that Work: Task-centred Fluency Practice*. Cambridge University Press.
5. A weakness in a particular area need not mean that person should not address that area: often someone who finds a subject or topic difficult will bring a new light to it for everyone, and learn from this themselves. Much depends, it seems to me, on acknowledging the fact that all teachers are learners, and that we all have a lot to learn.
6. The Lothian Series consisted of materials produced in the time of GLAFLL and later published by Macmillan, which offered the kind of activities which, it was hoped, would encourage the learners to use language in a communicative way. They included Penfriend letters, Pairwork exercises with information and affect gaps, Reading 'for Real', a Writing 'folio' and a multi-skill listening package. All of these were produced in three or four languages. See Part 2, Note 23.

7. Stenhouse, L. (1975) *An Introduction to Curriculum Research and Development.* Heinemann.
8. I will try to explain in more detail in this note how this operated. Most teachers used the same kind of approach and the workbooks contained many examples of this view of language which is based on encouraging the development of the pupils' own grammar as French was being encountered, rather than explaining what was being encountered in terms of standard grammar. Beginners would meet as set phrases 'j'ai oublié mon cahier' along with 'je peux aller aux toilettes?' and 'je peux tailler mon crayon?' (either because these occurred as they arose normally in class or because they encountered them in their workbooks). As far as they knew there was no difference between the infinitive and the past participle. This was introduced in GLAFLL by John Clark as the '-eeks-ay system' – what was learnt in terms of structure was the use of the following language structure: 'je' plus word 'x' (French pronunciation 'eeks') and the " sound – 'eeks-ay'. The 'je peux' was followed quickly by 'on peut?' when groups or the class were involved. 'Vous voulez aller ...?' was normal teacher talk in a classroom where pupils decided for themselves what to do. 'Bon, c'est décidé?' would be said when pupils in a group worked out what they were going to do. The PALE units allowed the teacher to say such things as 'tu as écouté ou tu as paré when presented with a cassette, and when asked for one 'tu vas/veux écouter ou parler?'. New sentences followed such as 'tu voudrais x?/vous voudriez travailler en groupe?' and these were no different from 'on pourrait aller au studio' or indeed 'tu as oublié?' Such exceptions as 'je suis allé' were taken in their stride without murmur – and as is usual this would be reproduced incorrectly from time to time. Since things were always being mislaid, 'j'ai perdu' and 'tu as perdu?', 'j'ai pris..' were part of the normal classroom language. Attitude to error can best be described by example: 'Qu'est-ce que tu as/vous avez fait?' was a question often required by the teacher which resulted usually in the production of what might be described as something ending in the sound 'é'. However, if in response to 'qu'est-ce que tu vas faire?' the teacher heard 'j'ai....' she would likely stress 'j'ai dit *vas* faire – pas *as* fait', since the error had the potential to confuse. This made for a rapid progress in terms of variety of structures which were likely to be understood. These were mainly met in the first and second persons (while 'vous' would be heard regularly, 'nous' was replaced by 'on'). Third person language is less frequent when dealing with the here and now. Pupils were also used to hearing language used about language and about learning, e.g. Vous avez compris? Vous écoutez? Concentrez! Consultez le dictionnaire! Maintenant on va aller ... Tu as fini? Qu'est-ce que tu as écrit l? Je me suis trompé ... (and for some) – C'est un verbe – il faut chercher l'infinitif dans ton dico ... and so on.
9. Standard Grade conversation was tested both internally, with six examples of assessed pupil performance, and by means of a final proficiency test, set by the Scottish Examination Board, conducted and marked by the teacher. For this the pupils were given an outline of the test situation the day before they took the test, to enable them to prepare for it. The pupils were used to working collaboratively and organised all kinds of self-help groups before the examination.
10. I recommend to the reader interested in responsibility training Leni Dam's

article, Learning autonomy in practice, in *Autonomy in Language Learning*, Gathercole, I. (ed.) published by CILT, which contains much other useful material.

11. Those teachers who did trust their classes, did so within the parameters of what they had taught them. It was not the case that they had a belief in the innate goodness of teenagers – far from it; it was rather that they and the pupils understood the limits.

12. I allocated myself a first-year class whom I took for two years, and allowed myself the luxury of 'leaving the learning up to them'. They were a delight and the experience a great pleasure.

13. Up until then this teacher had only worked in the department as a replacement for a teacher who had left in the middle of a year – never an easy task.

14. The problem of the three very different feeder primary schools is an acute one at Balerno, as already indicated in Part 1. The secondary school is situated in the well-off suburb of Balerno, where Dean Park Primary is also situated. Dean Park sends over 90 pupils to the secondary, and it is no wonder that the minority from Ratho (perhaps 28–30) and Kirknewton (around 24), who are mostly from a rural, less affluent background, often seem to be swamped.

15. Once it took practically a year for two pupils in my class to produce anything worthwhile – I nearly abandoned hope. When they started to work, it was their own decision – probably like the example given by Dam, they had found that doing almost nothing was, after all, boring. The fact that they succeeded in the end quite well meant that they had 'picked up' a fair amount. Just because they had not appeared industrious had not meant that they were not learning. Teachers of course know the corollary – just because they look as if they are hanging on your every word does not ensure they are hearing what you are saying!

16. Hamilton, J. and Reid S. (1991) *In Play*. Nelson; and Hamilton, J. and McLeod, A. (1993) *Drama in the Language Classroom*. CILT.

17. Guessing was 'taught' and rewarded, even if the guess was incorrect. The more pupils were adventurous with language, the more they were likely to guess correctly. Certain strategies were taught. Gender, for example, in German. When pupils eventually asked how to tell if a word was der, die, das, they would be told they could find out for themselves: all they had to do was, in a group, go through a few pages of a dictionary listing nouns under each heading. Of course there are almost twice as many masculine nouns as the other two. They would then see that many of the feminine ones ended in – e or – ung, and perhaps that quite a few neuter ones began with Ge-. This gave them a 'rule' they could see the sense of applying, which they were unlikely to forget because they had discovered it for themselves.

18. Taking pupils out of the environment of the classroom not only did wonders for motivation, it offered scope for teachers (and not just Modern Languages teachers) and foreign assistants to talk about things not seen within the confines of the school. It also gave relevance to such activities as 'finding the way' when this consisted of instructions sending pupils all round the centre of Edinburgh, collecting a variety of information and ending up, much to their surprise at a German cafe for 'Kaffee und Kuchen'.

19. *Upgrading New Zealand's Competitive Advantage*, Graham T. Crocombe,

Michael J. Enright, Michael E. Porter, (1991). Oxford University Press.

20. The 1981 'Parents Charter' gave parents the right to send their children to the school of their choice as long as there were places available. Previously it had been compulsory for children to attend their neighbourhood school.

21. *In Play, A Drama Resource Kit for Modern Languages*, Judith Hamilton and Sandra Reid. Nelson, (1991).

22. New York's schools – Begin again, *The Economist*, 4–10 September 1993.

23. The Board of Education consists of seven members who are in effect answerable to no one. Its appointments are criticised as being blatantly political, for which reason it has lost the support of the teaching unions and scandals abound about its running of the system.

24. *Miracle in East Harlem*, Seymour Fliegel and James MacGuire, Times Books (1993).

25. Zaltmann *et al.* (1973) found that a high degree of centralisation inhibits the initiation of innovation. Kanter (1983) similarly found that high stratification – too many levels within an organisation – leads to preoccupation with status and insufficient freedom for creative thinking, which she calls 'the elevator mentality'.

26. In many schools the entire school timetable and decisions about who teaches which class are made by a deputy head or other member of the senior management team. This seems to me both unnecessary and counter-productive, as well as wasting a potential opportunity for staff training.

Part 4
The Right People for Innovation

Introduction to Part 4: More than Intellect

Harnessing the social forces already present in society is more likely to promote innovative capacity than any management system. Inspiration stems from links between people, and inspiration requires passion.

We have been brain-washed by the doctrine of management. One would think that the management industry had invented the idea that people must be taught to work together in order to get things done, as if somewhere along the line we lost the ability to share tasks and the social skills necessary for the smooth conduct of relationships. A few years ago, I recall, my colleagues and I regarded with mild amusement a glossy brochure advertising a new service to industry by our tertiary institution which was embarking on income generation as part of the great entrepreneurial *Zeitgeist*. This service claimed to teach, of all things, 'People Skills'. I have since tried to imagine explaining 'People Skills' to Cook Islanders, who must be world leaders in the conduct of personal relations and social organisation. Have we in Britain really reached the stage where we have to be *taught* how to be human?

The social system used to take care of such things, and in addition could be relied upon for the dissemination of ideas. Even before mass communication, 'networking' was a function carried out by the Church and the early universities, though we must not forget that the troubadours, too, played a role here. People have an appetite for news, for ideas, for word of different worlds.

Rural and other small communities such as Dumfries and Galloway, know how to harness the forces within their area and how to build on existing links. When there is a need to come together in order to move forward, existing links become strengthened, such as the links with parents described in the case of the foreign visits organised at Balerno High School. We also saw in Part 1, Chapter 4, how teachers, teacher trainers and student teachers in Western Samoa came together to heighten awareness of code-switching in English medium classes. Samoan communities, village-based and family oriented, are also close-knit and organised along social lines. It is easy to imagine that such an arrangement would fit naturally into the existing social pattern.

The main feature of the links mentioned above is that they all derive from a perceived need. Just as the idea of the language task has helped teachers provide a wider range of communicative activities for their pupils to engage in, so the task provides a useful focus for teacher development. Teachers seem to prefer In-Service training sessions where there is something for them to actually do or to create, particularly when they share in the results. 'Swop-shops' are a useful source of ideas and can, when appropriately organised, produce more than simply an exchange of materials. Whatever the linkages, those which work well are mostly created by people who get along well together. Linkages seem to work less well when outsiders decide on grounds of rationality to bring together two institutions or two sets of people.

Harnessing forces which already exist in society to foster the spread of innovation may make more sense than to invent additional institutions and systems to do this artificially for us. Teachers like to be made to think, and for this they rely on those whom we might call professional teacher developers – the academics, researchers and writers, the conference speakers and course leaders, many of them classroom teachers themselves, who, thanks to advisory services and to institutions such as CILT and ALL have played an important part in disseminating information and ideas. Those who can write and speak with clarity and distil ideas without adulterating them play a key role in the spread of innovation. Language associations and institutions, through the organisation of meetings, conferences and newsletters, and through publishing ventures, succeed in making many teachers aware of what is going on in other places, by coordinating efforts and providing a back-up to the work done. There are modern troubadours as well, drama groups like Pilgrims and others, that bring a new dimension to the work of teachers.

Taking up what is available is still mostly left to individuals, and in Part 3 I suggested that one way round this was to regard Modern Languages departments as a suitable base for teacher development. The problem still arises of how to find ways of disseminating ideas from department to department, particularly in the absence of local authority advisers. If there is a real reason for coming together, as in the case of the primary language teaching pilots or the GLAFLL project, and where teachers see the need to produce something which they will be using themselves, the result can be extremely productive. Meeting for the sake of it never seems to get anyone very far. Even meeting to discuss needs schools have in common often ends up in disappointment. There is, however, one area in which schools can be said to have needs in common and where they can be the direct beneficiaries of working together, and that is in the area of pre-service training.

Institutions with responsibility for teacher training, because they belong to the tertiary education sector, may find themselves cut off from schools, which come under a different department or ministry. Most teacher training institutions deal only with pre-service training and, with a few notable exceptions, have had little or no responsibility for In-Service work with practising teachers and few concrete links with local authorities and schools. This is now changing. The next section of the book describes how one such institution has come to work in partnership with the local authority advisory service, teachers and departments, basing its course on shared beliefs about the need for a thinking, innovating teaching force.

Prose and Passion

All those who work in the innovative area know that what they are doing is relating idea to idea. It is, as Forster puts it, a question of whether we can or not 'only connect'. Forster's heroine knows how this can be done. The quote in full reads:

> *Only connect! That was the whole of her sermon. Only connect the prose and the passion, and both will be exalted, and human love will be seen at its highest.*[1]

Little wonder that we usually only hear part of it – those who would have us 'connect' usually have in mind that we use only the intellect, not the emotions when we do so. Yet in a book dealing with inspiration, we cannot ignore the realm of the emotions – how else do we become inspired if not through our passions? It is a mistake to assume that all that is lacking in order to encourage more teachers to innovate for themselves is an efficient means of disseminating information, or a common task in the execution of which they can combine. This is to ignore the fact that we need to lift our eyes from time to time from the here and now, that along with the monasteries and universities, there also came the troubadours.

Magic and mystery

This brings me to the crucial question of inspiration and its sources. Here we enter the world of magic and mystery, and need to consult with those who understand such things. As a guide to the mystery, there is, in my view, none more skilled than Earl Stevick, whose works have influenced me personally more than those of any other writer. Drawing from what he has to say, I have attempted to relate what he writes to the theme of this book and address, if only at one remove, the mystery of it all.

14 Partners in Training

A teacher training course aims at creating a three-way partnership between training institution, teachers in local schools, and the trainees themselves.

In 1989, Moray House College, as it was then called, welcomed its first batch of new recruits to Modern Language teaching after closing down the department some years previously. The fact that there was nothing left of the earlier course – they had even given away the Modern Language books in the library – allowed the college to make a complete reappraisal of the role of teacher training in the subject. The previous year, 1988–89, Lothian Region agreed that I be seconded part-time to work out a framework for the new course starting from scratch. This first year was a year for consultation, research and informal exchanges of ideas, involving visits to many other teacher training institutions and discussions with those working there. Finally a team of experienced teachers from Lothian Region, many of whom had worked together in the GLAFLL project, together with the Adviser and myself as newly appointed lecturer in Modern Languages at Moray House, drew up a programme of teacher development. This group was eventually known as the 'Steering Committee for Initial Teacher Training in Modern Languages'. It was to take responsibility for providing a new approach to the training of student teachers, one in which practising teachers in schools played a pro-active role. Later on, as student numbers increased, teachers were to be seconded from Lothian Region to Moray House on a part-time basis, thus maintaining the regional links. One of the committee's first tasks was the selection of new recruits.

Selection Day

Session 1: Getting to know you

The 20 young men and women eyed the figure in the middle with carefully fixed expressions of willingness and more than some suspicion, then plunged into action, greeting each other with 'bonjour's, 'Guten Morgen's, 'bongiorno's 'hola's and some 'sdrazvetie's'. From the sidelines a note was taken of those who failed to make eye contact – and of the man who seemed to need to grasp hold of every young woman before addressing her.

Selection procedures for teachers have traditionally consisted of the one-off interview. This is something that most language graduates find relatively simple. After all, they have chosen a field in which communication skills are essential – and have been having interviews in the form of 'orals', probably for many years. Selection procedures for the armed forces are harder by far, as are the screening procedures of some multi-nationals. Is teaching really so unimportant that we can accept people on the basis of a one-to-one interview which reveals only a tiny part of an individual's potential as future teacher and colleague?

Session 2: Logic puzzles – how well do you cooperate?

'Il y a comme un triangle au centre – non, pardon, un peu à gauche, oui, comme ça, et puis – zut, un instant, dans le coin à droite....' Julie wished she hadn't come. All the others seemed so confident. The chap opposite had so dominated the card puzzle that no one else got much of a chance to speak – though she had wanted to tell him that the instructions had clearly said that the order was ace, two, three – and that putting two aces on top of each other couldn't therefore be correct. When the instructor had pointed this out, the chap had found his mistake funny – she would have been mortified. She hoped her individual interview would be better – so far she hadn't given much of an account of herself. She did so desperately want to be accepted – she had never thought she wanted so much to teach until her year as a foreign assistant in France. Never mind the fact that the kids were an undisciplined mob – she had won them round, and used all the games and techniques she had learnt on the induction course. Come to think of it, the sort of thing they had been doing all morning wasn't so very different.

Teaching requires so much more than the technical skills that used to be listed, as they still are on driving test forms, as if 'relationship with class' were of the same importance as 'blackboard skills'. Over one half hour it is easy to miss qualities of persistence and calm doggedness, and not always easy to weed out the confident, urbane charmer whose total absorption with self makes him a good raconteur but would make a lousy colleague.

Individual interview – what do you think?

Herbert stretched back confidently in the chair, smiled winningly, and proceeded to expand on his ideas on education.

'You see, what you have to do is win them over, motivate them. Of course, when I was in the navy, we had a similar approach with the new recruits. Stick and carrot. It always worked – not that I ever had any difficulty, you understand. Discipline doesn't worry me. I suppose I'd have a bit to learn about all the new courses and things, but you are quite right, you know, about talking French all the time – really it's the only way. And group teaching – well, that's how it's done these days, isn't it?'

The two interviewers glanced at each other – let him get on with it – he was digging such a hole for himself, it was almost a shame. Almost, thought the woman; if she hadn't felt his arm slide round her waist when he volunteered himself as her partner in the second activity, she might even have felt sorry for him. Mentally listing him as 'the groper', she thought about the girl they had just seen. Awfully quiet in the morning – but what a difference in the individual interview – and she had come out fighting when challenged about her commitment... Julie, that was her name. She'd make a good teacher, that one. Plenty of 'smeddum'.[2]

While the 'Herberts' of this world, thankfully, mostly rule themselves out, some of those who present themselves for interview fail to do themselves justice for a variety of reasons. This is why a whole day is taken up with selection procedures in the Language Studies department at Moray House Institute of Education.

Later that afternoon in Pamela's flat

Mark thought Pamela looked just fantastic. What a great pair of legs. And now she was telling him that the chap in the interview for teacher training college had had the nerve to ask her whether she thought she could go on teaching practice dressed like that! Some cheek. Whatever had she told him. 'I told him the truth – that I'd spent so much on the jacket for the interview, I'd no money left to buy a new skirt – honestly, Mark, I was mortified.'

Meanwhile, back in college ...

'You said what?'

'I asked her if she'd go to school dressed in that skirt – I mean, come on, think of that heidie at Braehead – he'd take a fit! Then send her home to change ... remember that French assistant and the trousers ... I have to say I was impressed by how she took it. I think she'll be great, actually, lots of 'go' and a good straight answer. She'll buy a new skirt, too, I bet.'

One of the best she did indeed turn out to be. Personal qualities like honesty and integrity are what we would all like to see in teaching colleagues. It is not a profession for smooth talkers and self-servers – the young have a way of identifying those who talk a good line and fail to deliver.

The justification

'Handknitted yoghurt sweater, hair all over the place, petticoat showing. Heavens above, if they can't even get their clothes on in the morning, how on earth do they think they can organise a class! Can't you just hear the noise from that one's classroom?'

'You really are hard on them, aren't you?'

'Not a bit – just think of the poor school that has to cope with that for the rest of her teaching career. It's a waste of time being sorry for them. If they are not up to it, you're doing them a favour rejecting them.'

The selection of new recruits requires both sensitivity and courage on the part of the selection team, who have a very real responsibility to the profession. It makes good sense to involve those who have eventually to work with new teachers. Teachers in departments who have to 'nurse along' colleagues who clearly are in the wrong job, regularly bemoan the fact that no one seems prepared to protect them from this. Not all training institutions are supportive to the idea of failing a student teacher, or refusing to endorse a probationer's certificate.[3] Once a relationship is formed, lecturers understandably find it hard to take personal responsibility for removing someone from a course, and indeed most training institutions make it practically impossible for them to do so, which is why the selection procedures conducted at Moray House Institute of Education by an experienced team of practising Principal Teachers, along with the regional Adviser and college staff, are deliberately designed to be so stretching. Not only do they give an opportunity to candidates to demonstrate a variety of characteristics which an interview on its own would miss, they set the tone for what is to come in the college course – the use of the target languages as part of the methodology, the importance of colleagues and teamwork, the fact that teaching is anything but a soft option.

Hitting the Ground Running

'You have to walk before you can run' is an adage that suggests that in learning there is a strictly linear path and, if you fail to follow it, you will end up by coming a cropper. This rule may do very well for training athletes, but it is unsuitable for the training of student teachers, many of whom hit the ground in college already running. Student teachers come from all kinds of backgrounds, more and more of them already have some experience of teaching, and while many still do come straight from university, some are in the 40–50 year old bracket and have worked all their lives in industry or commerce.

These trainee teachers have the potential to be the front runners of innovation in schools. Not knowing that certain things are 'impossible' is a distinct advantage. If courage is not encouraged and rewarded early on, the chance can be missed, because inevitably student teachers will imitate those they see as being successful. Once patterns are established – and these can be established very quickly – people are reluctant to alter things, particularly if they have worked. There is a danger that the potential of a person to develop a whole range as a teacher can be shut off early on, which is one of the concerns the profession voices about the notion of purely on-the-job training.

In at the deep end

To encourage confidence, it helps to have a sense of belonging to a group. The Moray House course starts with games and activities aimed at team-building and getting people to know each other in a stress-free atmosphere. Whole group games such as 'Find someone who...', 'Do you like your neighbour?', 'In my grandmother's suitcase', and so on which one can also play with pupils, can be used for a two-fold purpose – relaxing the group and demonstrating a useful classroom activity. This then sets the pattern for future sessions, where students, individually or in small groups, are encouraged to lead the session with activities suitable to the session's topic, in whatever language they choose.[4]

For example, in 'Find someone who....'[5] on their first day in college the new student teachers are each given a sheet asking them to find within the group someone who, for example, has been to the same place during their year abroad, someone who voted 'green' in the last election, someone who is not wearing something bought in Marks and Spencer's, and to write down their name.

This serves two purposes: it enables the new group to get to know each other in a swift and relaxed way, and it lets them see a real communicative activity in action – and a mixed-skill one at that. It also establishes a pattern of group activity using suitable material for adults, followed by an adaptation of the activity for use with pupils.

Much of the start of the course aims at getting the student teachers used to leading activities and learning how to make themselves understood. Mime, gesture and voice can be worked on and improved within the training institution before they are needed in schools. For each technique learnt and practised within a working group, there is a subsequent visit to a school where there is an opportunity for the group to team-teach classes and analyse the results. Clearly some protection of the ego is necessary, and groups themselves work out who will lead and who will follow. Moreover, not everyone is comfortable in the 'teacher as leader' mode, though all have to do it at some time. Those less extrovert types are often happier in a less dominant role, and this can result in their using their strengths as facilitators in later sessions dealing with responsibility training and so on. Some unusual and thought-provoking methods explored in the course, such as Suggestopedia and Community Language Learning call for a sympathetic and supportive approach which suits some people very well.

If student teachers are not exposed to such things, they may be sidetracked from finding the teacher within themselves. If they concentrate on a particular model, however effective it may be, they may fail to do themselves justice. While most start off imitating someone, it is the job of the trainers to ensure that each individual fulfils their potential to develop as a complete person in the classroom.

Applying the same principle

The focus of our thinking about how pupils can be brought to cope with language learning has shifted over the last 20 to 30 years. Language teachers have a greater awareness of language, not just as a system which can be analysed and described in terms of parts of speech, but as a useful tool which can be seen as relevant to the needs both of individuals and the country as a whole. This view encompasses essentially a pragmatic, ends-means, input-output approach, which encourages the learning of much that is deemed useful and relevant to the European citizen. It rarely, however, seriously encompasses the notion of language learning in humanistic terms, as being concerned with the whole person, who in order to learn, requires to have control over their own learning as an active participant in a development of self where the processes of learning are as important, if not more important, than the products.

To those who hold the latter view, there is no great difference between teaching a language effectively to pupils in a class and training teachers for the future. The same principles will apply because what is involved is a change in behaviour as well as attitude:

- learners require to be involved and active
- they learn best when experiencing things for themselves
- responsibility for learning rests with the learner
- each learner has a preferred style of learning
- as members of a social group, the ethos, values and health of that group have to be considered as contributing to the learning processes of individuals

Any programme which seeks to turn out teachers who themselves will be concerned with their pupils as whole people has to take the learner as the starting point. This approach requires a flexibility which is often at variance with the institution itself, because each year's intake will differ from the previous year's, and the needs of individuals will have to be met in ways that rule out a prescribed and definitive syllabus. It also requires a framework which allows the monitoring of progress and room for consultation, in order that people do not become lost within a system which offers too much choice and too little guidance.

Working towards a consultative model

No institution in Britain is able to staff to a level which makes the consultative role a possibility. Yet the consultative model is the one that is most likely to get the best out of individual trainees. Logic suggests that one should look beyond the college to find a system that can offer more personal attention than is possible within an understaffed institution. At Moray House logic suggested the utilisation of existing resources and a recourse to the informal groups of teachers who already had experience of working together in the days of the GLAFLL project, along with some 'new blood' of a later vintage.

Designing a Course

Teacher trainers do not work in isolation from the communities of teachers on whom they rely to give new recruits the right start in the profession. In order to ensure a coherent experience for new recruits, the training institution has to take into account that it is only one-third of the team involved. Providing a framework for initial teacher training means providing a framework for a three-part collaboration, involving the training institution, the schools and the student teachers themselves.

The point has already been made about the fact that power and responsibility lie at the heart of problems of teacher development. If teachers have no say in the nature of the training of recruits to the profession, it is hardly fair to expect them to take the responsibility for it, even less so to ask them to carry the failures of the training system. As already said, the first step towards the development of the new course at Moray House was a prolonged series of discussions about what teaching Modern Languages consists of and requires, undertaken with many people, some of whom were later to form the Steering Committee for Initial Teacher Training, incorporating Lothian's Adviser for Modern Languages and staff from Moray House Language Studies Department.

Most models devised under new schemes for more extensive school involvement in pre-service training still see 'theory' as something which belongs to the academic institution – not something with which the teachers have to do. This is to underutilise and underestimate teachers drastically. As Figure 14.1 gradually took shape, as the various people analysed what the classroom teacher actually had to do and be in order to be successful, what emerged in discussions was the importance of a wide range of features some of which were a matter of knowledge – e.g. of the subject, of aspects of pedagogy, psychology, sociology and linguistics. Some of these features were a question of training, such as technical skills, and others less susceptible to intervention like a person's beliefs – about language and how it is learnt, about children and how they learn, about life in general, and things which have to be taken as already set in adults, like sociability and a sense of humour. When we judge someone's effectiveness as a teacher and their suitability as a colleague, the group decided, we consciously or unconsciously rely on a combination of such features which we may not articulate, but which form the basis of our judgement. The course was aimed at addressing all of these features. Some of the features will have to be developed through training, others may change during the course.

Each Teacher in Training Comes with:

Personal Qualities

judgement
responsiveness
self-confidence
smeddum
enthusiasm
resilience
endurance
diligence
responsiveness to ideas
sense of humour
risk-taking propensity
balance
clarity of thought
powers of analysis

Beliefs About

themselves
life
politics
learners
learning
the TT institution
the subject

Affects/Dispositions

positive
helpful
acceptance of others
tolerance
supportive
adaptive

Knowledge About

Learners: psychology, sociology,
psycho-linguistics
Foreign language: descriptive
(grammar, phonology etc)/in action
Education system: historical, political,
exams, organisation
Linguistic theory
Methods and types of assessment
How they learnt the FL

Proficiency In

(a) Techniques (long term)

assessment
drama
eliciting response
preparing for learning

(b) Strategies (short term)

discipline
monitoring
attention getting/maintaining

Abilities/Skills

(a) Personal
application of common sense
negotiatory
communicative/
interactive: demeanour, dress,
voice, body language,
empathy
manner(s)

(b) Professional
(i) **Materials production**
conceptual
practical: paper-based,
word-processing, audio,
video, mixed packages
(ii) **Managerial**
of resources
of materials
of classroom
of records
(iii) **Technology**
computer
word-processor
audio
video
camcorder
OHP
language learning equipment
(e.g. PALE)
(iv) **Foreign language proficiency**
FL1
FL2

Figure 14.1 Some desirable features in trainee teachers

Plotting progress

The outline depicted in Figure 14.1 appeared initially as a rough diagram, in which the trainee teacher figured in the centre around whom people scribbled in the things they thought important. It grew, as ideas were added and it became the basis for the planning of the course and the materials used on it. In order to make clear to the student teachers how the Committee viewed the demands of the profession, a 'progress card' was developed based on the diagram. All new student teachers are given this document on which they are asked to plot their position. As they gain experience, master certain skills, acquire additional knowledge and perhaps develop certain facets of their personality, student teachers can see themselves move from left to right on the sheet. Thus they see what they have achieved as well as what is still to be addressed. They can, if they wish, show this to staff in schools so that they can be helped in those areas they themselves have identified as needing development. This document can be seen as a kind of operational syllabus which, because it is different for each individual, has to be the responsibility of each individual. It is the focus for discussion about needs and progress, and it is against the 'progress card' that student teachers know they will eventually be judged by those who know them best in the schools.

In addition to the 'progress card', which is an essentially private document, the Steering Committee drew up an 'activity sheet' in order to help teachers in schools make a focussed contribution to training. A copy of this is given to all student teachers and sent in advance to all receiving schools. This lists mostly short-term objectives of a mainly technical nature which student teachers should be expected to master in the course of a term. These are things like playing language games, marking Standard Grade Speaking Tests, using the Pale units, modifying the use of the target language to make it more comprehensible to learners and so on.

Involving school departments

In setting up college-school liaison, the Steering Committee wanted to ensure that the schools were properly briefed about the course so that misunderstandings did not arise. As a result, college staff attend regional meetings of Principal Teachers at the Teachers' Centres in Lothian and other regions, as well as departmental meetings in schools; to the teachers in schools to which trainees are sent there are invitations to termly consultations in college. A video has been made about the course, and sent to all schools which offer teaching practice – wherever they are. It was part of a 'pack' of materials, developed by Janetta Jeffreys-Jones, a Lothian Principal Teacher on secondment to Moray House. One of Jeffreys-Jones' tasks was to visit schools and draw together with the department and board of management a consensus about what the department was able and willing to contribute to the training.

Nursery slopes

One feature of the course is the visits which are made to a small number of schools during the part of the term usually reserved for work in college.[6] These are schools whose Principal Teachers volunteered to take an additional responsibility for monitoring a small group of trainees. The idea stems from the 'mentor' model, which is gradually becoming popular in ITT. It allows for individuals or small groups to have access to one person within a school (the mentor) who will advise and support them during their training. The arrangement developed by the Steering Committee is an informal one, and it is subject-based in a way in which many other schemes are not. The model uses college time taken from the normal timetabled tutorial sessions, giving additional time to school practice but under highly controlled conditions.

After the first year of the new course, the idea of giving each trainee an individual timetable was developed, so that by the second term, student teachers could opt into particular sessions and construct their own programmes for professional development. It became not unusual for individuals to go to their 'training department' rather than to attend a college Modern Language session.[7] Teachers from these 'training departments' maintain a close relationship with Moray House, where they conduct workshops and training sessions on their own areas of expertise.

What happens with respect to the 'nursery slopes' in Term 1 is as follows:

- presentation in college of particular techniques – games, drama warm-ups, mimes;
- student teachers provide more examples themselves and run sessions, usually in their second language, where they 'teach' something similar to another group
- student teachers visit the 'training departments' in groups to try out what they have learnt.

Quid pro quo

It is of course important that schools should benefit from links with the college as a result of the increased demands made on them. The Steering Committee suggested that each school hosting a student teacher should gain something useful and concrete as a result. Hence, each term the working groups at Moray House produce on word processor high-quality materials which the schools receive as a 'thank you': for example, a book of activities with accompanying materials, or a set of board games.

In the spring term, when schools are preoccupied with the requirements of the Standard Grade examinations, the Scottish Examinations Board kindly makes available the services of the examinations officer for Modern Languages, Veronica Smith, to conduct a session which introduces the student teachers to the operations of the Board, and outlines for them the restrictions and constraints under which the Board must operate. Detailed examples are given, in response to work done on actual examination papers by student teachers, of why certain examination papers and questions turn out as they do. Further sessions are then conducted by teachers who are employed as setters and markers by the Board, including a simulated Markers' Meeting, after which the examination papers of one Lothian school's entire cohort are marked by the student teachers according to official Board guidelines. Finally, the various language groups make up complete 'mock' Standard Grade examination papers which are distributed to participating schools.

Spin-off

As a result of their increasing involvement with Moray House, a group of Lothian teachers, many of whom were using, almost exclusively, their own materials in their schools, and quite a few of whom had worked either on GLAFLL or on the original Balerno team, decided to come together to promote the development of learner responsibility in their pupils. The main feature of the meetings initially was to arrive at a common understanding of the philosophy behind learner responsibility. It was not intended to provide simply a 'swopshop' of materials, but also to provide a forum for discussion of a process-based approach to learning. Teachers set up a base for the exchange of materials held on computer. Hard copy was held at Moray House, in the form of the school's pupil booklets, and teachers could bring in a disk and take a copy from the original disk. This meant that they could then edit themselves the materials made elsewhere, to fit their own school and its circumstances. Self-selected student teachers worked with the group, writing minutes, organising the storage and retrieval of hard and soft copy, adding materials and ideas of their own.

Evaluation

It is not always easy for people to see themselves as partners in a relationship where there is a one-way judge-and-jury role on which someone's employment opportunities may depend. In this respect the relationship is an unequal one. It is to be expected that things will from time to time go wrong and will need to be dealt with. The college staff attempts to involve student teachers as far as possible in the selection of course activities, sometimes using questionnaires to elicit responses to issues that seem to cause strain and worry. Representatives are elected to liaise with the college staff and determine the best course of action.[8] Alterations are made, suggestions taken up.

A yearly evaluation of the course is carried out by members of the Steering Committee who do this by means of discussions with the student teachers as well as through an end-of-course evaluation sheet. Thus, the course can be seen as something to which all three partners have an input, something dynamic which will continue to develop in the light of what is learnt from the experience.

15 Exemplifying Innovation

The following three examples give an idea of the nature of teaching practice and the kind of thinking about teaching, learning and language that student teachers did. The examples are based on work done by student teachers in connection with their professional projects. Some schools made videos of what happened in the classrooms and transcripts are printed here with kind permission of the teachers involved.

Example 1: Inspiration, Memory and Motivation

An exploration of the use of objects in the teaching of French to pupils of low ability[9]

Inspiration

- *It's a fertility symbol.*
- *I don't think so – it looks more like a kind of animal or bird to me.*
- *Middle East?*
- *Mm – what do you think, Mohammed?*
- *I was wondering if perhaps South America.*
- *Oh yes, that bird … what do you call it?*

The object went from hand to hand as all tried to add their own ideas. And in doing so each one revealed something about themselves and learnt something about the others. The tutorial run by the museum staff was always memorable; there was something about these objects that asked you to handle them. Strange how basic is the urge to touch new and unfamiliar things. Everyone for once participated in the hypothesising and debate. Would language pupils feel the same? What sort of things might one do? What objects might one use? What for?

Coincidentally, one of the student teachers at the workshop session, Corinne Bonnet, a former French Conversation Assistant, had herself been using realia to teach private pupils, including the very young. Because she was working with children who could not yet read, she was less interested in the uses of textual realia (the bus tickets and old receipts and programmes familiar from the Graded Objective days) than in the effect of objects themselves, which could be handled and examined. Could this be of benefit to older learners, and could it help create a natural learning environment in which real communication could take place with concrete referents and in which it was permitted to learners, as she puts it, 'to be a child again'?

Belief and background

Underlying Bonnet's work is a highly individual mixture of the intensely down-to-earth and practical and the esoteric and theoretical – what some would identify as a very 'French' combination. This exemplifies my own belief that teachers teach best and are happiest when teaching in ways that reflect their own complete selves. To be at our best as teachers we need to liberate aspects of our personality, not let ourselves be hemmed in by the convention or routine of the moment. Sadly, much of the teaching that takes place in classrooms is such that it diminishes individual teachers instead of liberating them.

Bonnet's previous experiences and her reading had established a theoretical position which served to underpin the work she did in the school and which she has since maintained in her teaching. Her starting point is the encouragement of natural communication, seeing her task as being one of 'helping students move away from the restraints of language usage into the wider perspective of language use'. Her previous experience as an FCA had been in classes where the only French used by the teacher as a means of communication was to ask pupils to 'ouvrez vos livres', to come to the 'bureau du professeur' or to 'crache ton chewing-gum' into the 'poubelle', as she puts it. She quotes Klippel[10] who talks of 'those rare and precious moments in foreign language teaching when the target language is actually used as a means of communication' – Bonnet's experience had convinced her that: 'these precious moments can be rare indeed'.

A survey of Strathclyde teachers on the use of the foreign language as the medium of instruction showed 'a general consensus of opinion that the only activity that could be easily conducted in French was the giving of classroom organisational instructions'.[11] Bonnet believed that far from being discouraging, this pointed to an aspect of interaction that could encourage the use of objects, namely the 'here-and-now' principle.[12] Her argument is that the 'here-and-now' principle should be exploited to a much greater extent by increasing the range of concrete referents available in the classroom and she uses the lessons learnt from museum education that teachers can 'easily teach themselves to teach with objects.[13]'

Objects have the following advantages;

- they are not subject bound – 'they cross curricular boundaries better than any other material; it all depends how you look at them';
- they are all around – 'When it comes to develop analysis skills it is ... efficient to use things commonly found in the classroom or at home';
- objects are attractive – she says of the pupils she taught with objects: 'objects never failed to attract their attention, or their fingers';
- objects reflect culture – and this helps teachers 'create situations where learners can experience a little of the foreign culture';
- everybody can use objects – because they are not tied to age or ability level – 'every child will be able to gain something from the experience' – and she quotes Burstall 'in the language learning context nothing succeeds like success'[14]

From experimental psychology she examines different learning styles and looks at work ranging from brain lateralisation through Suggestopedia to Neuro-Linguistic Programming and Accelerated Learning to show the effect on memory of 'multiple sense encoding'.[15]

To begin at the beginning

It was one of the occasions that teacher trainers dread. The late evening telephone call – 'can you help me?'. The school was in an area of high unemployment, the local pit had shut down and the outside of the school was covered in graffiti. A description of the class was enough to send one directly to the darkened room and the cold compress. Disaffected, unwilling to cooperate, a fair share of 'problem' pupils, large ... Their learning to date had been book-oriented and conducted at desks. Bonnet had been warned that whatever she did, 'these pupils must remain seated'. They were decidedly unpromising subjects for innovation and risk-taking, but Bonnet had announced her intention of using them for her 'teaching with objects' project.

Aims and lesson plans

One of the knotty problems of the lesson plan approach beloved of teacher training institutions,[16] where aims, objectives, ends, means, steps and stages are spelt out, is that the flexibility which is essential to pupil-centred teaching can be lost. While teachers need to be clear in their minds, this clarity ought by rights to reflect their thinking about the processes of learning as much, or more so, than the procedures of teaching. The aim in this case was not a linguistic one. It was to do with attitudes and affect: how to have the pupils feel that French had to do with them, so that they could succeed and rapidly benefit from an increased understanding of the language. The 'lesson' in this case consisted of a warm-up, involving movement round the classroom, two 'games' with the class split in two, and a multi-skill activity with the class in groups of four to six.

Whole class warm-up: grab a group

'Grab a group' calls for the formation of groups of various sizes according to numbers called out by the teacher while the pupils run around the room. This warm-up was chosen because Bonnet wanted to split the class and had identified two pupils who, she judged, should on no account be in the same group. When they were well apart, it was announced that the groups formed would be the groups for the next activity.

Logic puzzle

Pupils stood in two columns on individual squares of newspaper. At the front was a vacant square. At the back the pupil on the opposite corner to the vacant square was given a hat to wear. The aim was for the pupil with the hat to move to the square at the front in the least possible number of moves. Thus one of the people at the front had to move to occupy the blank square, his or her place then being taken by another and so on until the person with the hat was free to move. Each move was counted and the players were told it was a competition against the other group, whose moves also would be counted when it was their turn.

The instructions, as was the whole lesson, were in French. The pupils quickly got the idea. All the French they then required could be extracted from what the teacher had been saying: 'Toi, tu te mets là' and rendered by the pupils as 'toi (pointing) – là!' One learner commented afterwards: 'You had to stand on a bit of newspaper and someone would tell you to move on to another one. I thought it was good.'

There need have been no worry about movement and indiscipline. The video shows how the pupils were too busy working out their moves to bother finding out what their classmates were up to in the other part of the room. Indeed it is noticeable from the video that even fairly loud laughter from the other group passes totally ignored.

Kim's Game[17]

Objects were selected according to two criteria – ease of the French and the need to use the object later. Among the objects were:

- book, ruler, pencil (known vocabulary);
- éléphant, rose, enveloppe, dictionnaire (similarity to English);
- Prittstick, Blutack, Ambre solaire (brand names);
- string, matches, yoghurt cartons (needed later).

The idea was to take the pupils' attention away from the novelty of hearing only French spoken, and to have them quickly involved. These pupils had never heard of 'Kim's Game'. I had the distinct impression that they were unused to games playing altogether in a learning context. One previously disenchanted learner when asked about the lesson later in a questionnaire said: 'Someone took an object off the table and we had to guess what was missing. I thought it was good.'

Yoghurt carton telephones

This was an extremely ambitious group activity. I had cautioned against it in the form in which it had been devised, and I was wrong.

Groups of four pupils were given a dictionary and an envelope containing cut-up instructions. They had to put these in the correct order. Once they had done this, they had to assemble the materials and finally carry out the instructions. The instructions told them how to make a yoghurt carton telephone without in fact telling them that this was what they were making.

Because the pupils had no idea of what were going to be making I had predicted cries of 'it's too hard', when they were faced with the cut-up instructions in the envelope. Perhaps because of the warm-up activities, they set to with good will, and having sorted it all out, fetched the necessary objects and assembled them as instructed.

Having seen yoghurt carton phones used often before, I expected the pupils, once they saw the cartons, to recognise the activity from their primary school experience. This group did not seem to have any such experience to draw on, or perhaps they had forgotten it. It was funny, but also rather sad, having seen 10-year-olds take to this like ducks to water, to see these teenagers trying to work out what they had in fact made, and then how fascinated they were that they could actually hear each other on the 'phones'. Talking French to each other required no prompting, and the pupils searched their memories for things they could say. Characteristically they went all the way back to language learnt in SI. One lad, identified as having quite severe learning difficulties, and who had shown absolutely no interest in French, asked his partner: 'What's "what's your name?" in French'? Maybe this did not say much for three years of language classes, but at least, and possibly for the first time in a long while, he wanted to say it!

Follow-up

This first lesson had shown the pupils that understanding French would enable them to do things that in themselves could be interesting and worthwhile, and which they could enjoy. This gave Bonnet the necessary confidence to continue the approach throughout the rest of her time in the school. She devised a number of activities based on objects, the highlight of which was 'The wonder object' in which these same pupils mimed bizarre or unusual uses for some everyday things, turning the exercise '100 uses for ...' into a televised publicity slot.

> I told them to use me as a living dictionary ... After giving the instructions all I had to do was to wait for them to come to me and ask (in French) for 'words'. From then on the lesson was theirs. For me the lesson was the realisation of the potential of objects to enhance creative thought ... Observing these pupils I could see three elements at work; they felt free, they became more and more involved, more and more and more creative. A group started to tread the path of poetry:
>
> Avec l'objet magique on peut avoir une palette de peinture
> Avec l'objet magique on peut avoir une baignoire miniature.

The evidence of the eyes

The transformation in the pupils' behaviour was remarkable. On her arrival in the school Bonnet made a video of the behaviour of this group during their normal French lesson. They were then filmed during lessons where there were real objects available. The video testified to significant changes in the pupils' behaviour, as did the principal teacher who had been extremely keen to involve the department in the project.

First the video looks at what the pupils' 'off-task' behaviour is normally like, then a look at how it is during the activities involving objects in the course of the lesson described. 'Off-task' behaviour is defined here as that which has nothing to do with the task in hand. During the activities there are indeed movements, passing objects and cards over, leaning over to get a better view of the tray and so on. These are, however, to do with the task and have not been noted below.

The normal lesson (155 seconds)

Sitting in groups, with one lad on his own, all doing a task based on the book. Pupils can be seen:

Playing with pens; stretching; swinging on chair; looking at watch; leafing through book, stirring Tipp-Ex, talking; putting Tipp-Ex on friend's nose; pulling at each other's hands; reducing their erasers to shreds; describing to friends, with gestures, some game; arm-wrestling; fiddling constantly.

During Kim's Game (180 seconds)

Putting bag out the way; nodding head; picking up card; raising tray; looking at camera.

During Logic Puzzle (60 seconds)

Rubbing eyes.

Making telephones (120 seconds)

Hand passes in front of camera.

Also observable is a loosening up in pupils' posture, less concern about what others in the group are doing and increasing laughter, increased eye contact with both teacher and classmates. With the sound turned up, one is aware also of an increase in noise level, particularly when compared to the original 'normal' lesson, which is characterised not by ill-discipline or noise as such, but by an almost complete lack of attention to the book-based task, with a non-stop low hum of English. In the telephone extract, in contrast, there is some loud laughter, some enthusiastic calling out, but it is all focused on the activity.

What had happened in the course of the lesson?

The activities:

These were worthwhile.
They were taken seriously by the teacher.
There were things to handle and pass around.
A high standard of performance and rapid reactions were required.

The pupils:

They could behave as themselves – as 16-year-olds.
At the same time, they could 'be a child again' without losing face.
Their imaginations were engaged.
Their egos were protected.
They were at ease and comfortable.
There was sense of being a group and belonging.

The language:

Attention was not on the French itself but on the activity.
The French they were using was French they needed.
They chose it for themselves.
They found it for themselves.
They 'owned' it.
The language was always for a purpose.

Comment

Behind much successful foreign language teaching are some very matter-of-fact, common-sense principles. While it may seem to some teachers 'artificial' to introduce objects into classrooms, to have pupils make robot masks, as Bonnet later was to do most successfully with a first year class,[18] to turn yoghurt cartons into telephones and then speak to each other in pidgin French, precisely the opposite holds. Classrooms are not the ideal learning environment for languages, and certainly not the natural one. The obvious fact is that a language is learnt better, faster, in an environment with concrete referents where one is obliged to use it and is surrounded by it.

It is not necessary to pit one's mind against Chomsky's[19] and those others who believe that language learning is unlike any other type of learning, that language is separate from other cognitive systems and therefore cannot be explained by means of a general theory of human learning. This may well be the case – it is certainly one with which many language teachers intuitively agree. Nor is it is necessary to believe in the research results or relevance of the left-right hemisphere schools of thought, to embrace Accelerated Learning or Lozanov's Suggestopedia; we only have to think about what we remember ourselves from past learning experiences. As the much quoted Chinese proverb puts it:

> I forget what I hear,
> I remember what I see,
> I learn what I do.

Example 2: Creating the Context: Language Medium Teaching

From Pilton to Tokyo: A journey through the earth's crust

In order to get to Japan from Edinburgh, you could take a long-distance jet. Alternatively, if you hacked at the earth's crust, dynamiting your way through the toughest layers, sweating through the heat of the centre core, repeating the exercise in reverse and swimming to the surface, you could arrive in Tokyo having learnt a fair bit about how the earth is made up. If you did all this through the medium of a foreign language, you might learn even more.

In spite of recent exhortations to teachers of foreign languages to use the target language 'as much as possible', little attention has been given to what exactly it is to be used for. It seems to be assumed that the content of language lessons will be much the same – that is, teachers will continue to teach principally *about* the language, with meaningful messages limited to commands, suggestions and exhortations. The difference is that they will be teaching *about* the language *in* the language – and many teachers resist this approach, quite understandably, given that few textbooks make it easy for them to do this. Whatever the medium, wherever the real meanings in the teacher-pupil interaction meet the usually non-communicative text of the coursebook, there is likely to be some dislocation.

To date there has been little encouragement given in Britain to the teaching of other subjects through the foreign language, in spite of highly successful experiences in the Canadian immersion project, where pupils opt in to classes where they are taught all their history or geography in French. The argument against seems to be that Britain is not a country where a pool of bilingual teachers of subjects other than Modern Languages is available. Moreover, traditional subject boundaries are jealously guarded, in spite of an occasional foray into a one-off collaborative venture or some lip-service paid towards the cross-curricular in the shape of an afternoon's In-Service. The occasional.exception does occur, attracts some attention, makes the odd waves, then is set aside by those in a position to encourage such developments. There is hope of some spin-off from the initial positive experiences of the Scottish Primary Languages Pilot, as already described in Part 1. From south of the border, in England, Frances Morley, of Heathside School in Surrey, has, over a substantial period of time, enjoyed considerable success teaching Geography to 'O' level and GCSE. Her talk at the CILT 'Autonomy' conference was received with no small interest.

One of the problems associated with Language Medium Teaching is how to ensure effective teaching in both subjects, so that, for instance, the non-specialist French teacher does not revert to teaching the kind of geography she learnt at school in the way she learnt it, or that the non-language specialist geography teacher fails to modify his or her French or ensure that the input is indeed comprehensible. While a 'chalk and talk' lesson in French with OHP and map is perfectly imaginable, it would be a matter of concern if the considerable advances towards experiential learning in the social sciences were to be ignored.

In an attempt to investigate the potential of Language Medium Teaching within a secondary school, a small-scale project was set up between Moray House Institute of Education and Craigroyston High School. The school is not one of Edinburgh's many traditional bastions of privilege. Threatened with closure because of falling numbers, set in an area of high unemployment and considerable social problems, it has nevertheless distinct advantages from the point of view of innovation: preoccupations about 'we've got to get through the next unit' are secondary to concern for the pupils' overall educational experience; and genuine cooperation between departments and individual teachers, often a feature of schools at the tougher end of the chalk face, are evident.

There are other considerations that make Craigroyston a good school for innovation. Its Head Teacher, a legendary figure in Lothian education circles, unusually in these grey-suited, managerially driven times, sees his role in very different terms from simply that of 'implementing Education Department policies'. He encourages staff to work out their own programmes and does not burden them with the 'put it in writing' approach that is so stifling to initiative. Finally, from the point of view of the project, there was an interested Principal Teacher of Geography who was fluent in French, and a Principal Teacher of Modern Languages who was keen to collaborate.

Before going to Craigroyston on full-time teaching practice, Marie-Pierre Claret visited the school once or twice a week over a period of three to four weeks, to see the class (then in the second term of their first year) and to discuss with the teachers the kind of material she might prepare. Planning was also carried out with myself as course tutor. It was agreed that the PT Modern Languages would film on video as many lessons as possible.

At this point the reader might like to speculate as to what might be expected in such lessons. Use of target language, of course, group work, task sheets with perhaps dictionaries and probably the props of the usual geography lesson.

Such, indeed, there were; but what was so unexpected and astonishing was that not only was the entire project carried out using activity-based learning in geography, considerable use was made of techniques from another discipline, that of Drama. Movement, mime, dance – all played a part. There was even some Japanese! A transcript of part of one of the lessons with an outline of the proceedings is below.

The pupils are in a circle along with Claret. Claret outlines with arms the globe, while saying:

Voici la terre, grosse, grosse, grosse, grosse, grosse … et voici l'écorce terrestre, petite, petite, petite, petite, petite – l'écorce terrestre OK (both arms raised to either side, hands apart, tracing a circle) *et voici le manteau – grand, grand – très grand le manteau et* (hands forwards tracing a small circle) *au centre le noyau, le noyau. Alors donc voici la grande terre* (as above) *et on va traverser la terre* ('walking' motion with fingers of one hand diagonally through the large outlined circle towards outstretched left hand representing Japan) *on va partir de l'Ecosse* (small circle, continuous movement with fingers to indicate Scotland) *on va traverser la terre et arriver au Japon OK? D'accord?*

Alors, venez avec moi, nous allons creuser un trou dans l'écorce terrestre (whole body movement to lift spade from behind) *on prend la pelle – attention* (digging motions accompanied by whole circle moving to the right as feet are used for purchase while digging) *toc, toc, toc. L'écorce terrestre est très dure... toc, toc, toc – attention OK, – alors, attention on va soulever ça* (all bend over, fingers to ground, whole body slowly to upright position, arms outstretched, casting the block of earth out the way to their left) *ah ah ah ouf!* (wipe hands).

Bien, alors maintenant on plonge dans le manteau, on plonge dans le manteau. OK, attention (flex knees, jump, hands in the air – all land in middle of circle). *Nous voici dans le manteau. Oh, chaud* (first from pupils, wiping faces and shaking out tops of their T-shirts) *... très très très chaud ... et ça colle. Nous sommes dans le magma – il fait très chaud.... oh mou, très mou* (arms and legs indicate consistency as they walk ahead on the spot) *c'est très sale et voilà* (pointing and outlining small circle) *le noyau au centre, le noyau ici. Le noyau, c'est dur,* (teacher advances and hits the core hard with right hand, copied by pupils) *cling! cling! cling!... le noyau, très dur ... cling, cling, cling..* (ringing noise repeated) *– très dur.*

On va creuser un tunnel. On va dynamiter le noyau ... (All remove imaginary matches from back pockets, bend right down facing centre almost touching and retreat having laid the charges, still facing centre and bending over extending the rope – hissing noise, all jump high in the air, arms aloft and fully extended). *Boum! On a réussi! Attention to* (late-comer) *– tu te mets là, OK* ... (pupils walk round to the right in the circle with arm movements) *on a traversé le noyau* (hand outlines core and then crosses it) *voici le tunnel dans le noyau, et alors on est dans le manteau ... c'est chaud* (wiping brow and shaking T-shirts) *et puis c'est mou dans le manteau* (walking on the spot, arm movements indicating texture again). *Oh il fait chaud* (wiping brows again) *et ça colle. Voici l'écorce terrestre encore* (arms raised together and extended either side of the body forming a circle as before) *et on prend la pelle* (from behind) *et on va creuser, hein?* (this time they dig from below as they go round in the circle, arms raised and lowered in unison) *Toc, toc, toc, toc. Attention on va ..... là, et mettez vos pelles de côté* (sound not clear – spades are put aside, hands hold up the piece of earth dug out and with great effort) *attention, bien, on la met là, d'accord* (chunk of earth flung to side) *oh, c'est difficile... OK, et nous, on est dans l'océan pacifique maintenant* (swimming breaststroke as they go round in the circle) *gloub, gloub, gloub. Retournons dans l'écorce terrestre. Il faut creuser un nouveau trou. Toc, toc, toc.* (All stop, bent right down and raise bodies, arms extended to their sides in surprise) *ah nous voici au Japon* (now arms folded, they bow in traditional Japanese gesture first to the person on their right, then to the person on their left, across the circle several times). *Konichiwa,*

konichiwa. Voici la terre (gestures as before) très grosse, et nous avons traversé la terre et nous sommes au Japon. Konichiwa.

The video of the lessons does what a mere description cannot do, illustrating features of pupil behaviour which show them to be clearly involved, showing pride in their work – and it is obviously work, to them. They show their 'ownership' of what they are engaged in, there is no inattention, no 'off task' behaviour. Even when a pupil arrives late, he doesn't disrupt the sequence, but joins in, clearly knowing what he is about. The pupils take their cue from their teacher – whose own behaviour demonstrates that what they are doing is serious and real for her and that she can 'see' and 'feel' her way through the earth. The pupils respond with a high degree of commitment. It is normally inordinately difficult to achieve good miming from pupils. It can be a messy and uncoordinated business for the non-specialist in drama to undertake. Yet the pupils here are obviously digging, dynamiting, swimming and sweating.

This short-term project was the catalyst for further developments in collaboration with Moray House. Student teachers in the following year who had an interest in Language Medium Teaching were assigned to the school on teaching practice and contributed to the programme of work. Materials were purchased for the school through the research and development budget of the college. A further encouragement was undoubtedly given by the imaginative decision of the school's Head Teacher to celebrate 1992 by taking the whole school in June to a variety of other EC destinations, including of course a visit to France by the class concerned, then in SII, whose studies in geography and in French concentrated on the area to be visited.

As for Claret herself, she has continued to work in this area, using French to teach home economics and biology among other subjects.

Example 3: Finding the Way In

Creating a response to poems and songs

Background

This work stemmed from Angela Hirsch's interest in literature and poetry. A native speaker of German, she had already some experience of teaching adults, and while it was clear that she would be successful with abler pupils, she and everyone else could see that there would be problems at the other end of the spectrum. Hirsch was both a perfectionist and an idealist – a tricky combination for someone wanting to teach in a comprehensive school. She engagingly confessed when she filled in her 'profile', that she knew she rated low on 'sense of humour' and did not envisage anything short of a personality transplant changing this. Hirsch had, however, a strong belief that everyone was capable of learning a foreign language and one of her aims for herself was to learn how to work with pupils of low ability and motivation. She believed that the main reason such children failed to learn was because the curriculum itself made them stupid. She agreed with Leonardo da Vinci – 'true knowledge can only come through the senses'. Could her love of literature and especially poetry be used creatively as a way of linking her world and the world of the pupils? Was it not a question of finding the way in by stimulating the natural curiosity of young people? How might this be done?

Inspiration

This came in the form of material I encountered at a Goethe Institut seminar in Augsburg where one of the participants, Filip de Nys from Antwerp, demonstrated a whole range of imaginative and highly innovative techniques he used in his classroom. De Nys is co-author of *Lesekiste*, which was about to be published by Langenscheidt shortly after we met. While the material he demonstrated was of course under copyright, the principles underlying it could be used to present all kinds of things. These principles seemed tailor-made for Hirsch.

In essence, it was a question of taking a piece of writing and finding in it something to which a teenager could relate. This would come from the theme of the text. Before considering the text itself at all, using this theme as a starting point, a series of linguistically simple but interesting and worthwhile exercises, sometimes in the form of puzzles, with room for open-ended responses, would lead the learner towards the text itself. As Hirsch puts it: 'The students can use language playfully when exploring the themes ... They may identify with the persons, situations, views represented ... The units all provide 'room', possibilities for the students to express their own ideas and imaginations creatively.'

Let us take the example of the song 'Kinder' by Bettina Wegner. The worksheets are called: Große Leute – Kleine Leute. They are illustrated amusingly and it is clear from the visual cues what the pupils are supposed to do. The first exercise asks pupils to look at the contrasts

that exist in the world – and they are asked to draw arrows between the
words on the left and their opposites on the right (some of these words
are included because they appear in the song):

Große Leute	Süd
Nord	Kleine Leute
kalt	Katze
gigantisch	Lamm
Maus	warm
hart	winzig
Wolf	weich

Step two introduces the idea of similarities, and some more words
that will come up later:

Große Leute und Kinder haben sehr viele Kontraste. ABER: sie sind
auch ähnlich. Alle sind Menschen... Alle haben...:

Augen

Ohren

Mund

Hände und Finger

Füsse und Zehen

Rückgrat

Herz und Seele

Step three (illustrated with a cartoon of a huge, fierce woman shout-
ing at a small terrified child) comes close to the song's theme:

Aber es gibt einen sehr großen Konstrast bei großen Leuten und
Kindern:

Große Leute haben *Authorität*. Die großen Leute sagen zu den
Kindern:

'DAS DARF MAN NICHT!!!'

'DAS DARF MAN NIE!!!'

'DAS IST VERBOTEN!!!'

Pupils are invited to list and illustrate what they may or may not
do.

They are then asked: Was ist typisch für große Leute und für Kinder?

Große Leute   Kinder

spielen gerne Spiele
arbeiten viel
lesen und schreiben viel
schimpfen oft
sprechen oft laut
sind oft seriös
sind oft agressiv
haben fantastische Ideen

Step four introduces Bettina Wegner and her work:

Ihre Gedichte und Lieder sind kritisch. Ihr Lied 'Kinder' sagt:

Die großen Leute in der DDR sind viel zu autoritär.

The pupils then read and hear the song. They are then asked to tick some of the words Wegner uses in the song to refer to children:

Kinder haben: Hände   Ohren
                Füsse   Augen
                Zehen   Seelen
                Rückgrat   Münder

And after hearing the song again, they are asked what they think the singer is trying to say:

Was denkst du? Was sagt Bettina Wegner in ihrem Lied?

Kinder sind klein und delikat
Kinder sind authoritär
Große Leute sind zu strikt
Große Leute respektieren Kinder
Große Leute respektieren Kinder nicht
Kinder und große Leute sind gleich

And to add for themselves anything they may want to say:

Große Leute ... Kleine Leute ...

Stell dir vor... Du hast im Traum eine tolle Phantasie: Ich bin groß, große Leute sind klein:

Ich darf ... Du darfst ...

The material on its own was excellent and imaginative, but of course it was only a written version of classroom procedures for involving pupils.

In order to use the technique effectively, the teacher has to 'get under the skin' of a particular group of pupils. This for Hirsch was the challenge – to get out from behind the materials and engage the pupils directly.

Background

We have to go back to an earlier occasion at the very beginning of training in order to understand the changes that had been effected by Hirsch over a short period of time. The first lesson Hirsch gave was in the fourth week of the course where she took a class along with another student teacher for a period. Her half of the lesson was a well-prepared display of teacher-domination, a copy of something she had seen on observation which had worked well – for someone else. It involved beautifully prepared, humorous Overhead Projector Overlays based on the topic of 'the family'. It had all the ingredients of a traditionally well-prepared lesson. Classically for a beginner, the attention was on the content and presentation of the lesson, the pupils hardly got a look in. Much was extremely promising but this approach, based on someone else's work, was inauthentic in terms of the personal qualities, background and interests of Hirsch herself and she was clearly not at ease. It also distanced her considerably from the pupils. She had to find the teacher within herself, not try to turn herself into a replica of someone else.

In order to provide the opportunity to work with all kinds of learners and to try out a range of techniques, Hirsch's first teaching practice was in a school with a wide ability range and a strong training emphasis. In Queensferry High School, with Principal Teacher Anne McLeod, pupils were accustomed to an activity-based methodology with much use being made of drama. In such a positive environment, Hirsch was able to develop such things as mime, in which she was also interested. These things were relatively easy with the well-motivated Queensferry pupils.

Her next assignment was in a much tougher school – by design. The pupils tended to view outsiders with suspicion – including Hirsch – and when she persisted in talking to them in French and German, this only served to deepen the suspicion, and provoke some anti-German comments. The classes she had to work with, though small, contained several disaffected pupils who had all but given up. Fortunately the staff were extremely supportive, and although it was not their practice, they started using the target language themselves in order to let the pupils see that Hirsch had their backing.[20]

Meanwhile Hirsch had been selecting materials, recording songs, and producing workbooks with lavish illustrations on computer. It must have taken hours of work. Her courage failed, however, at the idea of using them straight away in this school. This is where the 'mentor' element came into its own. Hirsch arranged to return to Queensferry with her materials, to try them out with classes she already knew and who were likely to be well-disposed. This experience also helped her to iron out weaknesses in the materials and increased her confidence for their use in the second school where circumstances were less favourable. Could she persuade the pupils in the second school to do what had worked in the first?

The song she wanted to use was 'Vesoul', by Jaques Brel. The notion she took from it was 'compromising'. Hirsch wanted to pose the question: we all compromise – but up to which point is this a good thing? To quote Hirsch:

> I do not know the answer to such questions myself. The students will have to work these out themselves. We can explore the possibilities together. It is crucial that the students come to their very own understanding of the theme, the question and the fiction.... I would try to ensure that they then develop their *own* ideas and views.

Hirsch starts by 'tapping the students imagination and experience before introducing the fictional text'. Mostly for this she uses a combination of language and pictures – completing a drawing, creating new images, making logical conclusions. On this occasion, she decided that the notion of compromise would best be introduced through a direct approach involving one group of students at a time. This would allow her to modify what she was doing to suit the responses and abilities.

She started off at the blackboard and wrote up:

FAMILLE   COPAINS   COLLEGE

A rapid *ad hoc* survey of the group was done to find out, in the course of the last few days, where the majority of the teenagers had had problems or disagreements – and who had given in. English answers were accepted and sometimes restated, sometimes simply recorded as tallies. Some pupils assembled round the blackboard on which the tally was being kept, to watch the 'score' and help with the arithmetic involved. Their apparent superiority in this area seemed to make them feel good. They were all interested in each others' experiences, and would sometimes jog each others' memories. It turned out that siblings and parents were the greatest source of problems, and gratifyingly, school and teachers the least. That in itself was a subject for comment – even the pupils seemed surprised but acknowledged it to be true. In English or in fractured French examples came pouring in from the pupils and were noted down. At this point a lad who had been on the outskirts was dragged in by his friend – 'Come on, Danny, this is good'.

This for the pupils was probably the first time that a French lesson was not focusing on French itself as a language they had to learn for an examination, but on themselves and their experiences. It was not simply that Hirsch had found a theme with which the pupils could identify. She had also found a way of interacting with them, because on her side this was something *she* wanted to talk about – there were things about this group that she wanted to know. Hirsch points out:

> Vesoul is a song in which text and music complement each other particularly well. This mutual effect of the music and the poem can help in the understanding and interpretation of the theme. The repetitive/circular nature of the two partners' life together is reflected both in the monotonous poetic structure of the verses and in the musical rhythm – a waltz progressively gathering both volume and speed.

As far as the pupils were concerned, however, this 'music' was nothing like what they thought music ought to be. The gap between teacher and pupils had to be narrowed. Interestingly, Hirsch took the issue of the strange music straight to them and asked them to pay attention to it, much in the way a music teacher would ask pupils to characterise it: what was their impression – was it:

sérieuse	gaie
agressive	tendre
monotone	animée
passionante	superficielle
froide	chaude?

What instruments did they recognise from a given selection? Which one predominated? Which of the words they had ticked in the first task applied best to this instrument?

Then to the rhythm – from drawings showing a variety of rhythms, they had to select the ones they thought applied, and then work out what kind of dance music from a given selection might apply.

Possibly because the pupils had been taken seriously all along and their opinions sought, they were persuaded to give the material the benefit of the doubt. Once they discovered that they could actually understand some of the words of the song, they found their musical prejudices evaporating, at least a little. Subsequent evaluation of the lesson by questionnaires and interviews was positive and Hirsch continued to teach the class successfully.

The reasons for the success of the lesson and subsequent lessons using this technique were close to what occurred in Bonnet's lesson using objects in a similar school.

The activities were worthwhile; they would have made a good music or social education lesson; they were taken seriously by the teacher, who set the tone; there were things to think about and things to do – and time limits were set to each activity so nothing dragged on.

The pupils were being addressed as themselves and could behave as themselves; their egos were protected and they were at ease and comfortable; they were not forced to return to their desks when they wanted to stand round the board; there was a sense of being a group and belonging; there was no loss of face; their interest was first engaged in finding out where people had most problems and in learning what these were; their imagination and curiosity were engaged by the materials themselves.

The language was not the focus of attention but the activity itself; what they were using was what they needed – the language had a purpose; the new words had impact and context; because the initial activities covered much of what appeared later, they were enabled gradually to understand quite extended and complex French dealing with ideas with which they were by now familiar.

This experience had far-reaching effects. Firstly, it remotivated pupils who had lost confidence in themselves and their ability to learn a foreign language. Soon they accepted lessons in the target language without a murmur.

Secondly, the impact on the department was such that a move was made to teaching through the target language – a move long contemplated but never embarked upon. The move was made on purely 'human' motives: because the staff genuinely liked and admired Hirsch and wanted her to succeed,[21] they were prepared to inconvenience themselves on her account. They would work together with her, devising ways of saying things to pupils so as to make themselves more easily understood. With Hirsch they 'team-taught' the classes, and Hirsch's miming talents came into their own.

While the department benefited from Hirsch, the greatest impact of the experience was on her. There had always been a doubt in her mind as to how she would cope with pupils in this kind of school. She had to make a choice: to take on a role that was not 'her' – a role as disciplinarian, using defensive teaching techniques and barricading herself metaphorically against the pupils with all the usual panoply of authority to which teachers have recourse; or to allow her pupils an insight into who she was, and what she had to offer, and trust that she could still maintain discipline by providing them with worthwhile things to do, and setting them high standards by treating them with consideration and politeness.

The first route is one often taken by native-speaker teachers – out of necessity, they feel. The second requires courage and support. The German anti-authoritarian approach which works well in a *Gymnasium* is totally alien to many Scottish establishments, some of which are still strongly authoritarian. Pupils simply react to these ways by deciding the teacher is 'soft' and chaos is the usual result. What I think made things work for Hirsch in the classroom most of the time – and there were times as a beginning teacher when they did not always work as well as she hoped – was her conviction about how things ought to be and her refusal to be beaten. She had an aim for the type of classroom she wanted, a view as to how it might be achieved, and a determination not to settle to be less than she might be.

I would like to return here to something said by Anne McDonald at Balerno High School which underlines the importance of this: McDonald had been teaching for 18 years with perfect success and yet said:

> ... for the first time in teaching I felt that I was in control of what I was doing, that I wasn't acting out what someone else had written down... for me I am a real teacher here as I have never been before'.

I would like to think that Hirsch, who has returned to Germany after several successful years in an Edinburgh state school, feels that she too is 'a real teacher ... not acting out what someone else had written down'.

16 Looking Around: Desert Island Books

One source of inspiration for innovation is the written word. The work of a few key authors in the field formed my own 'Desert Island collection'.

The BBC radio programme 'Desert Island Discs', in which celebrities had to imagine themselves being castaway on a mythical desert island was very much in my mind as I packed my things to come to the place in which I have written most of this book – Rarotonga in the Cook Islands – as far from Scotland, just about, as it is possible to go. Limited weight allowance meant that my numerous books on language teaching had to be cut down to the barest essentials. The choice I made was based on those books which most inspired me and which I considered would sustain me in the absence of dialogue with my many much-missed colleagues and friends. As tribute to the inspirations I have received from the authors of these books and as encouragement to others to seek similar inspiration therein for themselves, I shall attempt here to convey some of the many messages I have received from them over the years.

I have already dealt in some detail with one of my 'desert island collection': N.S. Prahbu's *Second Language Pedagogy*, with its many insights into teachers, teaching and learning. John Clark's book, *Curriculum Renewal in School Foreign Language Learning* is another 'must', not only because of the sentimental value I attach to the days of working with the GLAFLL project, but because of what is to me the main message of the book, that curriculum development *is* teacher development, and to date I have not met anyone who does it better than the author, a view which *is* held by many in Britain who still lament the loss to the country of so talented an educator of teachers.

When we teachers look to experts for practical help in how to get the best from our pupils, we hit a nasty problem: the message we receive is that we have to look closely at the learners in the light of what we know about them, about learning in general and about language learning in particular; but we do not understand how people in general learn a language, let alone how a particular group of people, or an individual manages it – this is simply not an attainable goal.

The best we can do is to look for pointers which can help us analyze what is going on in the course of what we do in the classroom and use them to inform our procedures. We need to be challenged to think, but because time is limited, we also need ideas which are easily grasped and easily applied; and the fact that we do not always follow the precise logic of those who expressed the idea in the first place is not as important as that we have a view, or a hypothesis of some kind which is susceptible of development and further investigation.

The work of some of the experts in the field of applied linguistics offers ways of looking at language learning that can help teachers to analyse their practice and their materials so that they can learn to distinguish one kind of practice, or one kind of material from another. The question which has dogged language pedagogy since time immemorial is the distinction between two different kinds of learning, their outcomes and the kinds of teaching which promote them. A wide variety of terms have been used and distinctions made between them. Some of them are:

- language use/language usage;
- competence/performance;
- learning about/performing in;
- knowing about/knowing;
- explicit knowledge/implicit knowledge;
- language practice/communication;
- form-focused activities/meaning-focused activities;
- accuracy/fluency.

Arguing about what was, or was not communicative, and whether or when it actually mattered, was the way in which teachers in the GLAFLL project came to formulate their own ideas. These arguments led to the development of materials along particular, coherent lines, based on a more-or-less common view that 'communicative' and 'real meaning' were, for practical purposes, synonymous.

The GLAFLL period was influenced probably more by Stephen Krashen's work than by any other. His monitor model has, as Brumfit[22] says, 'an intuitive practicalness, partly because of its simplicity and partly because it clearly describes a process that all self-conscious learners will recognise'. All subsequent writers[23] have addressed Krashen's model, even if they, like Stevick, Swain, Rivers and Brumfit, find it inadequate. I still find it a good starting point for thinking about language learning. Of his books I took with me the co-authored 'Language Two',[24] which was written in conjunction with Heidi Dulay and Marina Burt, because it makes for exciting and not-too-strenuous reading. I have always found the teaching guidelines in the final chapter, 'From research to reality: implications for the teacher', to be a most useful summary and have given copies of these to numerous teachers and student teachers.

The classics of Wilga Rivers are a source of countless insights and revelations – and there is scarcely a page that does not question some belief or offer a new thought. In common with the other writers I have mentioned, Rivers writes for the teacher who wants to be addressed as someone capable of dealing with the world of ideas. Of her works I have found *Communicating Naturally in a Second Language – Theory and Practice in Language Teaching* the most useful over the years. Also among my desert island collection is a book with a deceptively simple title, *Communicative Methodology in Language Teaching* by Christopher Brumfit. While it is indeed about communicative methodology, at the heart of the book is the importance of the personal experience of the teacher. Unlike some books about methodology, it is not a book written for the technician.

Brumfit credits teachers with the ability to think for themselves and stresses the need to appeal to teachers' analytical capacities and to encourage and develop these throughout their careers. He argues convincingly on behalf of a profession which relishes theory and argument and sees it as the duty of teacher educators to oppose 'sloppy thinking'. In putting his own thoughts on paper he applies that academic rigour relentlessly – making the book a stimulating, if not an easy read.

Despite the measured case he makes, despite the balance and rigour, Brumfit writes at times passionately and with almost revolutionary fervour. He urges greater communication between members of the profession and highlights the need for 'administrative machinery for the activation of the profession'. He is clearly not thinking about the inspectorate at this point, nor is he making vaguely positive noises about supporting language associations and the like. He is on the side of an advisory service, which he sees as playing a crucial role in teacher development.

I have already used in this book his term 'an activist profession'. Being 'activist' requires discipline, study and hard work. An 'activist' profession needs access to a 'common language and system of concepts', and to have 'open and easy channels for communication, regularly used'. Hence in Brumfit's view there is a need for 'A really serious commitment to strong professional teachers' organisations, strong, subject-based advisory and support services, and fully utilised professional journals ...'. Not surprisingly he expresses a strong belief in the need for more research and for 'A true intercommunication (which) must consist both of those trained as researchers working as teachers and those trained as teachers engaging in research, and also of those who have had extensive experience of teaching exploring the significance of research and theoretical discussion.' His book represents one way through which teachers might well start such an exploration.

It has not been my intention in this book to make the case for any one view of language, language learning or language teaching. We teachers tend to operate intuitively rather than rationally in our classrooms, expressing views about our work and that of others in terms often of black and white. Jackson points out that this may be necessary in order to survive the 'ambiguity, unpredictability and occasional chaos created by each hour of 25 or 30 not-so-willing learners'.[25] I am grateful for that understanding, because I am all too conscious that in the course of the last 25 years I seem always to have had and to have voiced strong views, many of which I have subsequently altered with experience. Because my views and my practice have not always been consistent, although there have been some constants, I cannot claim that the discovery of 'Brand X' changed my life. But reading one particular author did.

Earl Stevick

Memory, Meaning and Method[26] begins thus:

> By speech we design great bridges and fight wars, we express our deep feelings and our spiritual aspirations, and even set forth our most subtle linguistic theories. We can talk, we can talk about talk, we can talk about talk about talk, and so on forever. Language is the special treasure of our race. It depends on what we call the mind but it comes out of the entire person. To learn a second language is to move from one mystery to another.

We do well to remember the mystery of it all. Those who have tried to tell us that language is this, or language is that, that teaching language is about teaching grammar, or drills, or situations, or communication, or even that teaching language is about children – have only told us a tiny part of the story. Beware those who know how to teach.

From decades, even centuries of apparent certainty, language teaching has moved to a state of constant and bewildering inexactitude, characterised by the attempts of educationalists to grasp and codify at least one of the prevailing theories and encapsulate it in some system or other. It is hard for us teachers who want to keep up to date to keep track of all the arguments, and sometimes reading those books designed to help only succeeds in convincing us of how little we know. Stevick's writing allows us to relax, to ponder and to consider. While always keeping his eye on the learner and the classroom, he takes the notion of the entire person as the basis for an approach to language teaching that is stimulating and at the same time threatening to many preconceived notions.

Memory

Stevick starts with memory, a subject to which he returns in his next book, *Teaching Language: A Way and Ways*.[27] He reminds us of a series of well-supported conclusions from the field of psychology that ought to make us pause. These have implications which subvert and destabilise much of current classroom practice. He casts doubt, for instance, on things that teachers tend to believe (or tend to behave as if they believe) and which influence what they do. We teachers are given to telling pupils that paying attention means that they will remember things – of course it doesn't – it doesn't work for teachers when they try to remember things they know are important, so why should it work for pupils? We also constantly use repetition as a device for promoting both understanding and memory; but what really helps people remember things are relationships between them, even when they make no conscious effort to do so. Stevick shows how efficient learners can be seen to make good use of association and mediators. 'Chunking' too can produce phenomenal results in the retainment of items. Most importantly, he demonstrates how crucial depth of processing is to learning, and depth of processing is tied to meaning.

The message

Stevick's message is not about the rights and wrongs of belief and practice, it is about meaning, of which memory is a by-product. Meaning depends on *'what happens inside and between people'*, and method should be subordinate to it. Consideration of this means questioning most of the things that conventionally take place in language classes. While what he says is challenging in the extreme, how he says it is a lesson in putting a point of view over in a way that takes effect. Stevick's gift as a writer is his ability to sustain a conversation with the reader, which leads to a feeling of well-being. This conversing with the reader is a form of 'stroking', and it makes us ready to engage in an internal dialogue.

Transactional analysis

Stroking, *'keeping the spinal chords from shrivelling up'*[28] is part of the theme of the middle of the book, which looks in some detail at the message of Transactional Analysis[29] for language teaching. The 'Parent', 'Child', 'Adult' categorisations of human interaction are an appealing way for teachers to look at the things we do, since we spend a great deal of time with children who may be in the 'Parent' disapproving mode, not to mention colleagues who may be in the 'Rebellious Child' mode. Analysing encounters with others enables us to understand, for example, why person X got the better of us, or why a certain behaviour does not work in a certain set of circumstances.

Now of course to those of us who remember the 1960s, this part of the book has been a trip down memory lane with a vengeance. Without doubt part of the appeal of Stevick's writing is that he makes no attempt to dissociate himself from his writing. The result is an intimate experience, also an unthreatening one. From such a prolonged 'stroke' the reader emerges ready to consider something new.

Introducing new ideas

The something new in this case is the description of some controversial methods of language teaching, along with many insights which call for some thought on the part of the reader. The ability through writing to challenge the reader, while stroking at the same time, appealing to the Child in the reader, in whom the creative mode is lodged, contains a lesson for all teacher developers. By the time we reach the third part, in which ideas start to bubble around us as we read about all kinds of new and sometimes weird ways in which languages can be taught, we have been put into a frame of mind that makes us open to think at the least 'there may be something in all this'.

Lozanov[30] calls a state which is the prerequisite of learning 'infantalisation' – the releasing of an openness to learn which we possess as young children and lose on the way to adulthood. A Suggestopedia session starts with a series of activities designed to release the 'infant', none of which are aimed at 'teaching' anything. Only when the participants are ready to learn is the actual material presented, accompanied by strains of Vivaldi and Beethoven. My own experience of a Suggestopedia session organised by SEAL (Society for Effective Affective Learning) left me, after an overnight train journey and one whole day's workshop, as fresh and relaxed as a holiday. The activities and even some of the actual texts remained fresh in my mind long after the event. Song, movement, smells, chants, touch, sights, dances, objects to hold, examine and exchange with others were all part of it.

Fortunately for those of us who lack the charm of Stevick, or the time available to Lozanov and others whose work Stevick describes, there are other ways in which we may be challenged. To return to the jargon of Transactional Analysis, one might say that the Adult also can be susceptible to challenge – in other words, our intellect may welcome the chance to wake up and have a go at new ideas which challenge previously held assumptions or offer something additional. It seems to be the case that any new notion is likely on first encounter to be instantly rejected – or at least sceptically filed away. As we re-encounter it in a variety of situations, we may reconsider, decide that under certain conditions, it might work – and slowly, usually very slowly, come to find it 'normal' and cease to fight it – we may even start to promote it with missionary fervour.

The message of Stevick, it seems to me, involves a different kind of response from that of those who write about methodology *per se*, and its effect is of a rather different nature. Messages about methodology, for instance, about changes in the direction of more natural language use, can in one sense be regarded as 'technical' messages. They only affect us as teachers. More disturbing ideas, such as those of Stevick, require a greater depth of processing, and hit the teacher in the solar plexus of her being, because they call into question not only her entire relationship with the subject, her pupils, and her job, but her beliefs about life and death, as well as *'what happens inside and between people'* inside and outwith the classroom. The result can be that her previous investment in her person is threatened – the self comes under attack. Threats to our carefully constructed image of ourselves as teacher show us up as particularly vulnerable – which is possibly why some of us will accept or at least tolerate changes 'imposed' by the authorities, its being to a certain extent our 'job' to do so, but often react negatively to the suggestions of colleagues. Perhaps this also explains in part why suggestions of parents, the general public, politicians speaking *ex tempore*, academics or even applied linguists fall often on apparently deaf ears.

Stress and anxiety

Our vulnerability is not something that is often addressed by those in charge of our development. Those individuals who are creative thinkers are described by Curran[31] as *'sick to teach'* – having a *'powerful and partially irrational craving to have people understand (them) on the intellectual level'*. Stevick goes on to say *'The passion to help one's students grow in their own individuality, becoming emotionally more whole and intellectually more self-sufficient (Lyon 1971: 197), is perhaps the most benign of teacher attitudes.'* To look at the teacher as in some way in thrall to powerful emotions goes against the current view of teacher as technician or as the tool of management – the dispassionate and non-questioning purveyor of regional or national policy, yet there are few other jobs which demand so much personal commitment and energy.

Of significant importance in considering the effects of innovation on teachers is the level and nature of the stresses involved. Stress and anxiety are all too often part of teachers' daily experience: Stevick quotes Jersild[32] *'many teachers and students have lived with anxiety day after day, scarcely knowing that the burden might be lightened ... Schools and colleges have usually offered them little in the way of help...'*.

Learners too have anxieties that impede learning, just as the teacher's anxieties may prevent her from realising her potential as a teacher. The notion of 'defensiveness' in terms of learning, in which the learner concentrates all efforts of not making mistakes, on adapting solely to the requirements of the teacher (or indeed the exam) also applies to 'defensive' teaching, where the teacher is so in thrall to her inadequacies that she ceases altogether to give of herself, keeping so close to the unit, the outcomes, the procedures, in other words the technicalities of teaching, that she fails to see the learners at all.

What goes on

What individuals reading Stevick take away with them must vary, but there is likely to be an awareness that so much other than the teaching of a language is taking place in the classroom, and that there is no one way, but many ways in which we might teach. What he offers through these insights into learning is the chance to select what we decide matters and to think of the way in which we and our pupils might benefit from what we know.

Stevick's conclusion in *Memory, Meaning and Method*, about what makes for success in language teaching and learning, was that success depends less on materials, techniques and linguistic analysis and more on what goes on inside and between the people in the classroom. In his next book, *Teaching Language: A Way and Ways*, he says:

> I have not changed my mind about the fundamental importance of 'what goes on inside and between', but I have been able to pursue this principle more deeply and at the same time to practice it more broadly, than before. As a result I have begun to suspect that the most important aspect of 'what goes on' is the presence or absence of harmony – it is the parts working with, or against, one another.

A little light

What Stevick is leading the reader towards is a view of the role of the teacher who, while in control of what is generally going on, is mainly concerned with the encouragement of the learners' creativity, sharing with the learners the functions both of the 'originator' and the 'evaluator'. Again we are not offered suggestions on how to teach, what to believe or anything resembling a series of procedures. On page 4 of the book Stevick makes it clear that readers are going to have to work things out for themselves:

> What I hope my readers will find in this book is not a map or a compass but only a little light.

Ways

It was through reading Stevick that I first gained an introduction into ways of teaching language to which the term innovative on first encounter seemed almost an understatement. The methods associated

with Counselling or Community Language Learning, The Silent Way
and Suggestopedia can indeed appear bizarre. These have certainly
never taken on in the context of normal school-based teaching – and one
can see why: to many teachers, they would seem the outside edge of
what one might call the 'hanging from the lights' type of methodology.
What they have in common, however, is the needs of the individual
learner to have more of themselves taken into account by the teacher
than the disembodied intellect which so often predominates. Considering these ways of teaching languages means considering ways of
viewing life – as well as 'other related matters'.

A taste of community language learning

It is not my intention to describe these methods here, and I have not
used them myself with classes. I have, however, seen a student teacher,
Kate Darrah, at Moray House Institute for Teacher Training, conduct
with others in her group an interesting short session based on Classical
Community Language Learning using Italian as the language to be
learnt. It was a first Italian lesson for the participants. Darrah's only
source was the account of this experience in Stevick's book. The experience allowed those involved to discuss how much they thought they
had learnt in Italian as compared with what they might reasonably have
expected a beginner to achieve in such a short time, what principles
were in operation and whether any of these, if not the method itself,
could be adapted to their future practice as teachers.

The learners sat in a circle in comfortable, upholstered chairs. A good
quality cassette recorder with extension microphone was in the centre
of the circle with someone not involved in the learning taking charge of
it. There were no distracting books or papers around, and bags, coats
and umbrellas had been put out of the way. Darrah explained what the
session would consist of: basically the learners were to say to each other
in English, one at a time, whatever they wanted, and Darrah, acting as
'knower' (to use the accepted term), would place her hands on their
shoulders and whisper an Italian translation for what they had said into
their ear. This the speaker would then repeat aloud. The Italian, and
only the Italian, would be recorded onto cassette at this point in the
learner's voice. After some 10 minutes of 'conversation', the cassette,
containing the whole 'conversation', was played back to the learners. A
period of reflection followed. Some things were then repeated on
request, learners tried to see how much they as a group could recall.

They also started to hypothesise about the new language. Immediately after the session, and indeed the next day, it came as some surprise to participants to see how much Italian they did in fact retain. In particular it was the confidence and the feeling of support which were the main substance of their remarks. (Stevick talks of people experiencing *'a blessed feeling of well-being and relief'* on encountering such techniques.)

Another interesting feature of the experience was the effect it had on Darrah's own teaching persona. Having seen her in classes as a lively stimulator of pupil participation in games, mime and other activities, it was interesting to see that she also possessed the ability to convey to learners a purposeful air of calm, soothing concentration. This is what I meant in the Introduction to this part of the book when I talked of learning 'to be 'at home' in a variety of modes' so that teachers find out 'how far in any direction they are capable of going as teachers'.[33]

The preservation of the self-image

Stevick has important things to say about the need for the teacher to be in control: humanistic teaching methods do not mean for him the abnegation of all responsibility by the teacher and the creation of what he calls a power vacuum. The patient, understanding, sometimes self-effacing teacher of Counselling-Learning does not *'let the students do just whatever they want'*.

Indeed, Stevick stresses the preservation of the self-image as the *'first law of psychological survival'*. In the many universes which intersect one another in a language class, each person sees his or her self in terms of *'an object of primary value in a world of meaningful action'*.[34] A humanistic approach therefore is concerned with the maintenance of the learners' and the teacher's self-image – which in no sense implies the free-for-all that many people consider is part of 'learner-centred' methodology.

This view of the language student is, in Stevick's words *'More comprehensive and more down-to-earth practical than a view which sees him as a combination of language aptitude, learning style, vocational goals and so on.'* Thus, the most important thing a teacher can do is to look closely at the class members in the light of this, not to psychoanalyse them, but to answer questions such as *'what attitudes do the students have to speakers of the target language, or toward language study in general? How are they reacting to the course as it progresses? What general and what specific pressures do these students feel from their parents or from their employers, from us, from one another, and from themselves?'*

Why innovate?

Stevick seems to me to go to the heart of the question of why teachers need to innovate when he addresses why a teacher should go to the trouble of becoming what he calls a humanistic teacher. There is clearly a close link between teaching 'humanistically' and teaching innovatively, as both entail looking at the learners before making any decisions about how to proceed. There is no question that the ways of teaching described by Stevick in these two books ask, as he says of the teacher '*a level of craftsmanship which must be unusually high and which must be maintained day after day*'. Why then do those teachers who use them nevertheless undertake something so demanding of skill and at the same time so risky? Stevick's answer seems to contain the essence of innovation and why it is not only important, but essential:

> *Perhaps the answer to this question is one of the permanent natural mysteries. For some people the answer to this question lies in the nature of life itself. In earlier chapters I said that when we say that something – a person, an animal, a vegetable, a microorganism even – is 'alive', we mean that it is able to take into itself new things that it needs, and to use them, and to get rid of what it no longer needs, and to grow (in size or in other ways) into the world around it; and that in doing all these things it continues to be itself even as it changes. 'Life' in this sense has not only length and breadth, but also depth. The same person who is physically sound and economically prosperous may on other levels have stopped taking in the new, and letting go of what no longer fits, and changing: may, for the sake of hanging onto the Self that is, have given up knowledge of, and further unfolding of, that very Self. This grinding to a halt, this digging into a permanent position, this inflexibility is a loss of life, therefore a kind of death on the one level – the symbolic level – which is available only to human beings and not to animals or plants.*

17 Pause for Thought: Extending the Partnership

Innovation is a social process. Given a creative spark, the freedom to operate and the right people, collaboration and collegiality can be relied upon to do a great deal. There is one role missing in all this – that of research. Ideas on how research and researchers might complete the partnership, and the crucial role of teachers' associations, are considered in this final chapter.

In this book I have written about my world. I have spent the bulk of my career in the classroom and this book is directed towards fellow teachers. We teach the way we do because of other people: and those who most enjoy teaching can usually cite a whole list of people who have inspired them over the years. However large or small the teaching community, some individuals stand out through their ability to convey their ideas to others.

More than the Sum of the Parts

We have considered how working together as a team or in a campaign not only enhances the professional experiences of individuals, but also produces social links which are sustainable and which means that such a team is permanently available for future deployment, and can be mobilised quickly to tackle new tasks and face new challenges. We have in particular considered the example of Lothian Region in some detail, where a loose and informal network can be identified, consisting of people who over the years have worked together and who continue to work together by choice, without the need for strong external control or centralised plan. There are teachers whose association goes back to the raising of the school-leaving age, who still recall the arguments which raged over the wisdom of teaching pupils to say 'je voudrais un pain' before they had met the entire conditional tense in all its glory, there are those who shared in the GLAFLL experience and those who started their teaching careers post-GLAFLL, but whose beliefs have been profoundly influenced by the debates which GLAFLL gave rise to.

The point I am making is that there is no system in operation in Lothian which is designed deliberately to bring this about, there is no Staff College. Such a group cannot be *ordered* to form and work together. There are no economic incentives, no prospects of promotion as a lure, in fact no obvious external motivational factors – nothing at all to attract the self-interested. What exists is a collection of individuals who know how to work together as a team and who are always ready to do so when there is a task to be performed which they judge worthwhile.

Lothian is not unique in this respect. Throughout Britain and in other parts of the world, similar groups can be identified who have shared in activities in the past and who can be relied upon to move things forward in the future.

Such groups do not function, however, in a vacuum. They require facilitators and leaders. Within an informal organisation, these roles may change, but there is always likely to be someone who is the focus of particular stages in the completion of a task. In the Graded Objectives movement in England there were key figures like Michael Buckby and Brian Page, and in Scotland many languages teachers acknowledge the contribution made by those such as John Clark, Richard Johnstone and Peter Wheeldon – all of whom have influenced a whole generation of teachers and all of whom at one time taught together in the same school, which suggests that propinquity and collegiality may have considerable knock-on effects. The same is true at the Center for Educational Innovation in New York, where I noted that the directors were, like the three above 'friends from way back'. In the case of New York it was deliberate policy to put them together to form the task-force to push aside the dead hand of bureaucracy and get things moving in schools which had completely lost heart. Such people are influential not for the 'clout' they possess in terms of their status – there are plenty of people with status in education these days – but for their integrity, and because of the message they convey, which is that ideas are there to be relentlessly questioned and pursued. The same goes for those who write about ideas, such as Stevick, Krashen, Rivers, Brumfit and Prahbu.

Earlier on in this book I mentioned risk-taking and courage as being essential for innovation. The refusal to accept something because it happens to be convenient, or because it is policy – or politic, to do so, marks out the person of principle. Personal qualities matter to all of us, not only in our private lives. As teachers we are more intimately connected to the lives of others than is the case in most other walks of life. Whereas in industry it may be sufficient for a manager simply to believe in the product, teachers need to believe in people. Lose that, and there is no justification for continuing to teach. Belief, to the extent of passion, in what they are engaged in is a characteristic of those who inspire. Their credibility stems from that, and from the fact that they also know when to make use of principled dissent.

We know that the combination of the right people in circumstances which give them freedom to operate enables the production of work well beyond the capacity of any one individual. The partnership scheme described in Chapter 14 represented the genuine desire of each partner to be involved more closely with the interests of the other two, so as to make the best possible use of all three. The notion of the effective utilisation of existing resources leads me to consider other ways in which individuals and groups might become more closely involved in focused work on innovation. We have already considered one kind of partnership. Let us now look at another role and another possible partner.

The Research Dimension

Successful teachers know how to work as a team and are applied researchers in their field. The innovative teacher has no option but to be a researcher, who differs only a small amount from the academic researcher. How else does an innovator proceed, if not by a series of hypotheses, tested and constantly refined. Of course innovative teachers would benefit from the increased rigour demanded of post-graduate work. That they know this is clear – for example, quite a number of languages teachers in Lothian Region have in their free time taken a part-time Master of Education degree at the University of Edinburgh, subsidised to some extent by the Region. This is another case of extra work undertaken by teachers which in itself has no particular monetary value, nor in fact is it seen as particularly career-enhancing. Most people claim to do it because it 'stretches' them. They like the challenge of being made to think and to have to put their ideas on paper. This is but one indication of the huge reservoir of potential within teachers which goes for the most part unused.

Industry knows that investment in research is essential if the product is to keep ahead of rivals. If those in authority in education could be convinced that innovation can be a means of improving the education service, and that part of the work of innovation requires a climate of enquiry and research, the next step would be to work out how to release teachers to carry out such research and enquiry in their own schools. There is nearly always some slack to be found in institutions – time can be created when it is a priority, and a reallocation of basic administrative tasks from teachers to administrative and clerical assistants would provide a starting point. If promoted posts can be created which release teachers from the classroom to run tuck-shops or book out the school minibus, if time can be found in departments to let teachers attend In-Service training outside the school, surely the opportunities can be created to accommodate some time for something so directly related to the purpose of education? The addition of a research remit to some promoted posts would be a start. The potential is certainly there. It is, as in all things, a question of defining priorities.

Researchers in residence

Another way to achieve a similar end would be to make use of an underutilised resource, the educational researcher, usually based at a university. What I would propose is to send, or indeed lease out post-graduate students or faculty staff to schools as consultants, in the same way as the scheme for 'writers in residence' operates. Such a scheme would have the advantage of providing both material and income for the researcher, and considerable spin-offs for the school. A researcher-in-residence would bring a healthy outside view of those things which teachers cannot see because they are too close to them, and at the same time would lead teachers to analyse with more rigour those things which they do see. All schools, all institutions, tend to look inwards, and to go through periods of stagnation. A researcher-in-residence would provide a splendid catalyst for innovative activity, particularly during those stagnant times when self-satisfaction beckons. While the appointment of researchers-in-residence might be an idea worth pursuing, it is possible to envisage a similar role being undertaken by a less exalted personage.

As already said, one of the many tasks student teachers in Moray House are asked to carry out is the completion of the professional project in which they are asked to provide a substantial piece of work relating to an educational theme. The work itself can be in the form of a traditional paper, a seminar or a video. For many of the student teachers in Modern Languages who chose to address a Modern Languages theme, it took up an amount of time quite disproportionate to the rewards which its successful completion would bring. It was, in point of fact, completely irrelevant to their employment prospects, and besides, marking tended to be remarkably lenient, certainly at the lower end, there being a great reluctance to penalise some of the non-Arts graduates for inability to perform on paper. While all this was known, it was a piece of work to which the student teachers dedicated themselves conscientiously and with enthusiasm. Some commented that they had put more into their professional project than they had into their final thesis at university. It was the same with those serving teachers mentioned above who decided to study for the M.Ed. degree. The fact that this kind of work is so intrinsically rewarding is surely something on which we could build. It seems a tremendous waste not to make use of people's potential in this area.

It is not a new idea to suggest that it would make a useful extension of a student teacher's task during on-the-job training to carry out on behalf of the department or school a mini-research task determined in conjunction with the department and related to that department's own work. It would also be useful in that it might encourage individual teachers to take a more proactive role as researchers themselves, and certain departments might even like to offer material and cooperation for research into a particular field.

An 'office' of innovation

What all this comes down to is the need for a freeing up of institutional boundaries, for creative thinking, not just about innovating within and across organisations but about organisation *as* innovation. To take one example of this, the 'Office of Innovation.'[35] This model can operate within or across firms, hence it can be made to operate within schools or departments, or across networks of schools. It need not involve the creation of new posts, although that would undoubtedly help, but would require redefinition of some existing remits. It need not involve a location, although it would benefit from access to a friendly institution. It would need resourcing, but it need not itself be the source of that resourcing. Translated from its commercial origins, I can imagine it operating in a variety of ways in education. It is essentially a process designed to deal with the development of complex ideas and innovations; it is, however, flexible enough to be used in a variety of settings. Much of it is how people operate already, formalised and given shape. Within the process are some identifiable stages and roles:

Stages	Roles
talent spotting	talent scouts
ideas creation/generation	originators
ideas facilitation	originators+facilitators
initial screening	originators+screeners
development	originators+facilitators
review	originators+reviewers
search for sponsorship/help	originators+facilitators
implementation	originators

Talent spotting may not always be necessary (the model on which I based this does not in fact envisage this role) but certain people – advisers, education lecturers, Head Teachers, inspectors – could be requested to note and report to the 'Office' examples of innovative potential which they encounter in their day-to-day work and which would profit from diffusion.

Those who create and generate ideas would have a 'direct line' to the 'Office', and the process would be set under way. The principle to be borne in mind is that the originators are the ones in control and it is they who must decide whether at any stage to take no further action.

At the beginning is the idea. The originators find a facilitator – someone with whom they can work and whose role is both advocate and guide through the structures necessary before implementation can take place. The facilitator's role is to examine the idea, assess with the originators its potential and discuss the various implications and knock-on effects.

Then comes some initial screening, which implies a short paper, drawn up by the originators in collaboration with the facilitator, followed by a presentation. Apart from anything else, it shows the degree of commitment to the idea of the originators that they have taken it to this stage. As we have already seen, innovation is not for the faint-hearted, it is not the 'flash in the pan'. Ideally the idea is screened by a group selected by the originator. This group would consists of experts in the field, and should come from a pool of volunteers within the organisation(s) involved. They are not seen as an executive group, but as consultants, whose role is to comment on the idea and make their own contribution to it.

After this, originators and facilitator come together to assess the likelihood of progress and decide how to proceed. If they decide to continue, further development, perhaps some experimentation and information gathering, lead eventually to the preparation of presentation material for a final review. If this goes well, then the search for what is required can be made with a maximum of backing.

What is attractive about the process is that at all times discretion rests with the originators – it is up to them to decide on viability or not. The others involved are in supporting roles, designed to stimulate ideas and encourage proper follow-through. The process itself is one likely to stimulate innovation and encourage the exploration of new ideas; it also has the merit of involving, if only in a consultative role, a wide variety of people. Although one can imagine its being formalised, one can also see that a limited version, within a school, say, across a number of school departments or indeed within a language association, could be made to work on a volunteer basis. Because teachers as a group would be putting forward any final proposal (for instance for funding), this proposal would benefit from the legitimacy of such a provenance.

Information brokers

There is another way in which existing resources are underutilised. One of the gaps which industry has to some extent plugged, but which is still a major problem in education, is the dissemination of research findings. The distance between classroom and university is not narrowed often enough, not through any lack of willingness on either side but more from the lack of a mechanism. Researchers have, however, a highly important role to play in schools. The study carried out by Rosalind Mitchell and Brian Partridge from Stirling University into the nature of classroom discourse was a case in point. This study took place at the time of the GLAFLL project in conjunction with the development of the SED sponsored coursebook, Tour de France and involved many schools. Its findings were widely circulated. The influence of this research *as it was being carried out*, caused teachers to question the nature of their interaction with pupils, and increased the willingness of individuals to experiment for themselves with new ways of using language in the classroom. The shock of discovering how little classroom time was taken up with initiation of target language speech by pupils (0.7%) was in itself instrumental in making teachers search for ways of remedying this. Research such as this can be a catalyst for stimulating educational changes. A similar example was seen in the case of teachers and trainee teachers in Western Samoa.

The information gap between research and those who would benefit from it highlights the need for the services of information brokers. Australia, as a world leader in information-brokerage about language teaching and learning, is likely to furnish interesting material on its effects. The network of institutions that has been set up ought to enable classroom teachers there to have easy access to the very best work. The challenge of running educational reform over so many languages in such a vast country has focused attention on the importance of the quality of the provision of back-up, both in terms of personnel and technology.

In Britain CILT is particularly well-positioned at present to offer teacher support and it is enjoying a high status in the eyes of the powers-that-be, underlined by new, smart premises and extensive facilities, as well as by the spreading reputation among teachers of the quality of its conferences and workshops. CILT's main business is information-brokerage, and its remit for the diffusion of research makes it the ideal centre for supporting new ventures in this area. CILT has now opened headquarters in Scotland, at Stirling University, where it is ideally situated to take up the role of promoting partnerships between researchers, teachers, teacher trainers and local authorities, one in which the University has already played a major role.

Greater use needs to be made of the potential of technology to extend our knowledge of progress elsewhere in our subject. If telephone conferences can be arranged for business people to save their companies the expense of overnight accommodation and travel costs, there is no reason for not exploring similar linkages of like-minded individuals in education. It should be possible for groups of teachers in one part of the world to share their findings with others similarly inclined in another part of the world relatively easily. International links, with the opening up of phone and fax lines to competition should be encouraged between teachers from country to country, as potentially greater in terms of cost benefit than foreign travel for the few. E-mail offers a cheap and simple way to communicate across the globe. If pupils can have satellite links across the world, teachers and researchers should benefit too. It is a question of using, or extending access to existing technology, not necessarily of investment in new technology. There is also an argument to be made for school departments to have a budget enabling them to benefit in this way, just as there is an argument to be made for encouraging them to take an active role in research. All of this is dependent, however, on a reappraisal of the role of the teacher, the nature of the job and the importance of innovation to the profession.

This is something that language associations can push for. Language associations, advisers, inspectors, teacher trainers all play the role of information brokers. Now more than ever the reach of language organisations needs to be extended and teachers need to be more actively aware of their importance. Christopher Brumfit calls for 'A really serious commitment to strong professional teachers' organisations, strong, subject-based advisory and support services, and fully utilised professional journals...'

Language associations

Language associations such as ALL and SALT have taken in recent years a more focused approach to teacher development and have also served to raise the profile of the teacher-as-researcher. Much happens in individual classrooms as a result of work first encountered at meetings or in journals and magazines. Through their associations, teachers can not only receive and pass on information, they can push for the authorities to change their minds about matters with which they disagree. There has been an increasing awareness of the need for these associations to move with the times – the old days of make do and mend, of accommodation in dubious and ill-smelling university halls of residence and appalling catering have been replaced by an experience akin to that not unfamiliar to middle management in industry. This has of course come with an increase in cost and teachers are having increasingly to meet these costs out of their own pockets. Christine Wilding,[36] Secretary General of the Association for Language Learning, expresses her concern that recent changes have made the job of associations harder:

> The teaching profession has changed enormously in the last ten years. Greater accountability means that education is more aware that time means money, time costs. This affects the amount of voluntary work which can be put into the subject teaching associations and other professional bodies. Many people such as advisers who were able to give time to associations are now freelance consultants and cannot do so. Because there are no advisers, there is an even greater need for teachers to exchange infor-

mation and support each other through associations. Associations in turn need to be more professional, and costs are rising because they need to pay for speakers and improve their image through appropriate publicity and promotions. No longer can postage costs be 'slipped through' and reliance be made on secretarial help in people's spare time.

Bearing in mind the need for the legitimising of innovation, there is an even greater need now for teachers to support these associations by means of which their voices can be heard. It may be that the most important task for language teachers at the moment is to provide a counter-balance to present doctrines which limit teachers' capacity to do their best work by tieing them into a narrow, bland, centrally-determined, efficiency-oriented plan, which uses up their energies by requiring them to be permanently busy on someone else's business, working to someone else's agenda. It is through associations and partnerships that teachers can use the campaign mode as a means of re-establishing themselves at the heart of the curriculum renewal process – convincing the powers-that-be that the sterile notion of 'efficiency' is not always effective. The development of campaigning capacity can enable teachers to take charge of determining and shaping the tasks to be performed, the research to be carried out, the direction of change. Language associations offer a possible campaign headquarters, a potential core 'staff,' and they have the undeniable benefit of legitimacy.

This book has been concerned not only with describing particular innovations, but also with identifying some of the conditions which encourage innovation to flourish. These conditions are linked to the notion of teachers as essentially social beings motivated by more than mere self-interest. To summarise finally what seem to be the most important points to arise out of the various experiences described:

Legitimacy is crucial to innovation: However, the balance of power between central authority and local autonomy requires to be maintained, so that domination by the centre does not stifle initiative and deskill teachers. Legitimacy can be conferred by movements and campaigns, by colleagues, and professional organisations.

Spread is crucial to innovation: Spread depends on legitimacy and hence on institutions. It is not just a case of enabling teachers to become informed about developments; it requires a teaching force which is sufficiently activist to react to new ideas and reject new ideologies.

Organisational structures are crucial to innovation: Informal structures allow for flexible responses and encourage initiative.

Individuals are crucial to innovation: We need to identify potential leaders; to support and encourage enquirers and risk-takers; to give a platform to those whose ideas inspire.

Envoi

False gods and snake charmers

When the missionaries first came to the Pacific, their phenomenal success was due to one thing more than anything else. When it came to the point, their god was stronger than all the other gods around. This was what impressed the 'pagan' to throw away and burn their graven images – and incidentally deny the world, and the descendants of these 'pagan', some of the finest examples of carving and art work; it was not the message of peace and redemption. The fact that the men of Jehovah, for it was Jehovah that they learnt to fear, could trample on the holy places, crush the sacred skulls of the ancestors, withstand the curses of the sorcerers and remain untouched, made them and therefore their god powerful above anything else the natives of these lands had ever encountered. The missionaries possessed other tricks, too, the trick of writing, of making light, of fire. And they could, if they needed to, call on guns in their support.

* * *

It is as important for teachers not to let the skulls of the ancestors be trampled on as it is for them not to let themselves be mesmerised by the latest trick of the snake-charmers. Nor should they go in fear of the big guns. When the old 'superstitions' were replaced with the new 'knowledge', many Pacific Island peoples lost the wisdom that was at the centre of a way of life. Once that had gone, the heart too, went out of them.

Notes to Part 4

1. *Howard's End*, Chapter 22.
2. 'Smeddum' is a short story by Lewis Grassic Gibbon set in the harsh farming country of the north-east of Scotland. Meg Menzies, raising a family of nine and working the unrewarding land, epitomises the quality which she sees as lacking in all her children bar her daughter Kath. The others Meg is quick to marry off, but of Kath she says: 'She's fit to be free and to make her own choice the same as myself and the same kind of choice. There was none of the rest of you fit to do that, you'd to marry or burn, so I

married you quick. But Kath and me could afford to find out. It all depends if you've smeddum or not.' Gordon Liddell, Head of the Language Studies Department at Moray House, uses the concept of 'smeddum' as a criterion in his selection of student teachers – one which Modern Languages was quick to borrow from him. It encapsulates the notion of self-determination, and the qualities of doggedness and discipline which distinguish the teacher who can last as well as set the pace from the one who shines merely at the 'one-offs' and crumbles under pressure.

3. The probationary period in Scotland lasts two years. It has been phased out in England.

4. Student teachers are encouraged to develop their second or third languages by the provision of foreign conversation assistant time, as well as by the requirement to work in 'language groups' based, where appropriate, on their weaker language.

5. This technique was first encountered in preliminary discussions about the new course with Vee Harris of Goldsmith's College, London. Moray House, in allowing a year for the preparation of the new course, provided funding for me to consult colleagues all over the country. The resulting course, as initially conceived, was a combination of a variety of inputs: from teacher educators in England Vee Harris, Barry Jones, Richard Johnstone, Michael Buckby and James Burch, from Advisers in Modern Languages in Scotland, such as Martin Prouse, John Fergusson and Peter Wheeldon, as well as innumerable friends and colleagues in the region.

6. The notion of using schools for short bursts of practice of individual techniques by groups of student teachers came initially from Barry Jones of Homerton College, University of Cambridge.

7. The use of the training department as a 'nursery slope' in the wake of any unfortunate experience in a first block teaching practice is particularly helpful. Student teachers, it is felt, should not have to face the Christmas break with the memory of failure hanging over them.

8. Questionnaires were used extensively with learners in Balerno High School in the early days, and the lesson learnt that those handing out the questions need to be able to deal with the answers, not all of which may be supportive to the originator's self-image.

9. Bonnet, C. (1990) *The Use of Objects in Language Teaching*. Moray House Institute of Education. Professional project.

10. Klippel, F. (1984) *Keep Talking*.

11. Franklin, C.E.M. (1990) Teaching in the target language: Problems and prospects. *Language Learning Journal*, September 20–7.

12. Dulay, H., Burt, M. and Kraschen, S. (1982) *Language Two*. Oxford: Oxford University Press.

13. Shuh, J.H. (1982) Teaching yourself to teach with objects. *Journal of Education*, 7(4), 8–15.

14. Burstall, C. Jamieson, M. Colen, S, and Hargreaves, M. (1974) *Primary French in the Balance*. Slough: National Foundation for Educational Research.

15. Budzynski, T. (1976) Biofeedback and the twilight state of consciousness. In Schwarz, G. and Shapiro, D. (eds) *Consciousness and Self Regulation*, Vol. 1. New York: Pieum Press; Bancroft, W.J. (1972) *The Psychology of Suggestopedia or Learning Without Stress*. Toronto: The Educational Courier. Rose; C. (1985) *Accelerated Learning*. Accelerated Learning Systems; Chall, J.S. and

Mirsky, A.F. (1978) *Education and the Brain*. NSSE; Jackson, P.W. (1968) *Life in Classrooms*. New York: Holt, Rinehart and Winston Inc.; Klippel, F. (1984) *Keep Talking*. Cambridge: Cambridge University Press; Kossuth, G.L., Carroll, W.R. and Rogers, C.A. (1971) Free recall of words and objects. *Developmental Psychology* 4 (3), 480; Russell, P. (1979) *The Brain Book*. Routledge and Kegan; Sutro, E. and Gross, R.E. 1983, The five senses – prime keys in the art and craft of teaching. *Social Studies*, 74(3), 118–24; Torres, C. and Katz, J.H. (1983) Neuro-linguistic programming: developing effective communication in the classroom. *Teacher Educator*, 19(2), 25–32.

16. Lesson plans as normally conceived, like defined syllabuses, do not really fit in with an approach to teaching that is not primarily concerned with 'outputs'. The term 'lesson planning' was used to indicate that it was important for each student teacher to define their own approach to their work, and to think through for themselves what they were trying to achieve, in terms that reflected their beliefs about learning and their understanding of how these could affect the learners.

17 In case the reader has never heard of Kim's Game, the version I played works like this: A tray of objects is placed in front of a group. They have a set time to view the objects and try to remember them. The objects are then covered with a cloth. An object is removed. The cloth is removed. The pupils take it in turn to name the missing object. A point is scored each time they are right.

18. This was a remarkable lesson which covered a double period. It started with 'Listen and read and do': Robot masks were made out of cardboard boxes and decorated. The classroom looked like an art and craft room. Bonnet had made a mask for herself as 'chef des robots'. She 'programmed' the class to obey her instructions and it was then a straightforward case of TPR – pupils had to obey instructions and then issue instructions to each other on the same lines.

19. Chomsky, N. (1986) *Knowledge of Language: Its Nature, Origin and Use*. New York: Praeger.

20. This bears out my intuition that teachers are as likely to change their behaviour for what might be called 'irrational' or 'social' reasons as they are as a result of theoretical arguments aimed at their intellect.

21. If I seem to keep returning to the importance of the human factor it is because there is no other explanation for some things. A change to target language use is unlikely to be achieved on the merits of intellectual persuasion – such a change is a change in behaviour and we only change our behaviour out of strong motives. These strong motives were present in this case. Hirsch represented to all those who were involved in her training a real challenge: here was someone with ideals which all teachers recognised and admired, someone who was prepared to work hard and try out all kinds of things, but who would not compromise personal convictions for expediency. Despite some miserable classroom experiences early on, Hirsch battled on, always polite to pupils, rarely taking the easy way out by sending for help. Those whom Hirsch influenced, and I include myself among them, recognised, I think, ideals of their own in her, remembered the compromises they had made themselves over the years and perhaps regretted, and were inspired by her example.

22. Brumfit, C. (1984) *Communicative Methodology in Language Teaching: The Roles*

of Fluency and Accuracy (p. 45).

23. Rivers (1983: 160) calls it an 'interesting, carefully elaborated metaphor of limited scope', while Stevick elaborates the model to produce his own version of it, the 'Levertov machine', to which he devotes a whole chapter of 'Teaching Languages, a Way and Ways'. Merrill Swain, who also finds Krashen's notion of 'meaningful input' useful in terms of immersion teaching, adds her own notion of 'meaningful output' to make up for the lack of a description in Krashen's model of what occurs when learners come to speak in the foreign language. Brumfit (1984: 42–9) takes Krashen to task on a variety of issues, and concludes that 'we cannot justifiably use it as a basis for language teaching methodology' – and this 'in spite of the influence of his work'. Krashen's work gained a great deal of currency in Britain through the BBC *Horizon* programme 'A child's view of language'.

24. Dulay, H., Burt, M. and Krashen, S. (1982) *Language Two*. New York and Oxford: Oxford University Press.

25. Jackson, P.W. (1968: 149) quoted in Brumfit, 67.

26. Stevick, E. (1976) *Memory, Meaning and Method*.

27. Stevick, E. (1980) *Teaching Languages: A Way and Ways*.

28. Berne, E. (1964) *Games People Play*. New York: Grove Press.

29. Transactional Analysis was popularised by Eric Berne in the 1960s and 1970s with the best-sellers, *Games People Play* (New York, Grove Press, 1964), and *What Do You Say After You Say Hello?* (New York, Bantam, 1972). In brief, it argues that we have three 'Ego states' – Parent, Adult and Child, which influence the way we behave and how we interact with each other. All interactions can be categorised under these headings. The Parent state controls – 'If I were you I would not do that' as well as nurtures and is referred to as the 'Natural' or the 'Controlling' Parent; the Child state is the emotional one, it is, in Berne's words, 'the most valuable part of the personality' because it is where 'intuition, creativity and spontaneous drive and enjoyment' reside – it is, according to Stevick, here that the qualities which make for language learning exist – but it can also cause problems, the Child being referred to as 'Natural', 'Adapted' or 'Rebellious'; the Adult is the state in which people try to make sense of the outside world, and is manifested by the asking of questions – it is also the one which reconciles the Child with the Parent. Keeping the states in balance is the key to a healthy personality.

30. Lozanov, G. (1979) *Suggestology and the Outlines of Suggestopedy*. New York: Gordon and Breach.

31. Curran, C.A. (1972) *Counseling-Learning. A Whole Person Approach for Education*, 144. Apple River Press.

32. Jersild, A.T. (1955: 8) *When Teachers Face Themselves*. New York: Teachers College Press.

33. Sad to relate, Darrah feels, since starting full-time teaching, that she has little scope to put her innovative talents into operation. The spirit of the times has caught up with her and she writes, echoing the words of far too many other formerly innovative student teachers: 'I have to confess that my present teaching is rarely as innovative. It seems to be such a sausage-machine of assessments sometimes, and it's incredibly difficult to go beyond teaching to them.'

34. Stevick here quotes Becker, E. who borrows the phrase from Adler.

35. I have adapted this from Robert Rosenfeld and Jenny Servo: Facilitating innovation in large organizations. In *Innovation and Creativity at Work*. 256–61.
36. Christine Wilding – personal communication.

Appendix 1: Matters of Management, Public Choice and Control

Market Forces and Managerialism

Virtually no country has been immune to the spread of the doctrine of 'market forces'. Among other things these are supposed to give a country more value for money in terms of the efficiency and effectiveness of its public organisations. Market forces have been responsible for the privatisation of state-owned enterprises such as power and telecommunications, and some consider that their role should be extended to cover all of state education. This is something that most of those working within state education instinctively reject. The doctrine of market forces, "capitalism without a human face", did not rise like Venus, fully formed from out of the sea. It is the product of a theory – I hesitate to award it the label 'philosophy' – which the literature refers to as 'public choice theory: the terms 'managerialist' and 'new public management' are also used. The genesis of these theories is the discipline of economics. Some understanding of these theories has more than a passing relevance to the whole issue of innovation because they have greatly influenced the conditions under which teachers now operate.

Public choice theory sees the solution to problems within the health and education services as lying in competition. By this is meant not only that public service institutions should imitate private sector models and techniques and compete *against each other*, but also that they should be run along similar lines to those of successful private companies and encourage competition *within the organisation*. This means that incentives such as promotion and increased salaries are used in order to bring out the best performances in people; that 'management skills' are valued over social and professional skills; that the setting of targets and the monitoring of performance is held to make for the better, that is the *more efficient* running of the institution. Of course it can be argued that the possibility of promotion does improve performance, that clear targets make for more efficiency and that management skills, more than social skills are needed where large units are the norm, now that the small local school seems to be a thing of the past. The other side of the coin is, however, that competition for promotion can destroy cooperation between colleagues, that clear targets often mean there is no room for divergent thinking, new ideas or principled dissent, that the technical skills of 'management' as some kind of discipline in itself do not replace the social skills which are essential for the pleasant conduct of human relationships. Competition, efficiency, targets and management skills of themselves may do little to enhance the feeling of *self-value* of individual teachers, who are rightly concerned with classroom performance. They can, however, be made to appeal by means more or less subtle, to the *self-interest* of teachers.

Critics of public choice theory say that it fails to take account of things people do for which there is no obvious reward, and those involved in education would probably agree that a view of teachers as moved only by self-interest does not explain all the things teachers for years have been known for doing: little things like taking clubs after school and at weekends, and big things like not making a career move because of loyalty to a school or to a particular group of pupils. Nevertheless, public and teachers alike seem to agree that such behaviour is on the decrease. This is perhaps because a sense of service within an institution is one of the first casualties of the promotion of self-interested behaviour.

Naturally, public choice theory rules out such a thing as vocation – even apparently disinterested acts are 'explicable' in terms of one or other kind of self-interest: public choice, to quote one writer, rejects *'notions such as "public spirit", "the public interest", "working for the common good", either on the grounds that they have little, if any meaning or relevance or because they are often used to give legitimacy to the demands of sectional interest groups'.*[1] Thus, in place of the belief that it is a sense of service which characterises a well-run public institution, we have the belief that what really counts is the efficiency of procedures within that institution. Efficiency can of course be measured – in terms of examination results, league tables, truancy figures, number of staff promotions, etc. What the theorists fail to see is that while efficiency is something which can be imposed on an institution relatively quickly, a sense of service, once lost, is not something which is easily re-established. A sense of service of course depends on people, while efficiency has to do with structures. Public choice theorists and economists, who hold efficiency as the main target, tend to see people as 'rational utility maximizers of all their behavioural capacities'[2] – not a view with which those familiar with the works of Mann, Marquez or Camus, say, would feel a great deal of sympathy.

In most countries, the full impact of this way of thinking has still to be experienced, but in New Zealand public choice is the ideology responsible for inflicting what many regard as irreparable damage to the public education system, while others see it as its salvation. In New Zealand there is no such thing as a 'small helping' of public choice, although even there the government has been forced by a near-defeat in the 1993 elections to mitigate at least some of the effects of its 'brave new world'.

In New Zealand, and now in Britain, the reliance on 'market forces' has led increasingly to the replacement of local educational advisers by contracted experts who are in possession of specific technological skills and know-how, who inform and hand down to teachers those things deemed necessary to effect changes along the lines of the model approved by the centre. Implementation, certainly not instigation, is seen as the teachers' role. Of course 'consultation' must be seen to take place, as long as the end result is the acquiescence of the teachers with the latest policy. This does nothing for teachers' self-respect. Self-respect and respect for colleagues are often the next casualties of the public choice ideology.

The need to control

No one has so far found the ideal 'method' of teaching languages, but even if there were one, a quiescent teaching force never would find it. There is a need for what Christopher Brumfit calls 'an activist profession'[3], where teachers are in charge of their own development. Yet teachers all over the world complain that they have enjoyed less and less trust over the years. The devices for control are numerous. From 'assessment instruments' to 'mission statements', we have seen management terminology shift from the scientific to the evangelical. Basically it means that all teachers should now be using this technique, following those guidelines, aiming at this or that attainment target –

hardly anyone ever seems to suggest that instead of simply implementing someone else's designs, what teachers should be encouraged to do
is to stop for a bit and think.

For it is not a neat and tidy world, the world of language teaching. In
many respects, when you look at all that is involved in the learning of
another language, it is a very messy business. Both how others learn it
and language *per se* are intrinsically not within our control. Naturally
we try to influence both of these. Our attempts to sanitise language for
school learners by neat packaging within curriculum guidelines,
defined syllabuses, fancy charts of input-outcomes, etc are totally
understandable, indeed essential. The problem is that these things look
good, but they disguise and distort the reality, by suggesting that all
will be well if only all teachers follow this or that plan, tick their way
through this or that list of functions, cover this or that grammar.

There is also, I believe, a link between views about how to manage
and how to train teachers and views on the nature of language, which
has to do with the notion of control. One of the reasons why teachers
teach the way most of them do is because they accept the way in which
language has been described for them. Describing a language in terms
of traditional Latin grammar, or structurally, functionally or whatever,
makes that language controllable and is likely to influence the way that
language will subsequently be taught. Real language, is of course, like
life, dynamic, and totally uncontrollable. 'Nothing remains the same
after someone has spoken.' Therein lies the excitement which attracts
some of us to the profession, and also no small degree of frustration. It
is little wonder then that teachers accept the rules, the nice safe
dialogues and someone else's idea of a syllabus only too readily.
Without such props, the question of what to teach becomes one the
teacher has to answer for her/himself. This is so far from what their
training has prepared them to do that few teachers consider altering the
content or even the sequencing of the set course.

Structuring the management and training of teachers is also a way of
controlling, or seeming to control, that which is of its nature, not really
controllable. While managers in education as elsewhere may obtain
token adherence to policies, they in fact can only influence things structural – things which have to do with efficiency, things which can be
measured. Most experienced managers in education know perfectly
well that the actual quality of teaching has nothing at all to do with
things like performance indicators. It is perhaps time for more of them
to say this – loudly.

Appendix 2: Scottish Campaign for Languages

In the autumn of 1987 a committee of advisers, teacher trainers and teachers who were members of SALT (Scottish Association of Language Teachers) was formed in order to have the learning of a foreign language made a part of the core curriculum in Scotland throughout the period of compulsory education. The committee was made up of the following:

Peter Wheeldon (Chairperson)
John Fergusson
William Dickson (University representative)
Danny Tierney
Edmund McFadden
Jean Nisbet
Irene Farrell
Sandy Wilson
Ann Carnachan
John McGuire (FE representative)
David Peat
Sharon Muir
Oonagh Aitken

The committee circulated a petition to all teachers of Modern Languages in secondary schools in Scotland, as well as to all FE colleges and universities: 78% of languages teachers in secondary schools and 86% of all languages lecturers signed the petition which was addressed to the then Secretary of State for Scotland, Malcolm Rifkind, MP. It read:

> We the undersigned are teachers of languages in .... (establishment)

> We deplore the proposals with regard to the learning of languages

in the CCC and SED reviews of the curriculum and urge you, as Secretary of State for Scotland, to include the learning of a foreign language as part of the core curriculum in Scotland throughout the period of compulsory secondary education.

The campaign was accompanied by press releases, letters to the press, attendance by teachers at their MPs' surgeries, and the circulating of briefing sheets to teachers wishing to take an active role. The response from MPs was heartening. The following quotes are examples of the kind of support received from prominent Scottish MPS:

Donald Dewar, MP:

I do have a good deal of sympathy with your plea ... There is certainly no good cause for complacency about our record here in Scotland and I am perfectly prepared to believe that we are so far behind the rest of Europe as to be almost out of sight.

Margaret Ewing, MP:

In conjunction with Parliamentary colleagues I have tabled Parliamentary Questions on the vital issue you raise.

Nigel Griffiths, MP:

I strongly support your views and I have written to the Secretary of State about this.

Robert MacLennan, MP:

... I am very ready to support your campaign in any way I can.

Alex Salmond, MP:

I write to you on behalf of myself and my colleagues to assure you that the Scottish National Party is in full sympathy with your concerns and in full support of your recommendations.

(Subsequently the SNP debated the issue at their National Conference.)

On behalf of SCL and SALT, the petition was presented by Councillor Malcolm Green (Honorary President of SALT) to the Scottish Office on Friday 13 May. The delegation of 10 represented all sectors of secondary and tertiary education. The event was attended by reporters from all major Scottish newspapers, and a variety of articles duly followed.

Peter Wheeldon and Christine Wilding (Chairperson of JCLA – Joint Conference of Language Associations, now known as ALL) were interviewed on BBC radio's *Head On* programme, 'head on' to the Chairperson of the CCC, Sister Maire Gallagher.

The points made on behalf of the CCC were roughly as follows:

(a) Teachers do not want languages in the core. This was based on the 1977 poll conducted by SCCML (Scottish Central Committee for Modern Languages).

(b) Coercion is a bad thing. The country will only prosper if it has potential linguists who *opt in* to study at school.

(c) Most schools are not ready yet for Standard Grade French.

(d) The SCC is recommending to the Secretary of State that study during S3 and S4 is not necessarily the best time to be studying languages.

This, as it turned out, was not the line the Secretary of State chose to take.

Notes

1. Kelman (1987); Mansbridge (1990); Tulloch (1984) quoted in *Reshaping the State – New Zealand's Bureaucratic Revolution* (1991) J. Boston, J. Martin, J. Pallot and P. Walsh (eds). Oxford: Oxford University Press.
2. Buchanan (1978) *From Private Preferences to Public Philosophy: The Development of Public Choice* (p. 17). London: Institute of Economic Affairs.
3. Brumfit, C.J. (1984) *Communicative Methodology in Language Teaching.* Cambridge: Cambridge University Press.

Bibliography

Asher, J.J. (1969) The total physical response approach to second language learning. *The Modern Language Journal*, 53.

Austin, L. (1993) Science curriculum, science catastrophe. *New Zealand Herald*, 8 September.

Bancroft, W.J. (1972) The psychology of Suggestopedia or learning without stress. Toronto: The Educational Courier.

Becker, E. (1973) *The Denial of Death*. New York: The Free Press.

Berne, E. (1964) *Games People Play*. New York: Grove Press.

—(1972) *What Do You Say After You Say Hello?* New York: Bantam.

Bonnet, C. (1990) *The Use of Objects in Language Teaching*. Professional project. Moray House Institute of Education.

Boston J., Martin J., Pallot J., Walsh P. (eds) (1991) *Reshaping the State – New Zealand's Bureaucratic Revolution*. Oxford: Oxford University Press.

Brumfit, C.J. and Johnson, K. (eds) (1979) *The Communicative Approach to Language Teaching*. Oxford: Oxford University Press.

Brumfit, C.J. (1984) *Communicative Methodology in Language Teaching – The Roles of Fluency and Accuracy*. Cambridge: Cambridge University Press.

Buchanan, (1978) *From Private Preferences to Public Philosophy: The Development of Public Choice*. London: Institute of Economic Affairs.

Budzynski, T. (1976) Biofeedback and the twilight state of consciousness. In G. Schwarz and D. Shapiro (eds) *Consciousness and Self Regulation*, Vol. 1. New York: Pieum Press.

Burns, T. and Stalker, G.M. (1961) *The Management of Innovation*. London: Tavistock.

Burstall, C., Jamieson, M., Colen, S. and Hargreaves, M. (1974) *Primary French in the Balance*. Slough: National Foundation for Educational Research.

Canale, M. and Swain, M. (1980) Theoretical bases of communicative approaches to second language teaching and testing. *Applied Linguistics* 1(1), 1–47.

Chall, J.S. and Mirsky, A.F. (1978) *Education and the Brain*. (Yearbook Part 2). National Society for the Study of Education. Chicago: Chicago University Press.

Chomsky, N. (1986) *Knowledge of Language: Its Nature, Origin and Use*. New York: Praeger.

Claret, M-P. (1990) *Language Medium Teaching*. Professional Project. Moray House Institute of Education.

Clark, J.L. (1987a) Communicative competence and foreign language learning. In *Annual Review of Applied Linguistics* Vol. 8 (1988), Cambridge University Press (pp. 85–96).

—(1988a) Curriculum development across languages and across sectors of education. In V. Bickley (ed.) (1988) *Languages in Education in a Bilingual or Multilingual Setting*. Institute of Language in Education, Education Department, Hong Kong (pp. 438–49).

—(1988b) *Curriculum Renewal in School Foreign Language Learning*. Oxford: Oxford University Press.

—(1988b) *Teacher Development is Curriculum Development*. Paper given at the Symposium on Curriculum Development and Continuing Teacher Education, Hong Kong University.

Clark, J.L. and Hamilton, J. (1984) *Syllabus Guidelines Parts 1, 2 and 3: A Graded Communicative Approach Towards School Foreign Language Learning*. London: Centre for Information on Language Teaching and Research (CILT).

Cochrane, G. (1987) *Reforming National Institutions*. Westview, Boulder, Colorado, for the World Bank.

—(forthcoming) *Management by Seclusion*.

Cooksey, B. and Ishumi, A. (1986) *A Critical Review of Policy and Practice in Tanzanian Secondary Education Since 1967*. The Rockefeller Foundation: Nairobi

Corder, S.P. (1981) *Error Analysis and Interlanguage*. Oxford: Oxford University Press.

Corson, D. (1985) *The Lexical Bar*. Oxford: Pergamon.

Council of Europe (1981) *Modern Languages (1971–1981)*. Strasbourg: Council of Europe.

Criper, C. and Dodd, W.A. (1984) *Report on the Teaching of English Language and its use as a Medium in Education in Tanzania*. Dar es Salaam. The British Council.

Crocombe, G.T., Enright, M.J., and Porter, M.E. (1991) *Upgrading New Zealand's Competitive Advantage*. Oxford: Oxford University Press.

Cumming, M. (1986) *Hear Say: Listening Tasks for French, German and Spanish*. Basingstoke: Macmillan Education.

Cummins, J. (1980a) The cross-lingual dimensions of language proficiency: implications for bilingual education and the optimal age issue. *TESOL Quarterly* 14, 175–87.

Cummins, J. and Swain, M. (1986) *Bilingualism in Education*. London and New York: Longman.

Curran, C.A. (1972) *Counseling-Learning: A Whole Person Approach for Education* (p. 144). Apple River, IL: Apple River Press.

De Nys *et al.* (1991) *Lesekiste*. Langenscheidt.

Drucker, P.F. (1985) *Innovation and Entrepreneurship – Practice and Principles*. London: Pan Books.

Dulay, H., Burt, M. and Krashen, S. (1982) *Language Two*. Oxford and New York: Oxford University Press.

Ferguson, A. (1984) A probationer's frantic reflections. *Modern Languages in Scotland*.

Firth, R. (1963) *We, the Tikopia*. Boston: Beacon Press.

Fliegel, S. and Macguire, J. (1993) *Miracle in East Harlem*. Times Books.

Franklin, C.E.M. (1990) Teaching in the target language: problems and prospects. *Language Learning Journal*.

Gathercole, I. (ed.) (1990) *Autonomy in Language Learning*. London: CILT.

Gringas, R.C. (ed.) (1978) *Second Language Acquisition and Foreign Language*

Teaching. Arlington, VA.: Center for Applied Linguistics.

Halliday, M.A.K. (1975) *Learning How to Mean: Explorations in the Development of Language*. London: Edward Arnold.

Hamilton, J. (1984a) A hornet's nest – Consultation and partnership in the classroom. *Modern Languages in Scotland*.

—(1984b) *Corresponding with a French Penfriend*. Basingstoke: Macmillan Education.

—(1984c) *Corresponding with a German Penfriend*. Basingstoke: Macmillan Education.

—(1987) The changing role of the classroom teacher. Joint Conference of Language Associations, Conference paper.

—(1990) Exploring language learning processes across the age and ability range. In *Language Continuity Opportunity*. ALL and CILT.

Hamilton, J. and Clearie, J. (1985) *Take your Partners, French Pairwork Exercises*. Basingstoke: Macmillan Education.

Hamilton, J. and Cumming, M. (1984) *Corresponding with a Spanish Penfriend*. Basingstoke: Macmillan Education.

—(1985) *Take your Partners, Pictorial Pairwork Exercises*. Basingstoke: Macmillan Education.

Hamilton, J. and McLeod, A. (1993) *Drama in the Language Classroom*. London: CILT.

Hamilton, J. and Reid, S. (1991) *In Play: A Drama Resource Kit for Modern Languages*. Nelson.

Hamilton, J. and Wheeldon, P. (1985) *Take your Partners, German Pairwork Exercises*. Basingstoke: Macmillan Education.

—(1986a) *The French Writing Folio*. Basingstoke: Macmillan Education.

—(1986b) *The German Writing Folio*. Basingstoke: Macmillan Education.

—(1989) *Italian for Real*. Basingstoke: Macmillan Education.

Hamilton, J., Cumming, M. and Wheeldon, P. (1988) *The Spanish Writing Folio*. Basingstoke: Macmillan Education.

Hamilton, J., Harris, M. Jardine, K. and Meldrum, D. (1985) *French for Real*. Basingstoke: Macmillan Education.

Hamilton, J., Priester, J. Watkins, S. and Wheeldon, P. (1985) *German for Real*. Basingstoke: Macmillan Education.

Hancock G. (1989) *Lords of Poverty*. New York: The Atlantic Monthly Press.

Hirsch, A. (1990) *The Use of Fiction in Foreign Language Teaching*: Professional Project. Moray House Institute of Education.

Hirst, P. (1974) *Knowledge and the Curriculum*. London: Routledge.

Hood, D. (1993) Qualifications by the unit. *New Zealand Herald*. November 9.

Jackson, P.W. (1968) *Life in Classrooms*. New York: Holt, Rinehart and Winston Inc.

Jersild, A.T. (1955) *When Teachers Face Themselves*. New York: Teachers College Press.

Johnson, K. (1982) *Communicative Syllabus Design and Methodology*. Oxford: Pergamon Press.

Kanter, R.M. (1983) *The Change Masters*. New York: Simon and Schuster.

Klippel, F. (1984) *Keep Talking*. Cambridge: Cambridge University Press.

Kossuth, G.L., Carroll, W.R. and Rogers, C.A. (1971) Free recall of words and objects. *Developmental Psychology* 4(3).

Krashen, S. (1978) The monitor model for second language acquisition. *Gringras*, 1–26.

—(1981) *Second Language Acquisition and Second Language Learning*. Oxford: Pergamon Press.

—(1982) *Principles and Practice in Second Language Acquisition*. Oxford: Pergamon Press.

Krashen, S. and Terrell, T. (1983) *The Natural Approach*. Hayward, California: Alemany Press.

Lo Bianco, J. (1990) Language in bilingual classrooms – Samoa as an example. *In Vernacular Languages in South Pacific Education*. National Language Institute of Australia.

Lo Bianco, J. and Liddicoat, A. (1991) Language use in classrooms in Western Samoa. *Language and Language Education*. Working Papers of the National Language Institute of Australia. 1(1), NLIA.

Lozanov, G. (1979) *Suggestology and the Outlines of Suggestopedy*. New York: Gordon and Breach.

Maley and Duff (1978) *Drama Techniques in Language Teaching*. Cambridge: Cambridge University Press.

Mbilinya, M. and Mbughuni, P. (eds) (1991) *Education in Tanzania with a Gender Perspective*. Summary Report. Dar es Salaam: SIDA.

Ministry of Education (1982) *Basic Facts about Education in Tanzania*. Dar es Salaam.

Ministry for Employment, Education and Training (1990) *The National Policy on Languages, December 1987 – March 1990. Report to the Minister for Employment, Education and Training*. Australian Advisory Council on Languages and Multicultural Education, May 1990. Canberra: AACLAME Secretariat.

Mitchell, R., Parkinson, B. and Johnston, R. (1981) *The Foreign Language Classroom: An Observational Study*. Stirling: University of Stirling. (Stirling Educational Monographs 9).

New Zealand Employers Federation (Nov. 1992) *Human Resources: An Introduction to Best Practice*.

Peddie, R. (1992) *The Transformers: Control, Power and the Economics Model in Education* (in draft).

Peters, T.J. and Waterman, R.H. (1982) *In Search of Excellence: Lessons from America's Best-Run Companies*. New York: Harper and Row.

Porter, M.E. (1990) *The Competitive Advantage of Nations*. London: Macmillan.

Prahbu, N.S. (1987) *Second Language Pedagogy*. Oxford: Oxford University Press.

Rinvolucri, M. and Morgan, J. (1983) *Once Upon a Time – Using Stories in the Language Classroom*. Cambridge: Cambridge University Press.

Rivers, W.M. (1976) *Speaking in Many Tongues: Essays in Foreign Language Teaching*. Rowley, MA: Newbury House.

Rivers, W.M. (1983) *Communicating Naturally in a Second Language – Theory and Practice in Language Teaching*. New York: Cambridge University Press

Rose, C. (1989) *Accelerated Learning* (4th edn.) Aylesbury, Bucks: Accelerated Learning Systems.

Rosenfeld, R. and Servo, J. (1990) Facilitating innovation in large organisations. In *Innovation and Creativity at Work: Psychological and Organizational Strategies*. Chichester: John Wiley and Sons Ltd.

Rubagumya, C.M. (ed.) (1988) *Language in Education in Africa*. Clevedon, Avon: Multilingual Matters.

—(ed.) (1994) *Teaching and Researching Language in African Classrooms*. Clevedon, Avon: Multilingual Matters.

Russell, P. (1979) *The Brain Book*. Routledge and Kegan Paul.

Scarino, A. Vale, D. McKay, P. and Clark J.L. (1988) *Australian Language Level Guidelines*. Curriculum Development Centre, Canberra, Australia.

SCCC (1978) Survey of Scottish teacher opinion on the Munn and Dunning reports. *Modern Languages in Scotland*.

SED (1977) *The Structure of the Curriculum in the Third and Fourth Years of the Scottish Secondary School*. SCCC.

Schellendorf, von General B. (1905) *The Duties of the General Staff* (pp. 566–7) (4th edn). London: HMSO.

Shuh, J.H. (1982) Teaching yourself to teach with objects. *Journal of Education*.

Stenhouse, L. (1975) *An Introduction to Curriculum Research and Development*. Heinemann

Stern, H.H. (1975) What can we learn from the good language learner? *Canadian Modern Language Review*, 31, 308–18.

Stevick, E. (1976) *Memory, Meaning and Method*. Rowley, MA: Newbury House.

—(1980) *Teaching Languages, a Way and Ways*. Rowley, MA.: Newbury House.

Stewart, V. (1992) *Cows, Dogs and Playing Fields*. Paper given to the Institute of New Zealand Personnel Management Conference in 1991, quoted in *Human Resources: An Introduction to Best Practice*. New Zealand Employers Federation.

Sutro, E. and Gross, R.E. (1983) The five senses – prime keys in the art and craft of Teaching. *Social Studies*, 74(3).

Swain, M. 1986, Two ingredients to the successful use of a second language as a medium of instruction in Hong Kong. *Educational Research Journal* 1, 1–6.

—(1990) *The Immersion Experience in Canada: Is it Relevant to Hong Kong?* Toronto: The Ontario Institute for Studies in Education (OISE).

Swain, M. and Lapkin, S. (1982) *Evaluating Bilingual Education: A Canadian Case Study*. Clevedon, Avon: Multilingual Matters.

The Economist (1993) New York's schools – Begin again, 4th-10th September.

—(1993) The cash street kids. 28 August – 3 September.

Torres, C. and Katz, J.H. (1983) Neuro-linguistic programming: developing effective communication in the classroom. *Teacher Educator* 19(2).

UNESCO (1993) Final Report: International Conference on Education 43rd Session 14–19 September 1992. Paris: International Bureau of Education. Paris.

Ur, P. (1981) *Discussions that Work: Task-centred Fluency Practice*. London: Cambridge University Press.

West, M.A. and Farr, J.L. (eds) (1990) *Innovation and Creativity at Work: Psychological and Organizational Strategies*. Chichester: John Wiley and Sons Ltd.

Widdowson, H.G. (1978) *Teaching Language as Communication*. Oxford: Oxford University Press.

Wilkins, D.A. (1976) *Notional Syllabuses*. Oxford: Oxford University Press.

Wong Fillmore, L. (1980a) *Language Learning through Bilingual Instruction*. University of California, Berkeley.

Zaltmann, G., Duncan, R. and Holbek, J. (1973) *Innovation and Organizations*. New York: Wiley.

Index

DATE DUE

NOV 2 5 1998			
APR 0 4 1999			

GAYLORD   PRINTED IN U.S.A